WE NEED NEW STORIES

WE NEED NEW STORIES

Challenging the Toxic Myths Behind Our Age of Discontent

Nesrine Malik

W&N
WEIDENFELD & NICOLSON

First published in Great Britain in 2019 by Weidenfeld & Nicolson
an imprint of The Orion Publishing Group Ltd
Carmelite House, 50 Victoria Embankment
London EC4Y 0DZ

An Hachette UK Company

1 3 5 7 9 10 8 6 4 2

A CIP catalogue record for this book is
available from the British Library.

ISBN (hardback) 978 1 4746 1040 7
ISBN (trade paperback) 978 1 4746 1041 4
ISBN (ebook) 978 1 4746 1043 8

Typeset by Input Data Services Ltd, Somerset

Printed and bound in Great Britain by Clays Ltd, Elcograf S.p.A.

www.weidenfeldandnicolson.co.uk
www.orionbooks.co.uk

CONTENTS

To Hiba, who writes new stories every day

INTRODUCTION

When I was a child, my grandmother, a woman from a Sudanese rural uneducated farming family, used to tell me long, elaborate tales about the land and property her late husband owned. She would speak about how large their house was – The Fortress, it was called, because it was the biggest house in the village – and about my grandfather's largesse and business acumen. Her favourite detail, one she repeated often, was how one could not carry a hot drink from one end of the house to the other without it getting cold. While other children were told fairy tales, my sisters and I were fed a diet of hyperbolic stories about the difficulties of navigating a large family estate. In addition to the beverage cooling issues, visitors apparently often lost their way, children had to be on standby at meal times to make the long trip to the kitchen for any requests and, allegedly, guests staying in the house could manage not to run into each other for days. If this sounds implausible to you then you would be right. Even as a child, the whole unnavigable fortress business seemed to be, above anything else, a highly impractical arrangement.

Yet still, I wanted to believe it. When, in my teenage years, I finally visited the seat of the Maliks in northern Sudan, the treasures, the land and The Fortress, the tea cooling distances were in fact puny, deserted and crumbling. My grandmother, by now deceased and thus unavailable for interrogation, had lied. I obviously knew on some level that she had embellished her tales, but her fantasies were so removed from the reality (the mud dwellings in which I was standing) that I was angry at her but also a little angry at myself. I felt like the deluded greedy treasure hunter, carrying a map with an X marking the spot where the birthright jewels are buried, only to find that the rocks in the treasure chest held no precious stones. I was a dunce at the end of a morality tale about pride and gluttony.

It should have been obvious to me that there was no Malik loot. Along with my grandmother, we had two uncles and an aunt squatting in our Khartoum house throughout my childhood. Sometimes when the house was busy they were forced to sleep in the yard. It was either a non-existent, or very illiquid treasure. But after a wave of self-loathing at my own eagerness to believe that I was the descendant of some high-born woman, I felt sorry for her. She had lied – but also in a way she hadn't. She had spun and then believed her own inventions because she needed to. Her stature, severely diminished by her husband's untimely death and his poor economic planning, meant that at the age of twenty-five she was an impoverished widow with five children. The stories had to be woven to sustain her, to create a cushion on which to land, as her real status plummeted. All my childhood I was fed this ancestral myth that still remains fixed for many of my generation of Maliks. It is a sort of private family madness. The story of the tea growing cold is still told by people who were born years after the original fable was made up. It is a fantasy, but a harmless one.

I grew up in a household and culture swaddled in such myth. The first, most important, foundational story was of a Malik family rooted not just in wealth, but in honour, grace and a kind of nobility. In Sudan, so profound is this view of an exceptional provenance that the Arabic word *asl*, meaning 'origin', has taken on another meaning. To behave badly, to question convention or simply to hail from a small inconsequential family all falls under the umbrella of having no *asl*, no 'origin'. Growing up, my three sisters and I were terrified that we would be accused of any of this. My mother, who was actually from a small and inconsequential family where there were no fortress fables to be told, had scandalously married into the Maliks. My father was a rebel who refused an arranged marriage to several 'good origin' relatives and instead brought home a young university student whose father worked in a rural soda bottling plant. A father who, worst of all, had shown up in the village from nowhere, some twenty-five years ago, with only a bundle of clothes, a prayer mat and a rosary. My mother was an interloper in the fortress family and it never let her forget it, constantly bearing down on her lack of breeding, which she consequently became obsessed with, passing on that social and familial paranoia to her children. It took a long time for me to become not only educated out of this self-imposed sense of status via self-censorship, but re-educated into recognising the way history, society and family had leveraged this flattering sense of relative superiority to ensure that we, as women, not only did not question subordination, but competed at suffering it with perfect self-composure. I do not think it is hyperbole to say that it was akin to leaving a cult.

I moved to the UK in the mid-aughts from Saudi Arabia, where my family was living at the time, and it was at great personal cost. It was an escape of sorts, but not from a gilded-cage-behind-the-veil oppression, just from the certainty of slow suffocation. I knew I didn't have what it took

to stay and make a life in Sudan or Saudi Arabia. I didn't
know what 'it' was. Sometimes I felt it was a lack of moral
fibre because of my failure to take to religion or social conservatism in general; at other times, I flattered myself that
I was just too irrepressible a spirit to fit in. Whichever, I
felt compelled to work three jobs for three years and save
enough money to move to the UK to start a post-graduate
degree. I fantasised about what my life would be once I
left home to get me through those hard days. I remember
fixating on one single thought – being able to leave my
house and shut the door behind me without having to tell
anyone where I was going or when I was coming back.
That image did not disappoint when it finally happened,
although the house in the dream was, in reality, a series of
damp flat shares – and for a long time I couldn't afford to
go anywhere but to university and back. To this day, I still
get a kick out of it.

But my initial sense of relief, even euphoria as I enjoyed
simple basic freedoms after a life suffocated by the narcissism of propriety, soon melted away. I had naively built an
idealistic image of a West where sure, things weren't perfect,
but where the basics as far as social justice was concerned
had been ironed out, or at least where attempts to iron them
out were ongoing. I was not prepared for all the ways my
new home was different, but in other ways the same as the
one I had just left – with a different sort of tribalism, a
different manifestation of misogyny, a codified economic
system of injustice. The sexism, in particular, was overwhelming as well as pernicious. Here I was again, deluded,
with my treasure map.

I moved to the UK only two years after 9/11. And I was
Muslim, black, a woman and an immigrant. But I also
managed, through luck and chance (not meritocracy or any

outstanding talent, but more on that later), to secure jobs in finance and the media without the usual requisite networks and affiliations required to do so. So I became an outsider on the inside, without the self-reinforcing circles one would usually pick up through education and socialising, the cosy in-groups whose norms I could bask in. It was like having some magic combination, a full house of difference, while also securing insight to the way things worked, without being compromised (or comforted, many times it felt like a loss, rather than a gain) by any sort of loyalty or sense of belonging to a pack. It became clear to me that here was another fortress mirage. The patterns were familiar. It was just the technicalities that were different.

I realised the full extent of my disillusionment when I read Ayaan Hirsi Ali's *Infidel*, a memoir which tells the story of a migration to the West by a woman who suffered at the hands of a religiously and culturally motivated patriarchy in her native Somalia. Ali's response to her newfound freedom was to fasten on Islam as an evil against which 'war' must be waged, and to embrace a morally absolutist belief in Western values. I came to the book expecting to relate to it, but it became clear to me that to a great extent, the writer had swapped one set of certainties for another. She had taken her own suffering at the hands of her culture, which subjected her to female genital mutilation and arranged marriages, as a reason to embrace other supremacist norms that came with their own violence against Muslims, minorities and women. It seemed to me a colossal waste, to fight so hard to gain freedom from one harmful ideology, only to voluntarily embrace another. She was just telling herself stories, the same way my grandmother did, and the same way I did when mythologising my new life away from home.

*

Individually and collectively, we need stories. It is a universal impulse. We need some galvanising, sense-making framework, a narrative, in order to instil order and a sense of purpose to our lives. Some myths are not only useful, they are necessary. All political orders are based on useful fictions which have allowed groups of humans, from ancient Mesopotamia through to the Roman empire and modern capitalist societies, to cooperate in numbers far beyond the scope of any other species. Every social unit, from the family to the nation state, functions on the basis of mythology, stories that set them apart from others.

Some myths are less useful than others, and some are dangerously regressive. In Britain, I began to see these tales being told on a cultural, not just individual, level, to justify the way things were and preserve the status quo. But they were not harmless self-comforting bedtime stories; they were toxic delusions that had a purpose, to stymie change. And they broke the surface with the Brexit vote in the United Kingdom and the election of Donald Trump as president in the United States. My focus in this book is on the UK and the US, but I am keen to stress that myth-making is not confined to these two nations, and to demonstrate that with comparisons to my own and other cultural experiences.

Before these two significant events happened, a malignant thread had been running through Western history, and it is made of myths. These are not myths that animate believers into a shared sense of camaraderie and direction. They are myths that divide and instil a sense of superiority over others. Nations are susceptible to these impulses when going through times of instability or subordination or dictatorship and demagoguery. Again, myths are useful and comforting galvanisers. But when they take hold in

democratic ostensibly affluent societies, it is not a tempo-
rary madness, it is a culmination.

I started to write this book at a time of both political
awakening and despair, when it was becoming clear that
something was not working, where there was fear and
distress but also a healthy impulse to resist and mobilise.
But the effort is inchoate and still fixated on the idea of
returning to a time before it all went wrong, rather than
the recognition that things have been going wrong all
along.

I have chosen what I believe are the six most influential
myths behind our age of discontent. Each myth has what
I identify as a 'tool', an argumentative technique that advances it. These myths are spun by those who get to speak,
who have the platforms, those who have historically ac-
cumulated the influence and power, who, culturally, are
defined as its vessels. Myths are spun out of several skilfully
woven untruths that cumulatively tug the scales in favour of
not necessarily those who are in power – it is less calculated
than that – but those who benefit from power.

This is not a book about a 'culture war', a tussle between
conservative and liberal forces, or the erosion of the 'centre
ground', the staple of much media commentary. What I am
suggesting here is that there is no 'culture war' as such with
regard to the fundamental beliefs that underpin the status
quo and sow discontent. Both the political right and left
exist within a flawed system. This system is one that will
periodically revert to its basest fears and hatreds, voiding
all that went before it.

This book is not suggesting that we rewire or deny human
nature. We simply need to acknowledge that when perver-
sions in our collective storytelling happen, they should, and
can, be unwritten. This is not a paranoid attempt to 'red

pill'. It is not a structuralism, as argued by anthropologist Adam Kuper, that 'has something of the momentum of a millennial movement where some of its adherents felt that they formed a secret society of the seeing in a world of the blind'. It is an attempt to tackle specifically the very obvious ways in which history, race, gender and liberal values are being leveraged to halt in its tracks any progression towards disrupting a centuries-old establishment of hierarchy which is paying dividends for fewer and fewer people. This is not a 'resistance' book. It is not a guide to activism. It is not a reflection on 'how democracies die' or how authoritarianism is on the horizon. It is an exploration of how, without questioning the very context in which resistance takes place, it is futile.

My motivations come from a personal prejudice. To put it bluntly, I was damned if I was going to spend my youth taking apart the value systems that exchanged my independence of thought for the comfort of a higher status in the food chain, only to embrace other values that did the same elsewhere. I hope you will read me as a sort of witness to the way myths work, and join me in my hope that the most pernicious of them can be successfully challenged.

CHAPTER 1

The myth of gender equality

'*Revolutionary men with principles were not really different from the rest. They used their cleverness to get, in return for principles, what other men buy with their money.*'

Nawal El Saadawi

The social contract between the state and its female citizens is broken. This contract is a sort of bargain, where one gives up some rights voluntarily to create an order in which everyone can pursue individual happiness. Every day, women are giving up rights involuntarily to live in an order which is not optimised for the pursuit of their individual or collective happiness. It is not even optimised for their safety. As hard-won abortion rights in the US are rolled back, as the gender pay gap continues to persist and even widen, and as cyber sexual harassment and online abuse becomes an everyday part of a woman's life, women are told not only that things are fine, but that they have in fact, never been better. I was used to this logic, this myth of gender equality, but did not expect to see it spread in the boardrooms of London, the respectable media of Britain and the United States, and the polite society of ostensibly liberal circles in those two countries.

Growing up in a conservative family in the Middle East and North Africa, I was quick to learn of this system of bargaining, where the ultimate spoils were not happiness, but survival. Much of my life was conditional. My education in an English language school was conditional on the fact that it did not Westernise me too much – the threat of being pulled out and enrolled in a religious school always hovered. Later, my professional chances were conditional on how many of my natural interests I could jettison in order to study for an appropriate career in medicine or its derivatives. My social status was conditional on my deportment – ideally a sort of demure but knowing fragility.

This was my biggest failure, a pose I could not strike no matter how hard I tried. I was scrappy, unkempt, in awe of my sisters and female relatives who glided through life, Sphinx-like, Geisha-like, respected by the menfolk and orbited by other women. I could not, despite trying very hard, replace my inchoate natural temperament with a more gathered demeanour. I played too much football in the street with the neighbourhood boys and experimented with eating or smoking quite a lot of what was growing wild and poisonous in the garden and surrounding brush. I remember at least two stomach pumping incidents. I was constantly bruised and in trouble. My consistent failure to be the sort of daughter that shadows womenfolk in kitchens and salons frustrated my parents who threw everything at the problem – religion, physical punishment, threats of being withdrawn from school.

For my father, who once told me 'men are an axe, they break things; women are a bowl, they gather things', the problem was not that I could not be free to be who I was, but that I could not embrace the freedom that only my 'natural' role in life could provide. The only way to find any peace was to accept the norms of a society that I did not understand nor saw any logic to and try to be really good at them. The only way was to give myself up and excel at performing.

The bargain

To be a woman is to be in this constant state of bargaining, irrespective of her particular circumstances. Women bargain to balance their roles as caregivers with their role as workers. Women bargain to balance their sexual agency with the threat associated with that agency. The bargaining is an unconscious process that is assimilated from the moment a female child is aware of her gender. As tentatively as a toddler learns how to walk and then effortlessly run, a woman learns that her life is a series of trade-offs. The bargain secures relative freedoms in a world where absolute freedom is either impossible or hard to achieve. A woman's education is spontaneous, organic, uncoordinated but also coherent. A woman is told, through all the mediums of her socialisation – family, popular culture, marketing and social interactions – what her value is. She is handed her currency and taught how to exchange it in the marketplace and how far it will stretch.

To be a woman is akin to being a prisoner with something to trade – cigarettes, alcohol, sexual favours, anything you have at your disposal to earn you that extra half hour to stretch your legs in the exercise yard or save you from a beating. Anything that in the scarcity of incarceration will earn you some respite from the tyranny of a system in which your rights are enshrined in theory but can be rescinded at any time. One would, of course, rather not be in prison, but if you are, it is better to have something to trade. The most powerful woman to the naked eye – financially

independent, educated, fully employed and equally paid,
living in a society with robust laws protecting her rights to
freedom from gender discrimination – is not exempt from
this barter economy.

And so a woman starts to trade. She sometimes accepts a
certain benign degree of male dominion in order to secure
financial support in a world where her employment opportunities are compromised by child rearing. She sometimes
overplays physical attributes and downplays intellectual
ones to attract a partner. She sometimes actively supports
male violence against other women in order to secure a relative status over those women. She sometimes is less loud or
assertive than she would like to be, in order not to alienate
male colleagues. She sometimes is more inclined to settle for
a spouse who is less than ideal, rather than remain single
and childless. She sometimes is tolerant of sexual harassment, because she needs a job. Sometimes she is able to kill
her own daughter, because the child's honour is her only
capital.

The myth that she will be told throughout her life is that
she is equal to men and so has nothing to complain about.
In fact, she will be told that she is more than equal, she is
overprivileged, that there is no compromise she has to make
for being a woman that does not fall out of the scope of what
nature intended. She will be given her own version of my
father's advice if she is unhappy or frustrated – men are
axes, women are bowls. The cornerstone of the woman's
bargain is that women are free, or as free as they can possibly be. The same myths horizontally throughout time and
vertically throughout space are thrown at women: you are
not unequal, you are *complementary*. You are not subjugated, you are *ungrateful*. You are not excluded, you are
entitled.

The myth, or rather the con, is that in the West, if we are not there already, we are on our way to building a society in which women have secured all the rights, sexual freedom, contraception, maternity leave, marital choice, and so any inequality beyond that is just biology. Any hope for more is greedy or simply misunderstanding the science. This is thrown in the face of all calls for additional rights. All that can be done has been done. How can you rewire biology?

The myth of gender equality deploys three arguments. The first is *complementarity*, a socio-biological determinism which holds that biology dictates social roles and behaviour. The second is *progress*, positing that any advances in women's rights at any point in time are exhaustive. The third, *meritocracy*, argues that the reason that women are under-represented is because they just do not work hard enough, or are just not good enough. These arguments are then reinforced by an argumentative tool I call 'the set up', a way of constantly killing the question for more rights by indulging in comparative deflection; are things not better today? Do you not see how others elsewhere are faring?

The myth of gender equality is helped along by the fact that the woman's bargain is not quantifiable or measurable because it is a clandestine affair. It happens furtively in the shadows, unacknowledged even to the conscious mind of all the participants. It is not one a gender analyst could render in a spreadsheet, but it is the algorithm that lies behind all the other indices.

The United Nations compiles an annual inequality index – the GII, or Gender Inequality Index. It measures gender inequalities in three aspects of human development – reproductive health, measured by maternal mortality ratio and adolescent birth rates; empowerment, measured by proportion of parliamentary seats occupied by females and proportion of adult females and males aged twenty-five years and older with at least some secondary education; and economic status, expressed as labour market partici-pation and measured by labour force participation rate of female and male populations aged fifteen years and older. Measuring these three factors is the closest we can come to assessing how far a nation has progressed in advancing gender equality, but there is no way of measuring the daily and cumulative tithes of womanhood outside those that limit her access to healthcare, education and employment. In 2017, my adopted country, the United Kingdom, sits at number 25 on the GII; my country of birth, Sudan, is at 139, but in both those countries, there exists a Panglossian belief that things are as good as they are realistically going to get, with room only for some tinkering around the edges.

But the delusion of gender equality is even stronger in those cultures that have made significant progress towards the cause. In the UK and the US, technical legislation has enabled women to take control of their reproductive decisions, pro-vided protection against clear professional discrimination on the basis of gender and secured equal political rights. But this elides the two ways in which gender equality is being eroded; the indifference of the state to providing enough support to women so that they can climb up the career ladder and the cultural complacency which has facilitated and normalised a rise in violence against women. The former ensures that women are absent in critical mass where it really matters, the latter demonstrates that there is still a failure to separate the value of women from their sexual worth.

Ironically, there has been a retrenchment of gender in-equality, exacerbated by all the ways in which women are visibly empowered. This is propped up by all the ways women continue to barter their rights and rage for survival.

Complementarity

Complementarity is the belief that much of what women complain about cannot be legislated away because it is human nature. The playing field has been levelled and everything that happens on it now is just the cut and thrust of the two genders interacting. The shrugging default to the rules of biology is universal across cultures – almost comfortingly so. To object to anything from forced marriage in Omdurman, Sudan, to the ubiquity of sexual harassment in the workplace in the City of London is to be met with this defence. And with it a demand that a woman make the biggest trade-off of all – to accept that inequality is a function of biology. The only way to avoid the wild's reddened tooth and claw is never to step outside the bounds of nature's purdah.

Both Eastern and Western societies have their own myths that preach that women are protected from male predators, and that when they suffer sexual harassment or assault it is because they have somehow transgressed. In Sudan or Saudi Arabia, I was told that if I followed the rules, dressed modestly and availed myself of the protection that society had provided for me in the form of male guardianship, then no harm would befall me. In the UK, I was told while working in finance that the non-advancement of women was unconscious, unmalicious bias, that the severe attrition of women beyond a certain professional level was because they want to have children and, that again, the system had legislated for the progress of women. Everything else was biology, including sexual harassment. In fact, a common response when the burden of female modesty is challenged is 'it is what it is', we cannot question nature's engineering or civilise our way out of it. There is a wisdom to it which ensures that women, the weaker and more vulnerable sex, are not overburdened. Biology is our destiny.

In Western societies, we can easily dismiss this determinism as backward when it is dictated by religion or by mullah-led governments in countries that are 'other'. But the very same fallacy runs the logic of female subordination everywhere. From Tehran to New York, women will be told that they are asking for it if they wear a short skirt in a bar or a looser than acceptable burqa in the street. The preachers of the myth that bad male behaviour is inevitable and thus excusable if women provoke it aren't just restricted to religion. We have not made as much progress as we think. Sexual conservatism and slut-shaming (bizarrely wrapped up in a pornified culture), rigid heteronormativity and casual misogyny slapped me in the face when I settled in the UK, and continue to surprise me to this day. The regressive gender roles that we think we have left behind as society has secularised are still present in academia and science. They are hiding in plain sight in popular culture and our social mores and they inform our political legislation.

It has been alarming to see a resurgence in pop sociobiological determinism. In 2017, Jordan Peterson, a Canadian psychologist, became a best-selling author on Amazon with his book *12 Rules for Life*. In this self-help manual for alienated men, Peterson dispenses advice that urges them to toughen up and for everyone to accept genetic order in a sort of happy existential oblivion that comes from knowing that 'the pursuit of happiness is a pointless goal'. It's an almost Sufi position, an ascetic Muslim sect that seeks oneness with God and a higher spirituality in general by eschewing the material ambitions of brief earthly life. Peterson's position on women is that they also, because of their genetic make-up, should not wander from their natural perch in the order. He attributes their modern distress at being torn between the demands of work and home to the fact that women went walkabout off the nature reserve.

According to Peterson, the gender pay gap, the average difference between the remuneration for men and women in employment (around 20 per cent to the benefit of men in the US and the UK) is largely a natural reflection of existing differences between men and women. These differences are explained in his adaptation of the 'Big Five personality traits' taxonomy: openness to experience, conscientiousness, extraversion, agreeableness and neuroticism. Peterson is fixated on 'agreeableness' in general, a classic fondness conservative men have for women in what they perceive to be their natural state – fecund, comely, pliable. Other differences between the genders include 'neuroticism', a woman's higher likelihood to experience stress, depression and emotional volatility, and her need to be cooperative and compassionate. Women have preferred choices, one of which is to have less demanding careers (or none at all). Social pressure forcing women to work in higher-paying jobs, or any job at all when they would like to remain at home, would actually work against their interests by interfering with their preferred choices. This is all underscored by another trope, that of 'complementarity'. Men are not superior to women, they are 'complementary'.

More than a century ago, British biologists Patrick Geddes and Sir John Arthur Thomson made the same points (and managed to do so with a much more wholehearted attempt at scientific method than Peterson – so much for progress). They argued that social, psychological and behavioural traits were caused by the difference in metabolic state between men and women. Women supposedly conserve energy (by being 'anabolic') and this makes them passive, conservative, sluggish, stable and uninterested in politics. Men expend their surplus energy (by being 'katabolic'). This makes them eager, energetic, passionate and variable, thereby, interested in political and social matters.

It is rare that these pseudoscientific conclusions are just left at that. Often, they are, as with Peterson, a justification for a status quo where women are subordinate, a nostalgia for a status quo when they once were subordinate, or a warning against chaos when the status quo looks like it might be changing. Peterson is often hailed as an innovator, a truth teller, when all he does is repeat and repackage ancient traditional gender role conservatism. In Chapter 6, which focuses on unreliable narrators, there is more on why Peterson is not to be taken as anything other than an old-school morality preacher, recast for a new age.

Geddes and Thomson's biological 'facts' about metabolic states were used not only to explain behavioural differences between women and men but also to map out a path for social arrangements. They were used specifically to argue for withholding political rights from women because, they claimed, 'what was decided among the prehistoric Protozoa cannot be annulled by Act of Parliament'. And so women cannot be granted political rights because they are not built for that purpose – and it would be pointless anyway, as women would not be interested in exercising them. And if they were forced, as Geddes and Thomson's descendant in thought argued more than 130 years later, it would traumatise them. There is a rich history of leveraging 'science' and 'facts' to the end of arguing that inequality is in fact, hardwired.

In the 1970s, menstruation was used to argue that women should not become airline pilots since their monthly hormonal instability would render them unable to perform their duties as well as men (or at all). More recently, differences in male and female brains have been used to explain behavioural discrepancies. The anatomy of the corpus callosum, a knot of nerves that connects the two hemispheres of the brain was studied for a 1992 article in *Time* magazine. The article surveyed then popular biological explanations of differences between women and men, claiming that women's thicker corpus callosums could explain 'women's intuition' and what impairs women's ability to perform some specialised visual–spatial skills, such as map reading. A woman cannot have an advantage over a man biologically without it counting against her in some other way you see. Her 'intuition' must be at the cost of her motor skills. Even a woman who is a disembodied bundle of nerves on a laboratory slab is forced into a trade-off.

Scientific biological determinism has a tendency to reach for the comforting headline that we can blame it all on wiring and go home. In 2013, clinical psychologist Simon Baron-Cohen opened his book *The Essential Difference* with the hard assertion that 'the female brain is predominantly hard-wired for empathy. The male brain is predominantly hard-wired for understanding and building systems'. But he dilutes this later in the work by saying that one doesn't have to be a man to have a male brain or a woman to have a female brain, which surely is the whole point of his thesis.

In another Baron-Cohen headed study in 2018, claiming to be the largest ever analysis of psychological sex differences and autistic traits, there are more smoke and mirrors. The research got its headlines. 'MEN AND WOMEN REALLY DO THINK DIFFERENTLY, SAY SCIENTISTS', said *The Times*, 'The much-maligned but longstanding idea that women enjoy discussing their emotions while men are mostly ex- cited by cars may be true after all.'

Upon closer inspection of the data by neuroimaging professor Gina Rippon in the *New Statesman*, however, it emerged that 'differences in empathising and systemising account for 19 times more of the variance in autistic traits than other measures, such as sex'. So strong are the political and social motivations to label brains pink and blue that we end up with what Rippon, calls 'neurotrash'. In her 2019 book *The Gendered Brain: The New Neuroscience that Shatters the Myth of the Female Brain*, she calls these per- sistent attempts to gender brains at the expense of women 'Whac-a-Mole' myths. They keep turning up no matter how many times they are debunked.

It is one of the most persistent deflections, this justifi- cation of the way things are by looking for biological or genetic smoking guns. It is a way to discount bad male be- haviour and chastise women for demanding better. And it is promoted by people who would never think of themselves as having a regressive or biblical view of the world.

The appeal to nature based on rational scientific fact also fails to account for all the biases that inform scientific research into biological gender differences. That is not to suggest that scientific research can never be completely objective, just that there should be space to consider that socialisation can be severely limiting of analysis. The trust a society invests in a certain type of narrator is often a func- tion of the hierarchy within it. In Islamic jurisprudence, the Hadith, the sayings of the prophet Muhammad, constitute a significant portion of religious legislation and fatwa. Those who believe in the veracity of the Hadiths cite the allegedly airtight and disciplined process by which they were collected and tested by Hadith authenticators. The main method of verification is that of an unbroken chain of narrators that can stretch back to the original source, the prophet himself. It is remarkable how many edicts, taken as scripture, come from the Hadith and not the Quran. Where the Hadiths specifically address women, ordering them to wear the hijab or stating that women are deficient in intelligence, it does not occur to those that follow the literal texts, or their explanation, that their narration and extrapolation into religious law happened at the hands of a long unbroken chain of men throughout the past 1,400 years or so. It is one of the most deep-seated delusions in organised religion, which, vis-à-vis women's rights, assumes that texts written by men and handed down through the ages via men, have not been compromised or coloured to the benefit of men. Scriptures that warn us that men are lustful and not in control of their faculties when it comes to women (necessitating that women must maintain modesty so as to not inflame these feral creatures) are the very same texts we entrust these wild men to curate in their unquestionable wisdom and restraint.

And yet men, and the patriarchy in general, continue to be entrusted with the narration of the laws of nature.

In November 2017, after the Harvey Weinstein scandal broke, the premier BBC news programme, *Newsnight*, held a debate on sexual harassment calling it 'The problem with men'. It began with host Evan Davis, the first openly gay presenter of the show and a liberal with an ear piercing, standing in a zoo. As he walked past the animals he asked if sexual harassment was just in our nature as animals who must accept the cut and thrust of the genders mixing. Is it in the end, just biology? It was no surprise that the ensuing panel conversation, between fourteen angry men and three bewildered women, immediately careened into the territory of men expressing frustration that in this new world, natural dynamics where women are touched against their will are now being policed.

A deluge of responses to the #MeToo movement fell along these lines – that of biology being pushed up against the wall by a feminist movement drunk with power. Pundits, columnists and academics listened to stories of women being touched, professionally intimidated for sexual favours and even assaulted, and responded with a collective outcry against what they perceived was a violation of the benign status quo. Men must woo women in order to procreate and where, in that melee, sometimes things just get a little messy.

In the UK, the author Douglas Murray concluded that #MeToo, if allowed to grow unchecked, augured the end of the human race. Writing in the *Spectator* magazine he catastrophised: 'The rules are being redrawn with little idea of where the boundaries of this new sexual utopia will lie and less idea still of whether any sex will be allowed in the end.' The journalist Peter Hitchens went down the creative route of concluding that all that women gain from this 'squawking' about sex pests is a niqab. Other journalists helpfully weighed in. Giles Coren in *The Times* expressed ironically resigned confusion about how one is to navigate this scary new world without accidentally sexually assaulting someone. Rod Liddle, a man cautioned for kicking his pregnant girlfriend in the stomach, wondered if women are just hardwired to be attracted to powerful men. Brendan O'Neill of *Spiked Online* called #MeToo a 'sexual inquisition', saying it was a 'sinister menace to democracy'. The former *Guardian* journalist Michael White went on BBC radio to call Westminster female reporters, who had over-come years of self-doubt to step forward and accuse male Members of Parliament of touching them inappropriately, 'predators'. In the US, Bret Stephens of the *New York Times* concluded that it had all already gone too far, appealing for nuance between rape and other forms of sexual as-sault – a conflation no one was making. It was a corporeal spasm.

These are not reactionaries, provocateurs or trolls. They are mainstream journalists across the political divide. What they are exhibiting is a typical response to the challenging of a deep-seated myth, that biology was destiny, by resorting to deflection and hyperbole. If we are going to stick with the obsessive commitment to biology as explainer for all behaviour, a helpful way to look at this phenomenon would be to see these people less as thinking individuals with agency, but as organisms on top of a food chain reacting with instinctive self-preservation to what they perceive to be an existential threat. Judge by biology always, and you will be judged by it inevitably.

The set up

En masse, they represent strong cultural resistance to a counter narrative, no matter how obvious the claim or credible the source. In 2014, UN special rapporteur Rashida Manjoo said that sexism in the UK is more 'in your face' and generally worse than in other countries that she has vis-ited. The response was a howl of denial, protesting that the UK had come a long way, and that it was absurd to compare it to countries where women suffer FGM or forced mar-riage. But Manjoo had not compared the UK to Somalia or Saudi Arabia. She had made a rather obvious statement that described the pervasive 'old boys' network in the UK, and the aggressiveness and ubiquity of commercial sexualised depictions of women. She also said that 'violence against women needs to be addressed within the broader struggles against inequality and gender-based discrimination.'

More revealing was how the debate was then framed. Rather than engaging with what Manjoo said, which was anodyne and generic, the conversation became a comparative one. Was Britain better or worse than other countries? Was Britain better or worse than before with regard to gender equality? The answers could obviously only be that of course Britain was better than other countries and better than before. It was a set up. The set up is the main communication tool by which changing a culture is resisted. It is an argumentative device that distracts from discussing the issue at hand by diverting attention to something unrelated. Once its methods are identified, the pattern is obvious.

A statement about sexist culture in the UK by Manjoo, a gender expert diplomat is rebuffed by the worthy banality that at least women's genitals are safe from mutilation on the green and pleasant land. An attempt to have a discussion about the culture of violence against women becomes one about how safe women are compared to other countries. An attempt to understand why rapes in London rose by 20 per cent in 2017 becomes a conversation about the semantics of the statistics. Maybe incidents of rape have not gone up at all but they're just being reported more? Or what if in fact, all crime has gone up, not just rape?

It could be worse. It has been worse. And in fact, it is worse elsewhere. On a macro level, in the media and in politics, trying to appeal to facts and sympathy in order to have a meaningful excavation of rising and constant levels of sexual abuse and assault, high homicide rates of women or the epidemic of sexual harassment in the workplace, is like presenting in serious pain to a physician who immediately asks you to consider that at least you are not dead. The point of the set ups is to not engage with the primary malady while also avoiding explaining why. That way the set up allows you to maintain the moral high ground. It is far easier to filibuster on why rape reports are rising, than it is to say, simply, that you do not care about rape. It is dishonest.

These set ups develop, like sentient straw men defensively scrambling to prevent any real discussion, in order to preserve the way things are. A system of inequality must create its own illusion of justice, through which it is sustained. It is a common impulse, not unique to any culture. Set ups are stabilisers, low-key propaganda that things simply are not that bad. The starker and more graphic the injustice, the louder and more feverishly it is normalised and excused.

But look how far we've come

The set up always invokes the proof of 'progress', as if any progress is all progress. And as if progress in certain clearly improved areas means that misogyny and sexism are not continuously reborn in new and ever more sophisticated ways.

In Saudi Arabia, for example, extreme gender segregation and denial of basic women's rights is normalised by harnessing popular culture and education. Saudi Arabia is not the first country that comes to mind when compiling a league of nations where women's rights have made big advances, but a cursory look at one of the UN GII metrics, education, reveals a giant leap. The first Saudi girls' school opened in 1960. By 2015, according to the Saudi Ministry of Education, there were more women than men enrolled in universities – 551,000 women were studying for bachelor's degrees compared to 513,000 men. Fifty years ago, the vast majority of Saudi women were illiterate, and leaving the house to pursue a formal education was considered taboo.

And yet this has not had enough of an impact to grant Saudi women autonomy from strict male guardianship laws, for example. A female university professor would still need the permission of her husband to travel or obtain a passport. If unmarried, she needs the permission of her closest male relative, a mahram (that is, a relative whom she cannot marry due to closeness of blood bond). The result is a lopsided power dynamic, where a university professor would defer to a younger brother, sometimes barely out of puberty, for permission to travel. This is the case for a close friend, a double Emmy award-winning Saudi documentary maker who is estranged from her father due to her political scrutiny of the persecution of Shias in the country, and so has to cajole her younger brother to approve any Saudi documentation she requires.

The very curriculum that ushered Saudi women into mainstream education also carried within it the blueprint for a society in which they could never escape subordination to men. Saudi state curriculum bans physical education for girls, and sewing and home economics classes are compulsory for female students from the ages of twelve to sixteen. Mandatory religious education classes instruct that women's voices should never be raised within earshot of men, and that unless employment is necessary, a woman's place is in the home. The state also maintains a monopoly on education by providing high-quality facilities for free, obviating the need for private schools, and paying university female students a stipend to attend higher education. Captive in this state education system that instils in them their place from a young age, women emerge into society not as disruptors, but compliant believers in the system. Saudi Arabia has managed simultaneously to expand women's access to education while leveraging that education towards the end of reproducing the patterns of discrimination. It is an example of how sometimes metrics of progress can be meaningless, and should be resorted to with heavy caveat when used as a measure of female emancipation. Nagat El-Sanabary makes this point in 'Female Education in Saudi Arabia and the Reproduction of Gender Division', an article in which she explains the reproduction of gender divisions and power relations through education in Saudi Arabia. The country has drawn both upon Islam and its oil wealth to expand female education vastly within traditional boundaries. She concluded that the Saudi model proves previous research findings that female educational expansion does indeed increase women's social and occupational options, but does not necessarily alter gender and power relations.

The argument of progress can be used to mask the fact that advances are always relative, rarely absolute. Just because things were worse yesterday, does not mean that they are ideal today, or should not be improved upon. The argument also ignores the reproduction of social and cultural norms that continue to hold women back. When any complaint can be dismissed as ungratefulness, it is impossible to secure any further wins.

The first response for a demand for more rights is to look back and remonstrate, almost implicitly threaten, that it could all be so much worse. It is a reflex deployed against women's rights activists throughout history. It is also an impulse that we can easily shed when judging other societies,

dropping relativist perspectives. Few Westerners would
look at Saudi Arabia and observe that where the country is
now with women's rights is fine, considering women were
only allowed an education fifty years ago. But they might
smugly think that advancement in their own countries is
satisfactory, without considering that the most basic political right, that of universal suffrage, was granted in the
United States and United Kingdom less than 100 years ago.
In Switzerland, women's suffrage was only granted in 1971.
It is also just easier to acknowledge toxicity in a culture that
isn't our own. The murder of women by members of their
family in Pakistan or Jordan is easily identified as an honour
killing and traced back to deeply ingrained religious, social
and cultural norms that see women's lives as owned by their
families in general, and by their male relatives in particular.
The same line of reasoning is not made when considering
the fact that in the US, three women a day are killed by their
partners or ex-partners and that half of all homicides in the
country are committed by an intimate partner. According
to the World Health Organization, the global figure is high
but still less than in the United States, hovering around 38
per cent of homicide cases. In England and Wales, in the
first half of this decade, 64 per cent of all women killed by
men were murdered by their partners or ex-partners. An
entire project, 'Femicide – Counting the Dead', collated by
Women's Aid and feminist researcher Karen Ingala Smith
was founded because no official authority was making the
gender link. If these are not considered honour killings, then
no uncomfortable examination needs to be conducted into
what lies beneath. But they are honour killings, in that they
are committed in order to avenge a slight to a man and
restore the honour that a woman's disobedient behaviour
has taken away, because a woman is the property of her

partner. The only difference between Western and Eastern honour killings, is that the latter are sometimes perpetrated by extended male family members and sometimes mothers, but all that tells us is that in Western societies a woman's ownership has been transferred from her family, to her male partner.

But let us focus on the argument of progress. In general, invoking progress is irrelevant when discussing serious systemic female disempowerment or cultural failures to protect women from violence. Malcolm X, faced with his own version of the progress roadblock in the race debate (where the argument was that American negroes were not being lynched anymore), said, 'If you stick a knife in my back nine inches and pull it out six inches, there's no progress. If you pull it all the way out that's not progress. Progress is healing the wound that the blow made. And they haven't even pulled the knife out much less heal the wound . . .'

This fondness of measuring the present in terms of how much better it is than the past, rather than how bad it is objectively, is not merely a feature of conservative thinking. It is also beloved of a certain type of neo-liberal intellectual. Steven Pinker, a Harvard psychologist, is a promoter of an inexorable enlightenment. In his book *Enlightenment Now: The Case for Reason, Science, Humanism, and Progress* he coins any resistance or complaint as 'progressophobia'. By framing progressophobia as a hallmark of right-wing thinking, Pinker has managed to Trojan horse this deeply conservative view into the halls of Harvard and earn the praise of Bill Gates who called *Enlightenment Now* his 'new favourite book of all time'. But to Pinker, 'progressophobia' is not just prevalent on the right, where nostalgia for the 'good old days' leads to a rejection of modernity, but on the left as well, which denies or ignores much of the progress of the twentieth century. Pinker clearly quantifies the progress fallacy, by focusing on the fact that gender equality has improved by bombarding the reader with statistics showing improvement over the past 100 years. The Enlightenment is taking care of things nicely you see, the rest is all progressophobia.

The concerted effort to fix a starting point in the Enlightenment is part of a wider tendency to attribute any Western success to a noble set of ideas, following which started an inevitable march towards the better. At some point the West was 'born', it didn't just haphazardly develop. Its moral blueprint, its DNA, came to be during the Enlightenment and then the West grew into the adult success that it is today. This is an exceptionalism that would rather see progress as a function of values (rationalism, humanism, commitment to scientific inquiry, individualism), than the toil and struggle of the weak and disenfranchised throwing themselves into activism and martyrdom against the institutions that work to exclude them. With this exceptionalism comes a myopia that can only see prosperity as a function of a benign capitalism leveraged to the good of man, rather than local and global exploitation of free and cheap labour. Above all, Enlightenment fetishisation is an ahistorical perspective that, if it were to be applied to gender equality in particular, would suggest that the state of women before then was uniformly awful, hitting a good wind only when John Locke dipped his quill.

It does not take into account, just on a very simple level, how the laws of Hammurabi, a Babylonian king who encoded one of the earliest and most complete written codes circa 1800 BC, gave women some divorce and alimony rights, introduced the death penalty for some forms of rape, and upgraded women's business and property ownership rights. Most of Hammurabi's code vis-à-vis women saw their rights as derivative of men's, but nevertheless the new laws were also 'progress', and did not need a European Enlightenment to move them along. When Islam was introduced to the Arabian Peninsula, it eradicated the custom of burying female babies, gave women inheritance and divorce rights, and limited polygamy. You are almost certainly scoffing at these three examples as evidence of progress, but if you do, you must also be prepared to reassess what counts as progress today.

Backsliding

The fixation with progress overlooks the real danger of backsliding. Since Donald Trump took office, he revoked the 2014 Fair Pay and Safe Workplaces order which among other violations withheld taxpayer dollars from companies which did not provide pay cheque transparency, and included forced arbitration clauses (barring cases from going to court) for sexual harassment, sexual assault or discrimination claims. The Trump administration also reversed a directive that forced universities to quickly investigate on-campus sexual assault. Former president Barack Obama had enacted the requirement, which lowered the burden of proof and cut federal funding if schools weren't compliant, in 2011. Trump rolled back another Obamacare provision requiring employers to offer health insurance that covered birth control. He signed a law that lets local governments withhold federal funding from healthcare providers like Planned Parenthood that offer abortions, along with myriad other women's healthcare treatments like breast cancer screenings. One month later he proposed a federal budget that defunded Planned Parenthood – which is already barred from using federal funds for abortion services in most cases – completely. Up to June 2019, according to the Guttmacher Institute, twenty-seven abortion bans have been enacted across twelve states since Trump came to office, with more in the legislation pipeline. This rollback initiative does not only affect the United States. Immediately after his inauguration, Trump also instituted a policy known as the 'Global Gag Rule' that makes non-governmental organisations receiving US funds for global health issues prove they do not use their other funding to provide abortions or talk about the option with patients. NGOs could not use US aid for abortion services before this rule. Trump also stopped an Obama-crafted rule from going into effect that would make companies track payment data based on race and gender. The data was meant to help close the gender pay gap.

On a global level, according to the 2017 World Economic Forum report on gender equality, there has been a similar reversal in positive trends. Now in its eleventh year, the Global Gender Gap Report has given WEF an opportunity to identify long-term trends in gender equality, and the picture that is emerging shows that there is a sort of terminal velocity that has been reached. The global gender gap measures four overall areas of inequality between men and women – economic participation and opportunity, educational attainment, political empowerment, and health and survival. While the global gender gap has narrowed since 2006, it has done so at a glacial pace. Should that continue, it would take another 100 years for the world's women to be on an even footing with men. There has actually been a widening of the gender gap since last year's study. In 2017, progress towards gender parity shifted into reverse.

So even if one were to cite inexorable improvement in the

world's only superpower and the land of the free, and in aggregate on a global basis, it would appear that progress does not have its own momentum. It is not fuelled by the principles of the Enlightenment and oiled by the invisible hand of capitalism. It is a tentative and fragile state which is sustained by the effort of constant activism and vigilance, both on the ground and on the ideological battlefield. An appeal for context, to point out that the overall pattern is one of improvement, is an appeal for quietism.

And the complacency of progress does not account for the reactionary backlash that progress often triggers, which makes it doubly difficult for the dermal layer to be treated, for 'the wound to heal'.

Overcorrection and the death of meritocracy

The next stage of denialism that kicks in after the progress roadblock is the claim of overcorrection. Overcorrection is the assumption that feminism will guilt society into creating another system of unfairness, one which will steal from the industrious and deserving rich (men) to give to the feckless poor (women). Ironically, implicit in this response is the concession that a correction does need to be made. The system is so skewed to one party that if there is an opening for change there is a risk of a deluge.

'Has feminism gone too far?' is now a fixture in popular discourse. In 2018, a Sky poll on the question showed that 67 per cent of Britons thought feminism had gone too far or should not go any further. It's a point that has (very much like 'progress') been present at every stage of the history of gender activism. It seems that no matter how much or how little feminism achieves, there will always be someone poised to ask if things aren't already going too far. It is less about what is achieved and more about the perception. Feminism has been going too far from the very moment the first woman asked for a basic right that a man had been afforded by birth.

The question has not even been reframed over the decades, it hangs crude and unrefined by events or changes in popular culture, rebuking gender activism, scaling back ambition and stigmatising progress. The question alone and its persistence reflects the low point we are always starting from, the suspicion of gender equality as a gateway for something else, something sinister, something that will disturb the natural order.

In a 1995 PBS episode of *Thin Tank* entitled (you guessed it) 'Has Feminism Gone Too Far?', two feminist writers made the argument that feminism, or at least what they perceived to be the wrong type of feminism, has gone too far. They make the distinction between their school of equity feminism (that which seeks technical equality for women in civil, legal and professional matters) and the 'too far' school of 'gender feminism' (which aims to eliminate gender roles altogether). The interview is more than twenty years old but could have been aired today, so much does it chime with contemporary themes; accusations of ingratitude for how good things already are, trivialising of complaint as indulgence, down even to campus moral outrages and the pathetic victim culture of students. One of the guests, Christina Sommers, an academic who wrote a book called *Who Stole Feminism?*, says:

'No women have ever had more opportunities, more freedom, and more equality than contemporary American women. And at that moment the movement becomes more bitter and more angry. Why are they so angry?' She then went on to say that feminism had become 'a kind of totalitarianism. Many young women on campuses combine two very dangerous things: moral fervour and misinformation. On the campuses they're fed a kind of catechism of oppression.'

Change is not constant, but resistance to it is. The vitriol expressed by Sommers and her co-guest Camille Paglia, also an academic and writer, described as being the 'spokeswomen for the anti-feminist backlash', towards their generation's cohort of feminist activists ages very well. Here they speak about Anita Hill, an attorney who brought a non-physical sexual harassment case against the Supreme Court nominee Clarence Thomas. She lost the case.

Ms Paglia boasted that 'I was the only leading feminist that went out against Anita Hill. I think that that whole case was a pile of crap. I think it was absurd. First of all, again, totalitarian regime, okay, is where 10 years after the fact you're nominated now for a top position in your country and you are being asked to reconstruct lunch conversations that you had with someone who never uttered a peep. Okay? This is to Anita Hill: "All right, when he started to talk again about this [sic] pornographic films at lunch in the government cafeteria, what did you do?" "I tried to change the subject." Excuse me! I mean, that is ridiculous. I mean, so many of these cases . . .'

Sommers chimes in: 'He never touched her.'

'He never touched her. Okay?' Paglia seethes, 'That was such a trumped-up case by the feminist establishment. Good men say that this will create an imbalance.'

If this shocks you now, it likely would not have done so at the time.

The interview can be quoted in its entirety for its revealing insights into the evergreen tropes used against women. Harping on about not 'rape-rape' sexual harassment they say, teaches a lack of agency because it puts all the blame on men for their transgressions, be they verbal or physical, and not on women for failing to enforce boundaries. Male transgression is just a matter of bad wiring – they simply weren't told often enough that what they were doing is bad. This is a serious misreading of how male entitlement works and how often boundary-setting not only fails to discourage offensive behaviour, but inflames it. In a US publication, 'When Men Murder Women – An Analysis of 2015 Homicide Data', it was determined that 68 per cent of women murdered by intimate partners or ex-partners were targeted for a rejection or a challenge.

Another ancient theme is that moral frenzy is encroaching upon justice and tainting bewildered good men. Due process is at risk because once a woman makes an accusation, a man is assumed guilty. This is a dogged belief that is indifferent to two realities: low conviction rates of men accused of sexual assault; and lack of social censure of men convicted of sexual assault. Neither of these suggest a society in a hurry to lock men up or shun them for sexual offences. A study by the University of Chicago found that in the US, Australia, Canada, England, Wales and Scotland, only 7 per cent of cases resulted in a conviction for the original offence charged – and only 13 per cent led to a conviction of any sexual offence, despite there being a rise in reporting of such crimes. The main reason cited for this was attrition, the cases just lost steam before they came to court because women were intimidated, were not given enough support, or were legally left exposed by corroboration burdens that render victim statements alone (for a crime that usually occurs in private) insufficient. Due process for men is healthy and thriving.

Social censure seems also to not have been overly

aggressive if one takes into consideration how powerful men such as film director Roman Polanski are still celebrated, despite the fact that a charge of sexual assault of a 13-year-old girl in the United States still has not been prosecuted because Polanski fled the country. Professionally, there are other high-profile cases where moral fervour would be expected to take over, but has not. At the height of the #MeToo outpouring of pent-up accusations, Glenn Thrush, a senior White House correspondent at the *New York Times*, was accused of making unwelcome passes at female colleagues in a previous role and then, when rejected, taking a playground revenge by making up details of sexual encounters to his male colleagues that cast him in a desirable, flattering light at the expense of the women who spurned him. After a careful investigation the newspaper decided that he had behaved in a way that made his female colleagues feel professionally compromised. He was censured but not fired. If lack of 'due process' means that we are beginning to redefine inappropriate sexual behaviour outside of the brutally coercive (such as that which makes women feel professionally insecure because they must continuously have to rebuff male advances), this is not failing men, it is having a long overdue discourse.

The overcorrection argument works to trivialise women's grievances, either by disbelieving them or disrespecting them because they're pathetic. It paints women as both a sort of knowing lobby and a wretched helpless class of tattletales who cannot handle their business. Women are somehow both canny, steely agents of a grievance industry, secretly handshaking as they step into the vista of flashing camera shutters on their way to smear your man and also limp, passive and suffering due to their learnt victimhood. They are either manipulative or inviting of assault by not being assertive enough.

Discomfort with any corrective measures, or even the suggestion of such, is nourished by the illusion of meritocracy, the belief that people's chances in life are influenced only by their ability and work ethic, rather than gender, class, race or sexual orientation. A strident feminism threatens this pristine system by overcorrecting to the benefit of the disadvantaged (the author Lionel Shriver disparagingly calls this a process of 'privileging the disadvantaged'). But the assumption that everyone has the same starting points in life, as well as equal opportunities on the way, is one that is easily disproved by how income and opportunities are limited or boosted by one's class and identity profile. It follows then that the explanation for any disparity between men and women, any gender gap, must be down either to sociobiological determinism (biology as destiny) or the failure of meritocracy. There are only ever these two positions to explain away the difference. Either women are actually supposed to have different jobs that pay less, depressing their numbers in the ranks of decision makers, or meritocracy has failed. Either men dominate professionally because they are just built that way, or women's performance is being artifically depressed. So which is it?

So if one rejects the first explanation as obviously regressive, then how can meritocracy keep reproducing the same patterns if there was no tilt, no finger on the scales? Either men are inherently superior and/or distinctly qualified to take on senior professional roles, or meritocracy in an absolute form does not exist.

In that light, clinging to meritocracy (by both men and women) can be interpreted less as a commitment to ensuring that all are compensated commensurately for their effort, but as a protection of the inherent natural advantages that an unregulated market meritocracy affords those who have a head start by virtue of their class, gender and race. There is a natural synergy here between those who believe in biology as destiny and those who believe in a neoliberalism which holds that individual autonomy free of state intervention is the best way to achieve social harmony. They both posit that at heart, the law of the jungle and the brutal order that it establishes is the most efficient way of maintaining order and progress. Anything else is suboptimal.

An internal company memo entitled 'Google's Ideological Echo Chamber', written by then Google employee James Damore in 2017, summarises the overlap of these two views neatly. His 3,000-word text expands on his belief that 'differences in distributions of traits between men and women may in part explain why we don't have 50 per cent representation of women in tech and leadership' and that 'discrimination to reach equal representation is unfair, divisive, and bad for business'. Damore's memo is a list of all the ways society has inculcated itself against change with regard to gender equality. What is most striking about the memo is that the main premise on which his argument stands, that diversity measures are bad for business, is not proved nor is there much effort to do so. The focus is on the climate at Google, one of the more progressive companies in tech, and how it makes people 'feel' about the views that they hold. It is merely the climate to which he is objecting, rather than specific instances where a far left ideologically orthodox liberal company closed ranks against a white man for saying the truth. This is a microcosm of how, when small changes are introduced in order to encourage those from different backgrounds up the ladder, this is seen as inefficient, a race to the bottom.

Believing in meritocracy is also a way of owning one's success as something attributable to one's good qualities, rather than accident of birth. *Harvard Business Review* calls this 'advantage blindness' whereby relatively powerful people become unable to see the impact of their behaviour on those less privileged, and also unable to acknowledge the extent of their own privilege, as it is the norm. This advantage blindness manifests itself in refusing to acknowledge the playing field is not level (meritocracy), focusing on one's own disadvantages (lack of empathy, invoking progress) and claiming that inequality is justified by the innate superiority of some groups over others (social-biological determinism). The entire argument complex for the myth of gender equality.

The research found that many senior leaders were uncomfortable with the idea of being advantaged. The researchers interviewed David, 'a senior executive who recognizes both having benefited from unfair advantages and the injustice of bias. He's tall, middle-aged, well-educated, heterosexual, able-bodied, white, and male — and these qualities provide David with unearned advantages that he intellectually knows he has, but that in practice he barely notices. He tells us he feels an underlying sense of guilt. He wants to feel that his successes in life are down to his abilities and hard work, not unfair advantage. "I feel like a child who discovers that people have been letting him win a game all along," he says. "How can I feel good about myself succeeding if the game was never fair?"

This belief in the 'fairness' of the game can also explain why women in professions that are highly skewed towards male employment tend to resist efforts to introduce gender representation, out of a concern that it might look like they are there out of tokenism rather than ability. In 2018, research published in *Work and Occupations* in the fields of engineering and STEM found that women on those career paths frequently rejected both feminism and the idea of gender inequality. It concluded that women's embrace of the (false) belief that engineering is wholly meritocratic reduces the impetus for change. The non-meritocratic nature of these careers is evident in their own personal experiences, but the women surveyed do not use their own personal experiences as a tool to critique or revise the mistaken ideology of meritocracy.

Women in such jobs have been exposed in high doses to the belief that an artificially introduced diversity implies a drop in quality. This both instils in those women a sense of exceptional achievement (they were the ones who made it on merit alone) and also makes them less likely to recognise any negative experiences relating to their gender. When discussing the concept of the women's bargain with Wesleyan University associate professor Amy Butcher, she told me that one of the trade-offs she felt she had to make in the past was to be more aggressive, that it was necessary to secure the same benefits that were afforded to her male colleagues without the same degree of lobbying. In reward, she was told by one of her colleagues that he liked her because 'she acted like a man'. At the time, when she was rising through the ranks of academia, she took it as the highest compliment. Being one of a handful of women in a heavily male-dominated profession is subliminally to receive that 'compliment' every day.

But the perceived diversity–quality trade-off is not based on empirical evidence. In fact, one of the authors of the report, Professor Brian Rubineau, told me: 'the experimental evidence for the effects of increasing diversity is voluminous and growing. For every study that finds increasing diversity results in performance declines, there are multiple other studies that find increasing diversity has no negative performance effects, and not uncommonly, significant performance benefits.'

Assuming that the mere admission of a woman into a certain profession ends her competitive disadvantage is mistaking 'access' for 'arrival'; it does not take into account all the myriad ways that an individual woman is undermined, and how they stretch into a lattice that becomes a glass ceiling. It is what journalist Lucinda Franks calls 'gender degradation' and the psychologist Virginia Valian calls 'the accumulation of disadvantage'. Franks, the first woman to win the Pulitzer Prize for national reporting, reappraised her experience in the light of the #MeToo movement, saying: 'we, the earliest female newswomen, were tough, ambitious, even cocky about our talent, but over the years, our self-confidence was often irreparably harmed. Our generation might have been smart, but there was much we just didn't get. Grateful to win a place in the hierarchy of power, we didn't understand the ways that gender degradation still shaped our work lives.'

Gratitude is a common theme when women of older generations speak of their professional success. Not only did they trade their respect for a shot at a career, they were grateful for it.

The McGill researchers also identified a similar pattern to that isolated in Saudi Arabia, one by which education, even at the highest levels, can act as a tool of perpetuation. They concluded 'that engineering education successfully turns potential critics into agents of cultural reproduction'. The research contributed to 'ongoing debates concerning diversity in STEM professions by showing how professional culture can contribute to more general patterns of token behaviour – thus identifying mechanisms of cultural reproduction that thwart institutional change'.

These mechanisms of cultural reproduction make agents out of allies. The three arguments, complementarity, progress and meritocracy, continue to take hold because those who would be their natural opponents remain trapped in their own binaries. This includes those other allies who somehow never seem to come through – the 'good men'.

The good men

The myth of gender equality isn't just propped up by cartoonish bad men who hoard the spoils of patriarchy. It's held dearly by the 'good' men as well. The woke brothers, the 'I'm on your side' dudes, the 'I'm a father to daughters and I'm appalled' dads. This man doesn't quite exist in pure ally form, he is an apparition summoned to stall a deeper appraisal of gender dynamics by classifying men into good and bad. They are either alleyway rapists or they are well-meaning flirts – there is nothing in between.

But what is a 'good man'? Is it Eric Schneiderman, a former New York attorney general, a Democrat and a man who has raised his voice against sexual misconduct and who has been accused by four women of physical violence and abuse? Or is it Mike Pence, the monogamous, religious vice president, who will not be alone in a room with a woman other than his wife, but who supports the Trump administration's dismantling of Obama-era gender discrimination laws? There is no obvious partition between good and bad men, and certainly none that can be traced along ideological, religious or political lines.

The list of high-profile sexual abuse accusations continues to grow and it is populated equally by liberals and conservatives. From Charlie Rose and Matt Lauer to Roger Ailes and Bill O'Reilly, misogyny is secular and has no politics, ideology or religion. It is why we constantly fail to make the connection between male violence and any cultural or social norms that give men a sense of entitlement over women and their sexual compliance, the 'honour killings' that are so easily identifiable in other cultures. When a man 'snaps', and murders his partner and/or his children, it is seen as an unfortunate individual malfunction. A 2015 Birmingham University study, which compared reporting on domestic violence in the *Guardian* and the *Sun*, found that even though the two UK papers were different in their political orientation and target audience, they both were guilty of reporting crime by way of its trigger – that is – the female victim.

'Unless the man is framed as a "monster",' the report found, 'the focus is on the woman (either leaving or staying) rather than the perpetrator. There are some interesting exceptions to this, for example, where the woman is the perpetrator of the violence, she is the main focus of the article. Another exception is when the domestic violence perpetrator is a well-known person, as in much of the articles on celebrities – in these articles there is relatively little attention for their victim.'

The study also found that many articles mention issues that 'can be seen to reduce the blame of the male perpetrator – for example, alcohol, football results, depression, lack of employment or the women's behaviour'. It also cited articles which suggested that jury prejudice is one reason why so few men are convicted for rape and domestic violence, due to the belief that there may be some aspect of female culpability. In both the *Guardian* and the *Sun*, reporters made the point that many abusers have been maltreated in their childhood. Raising such issues suggests that they 'explain' why men are violent towards their partners, and infer that there's no further need to search for the reasons behind that violence or what can be done to prevent it. Female victims of male violence are, largely, presented as those who have been punished for failing to keep up their part of the women's bargain – in this instance, behaving or dressing in ways provocative to men. An entire online subculture has been built on the notion of 'involuntary celibacy', the inability to find a romantic partner despite desiring one. Incels (involuntary celibates) blame women for rejecting them and radicalising them to seek revenge through violence. At least four proven cases of murder in North America have referenced involuntary celibacy as a motivation or referenced incel culture, including the February 2018 Marjory Stoneman Douglas High School shootings in Florida. But the ensuing analysis is still about the 'redistribution of sex', rather than the entitlement to it.

Misogyny has no track record and is easily divisible from the rest of a man's behaviour. The 'good men' trope also fails to account for all the ways change is resisted by men who would never physically or sexually abuse a woman, men who are au fait with the boundaries of verbal transgression and would recognise even coercive control as a form of abuse. In her book *Why So Slow*, Virginia Valian found that while men can embrace the need for efforts that lead to fairness, such as equal pay, they have a much harder time with their own loss of centrality. To these men, the end of the patriarchy *is* actually the end of the world.

In her essay 'MIA: The Liberal Men We Love', Professor Amy Butcher writes about the wall erected by the good men. In a post-Trump world, she observes how men have begun to appear in a different light to their female partners, friends

and siblings who assumed they were on the right side of
the sexism debate. She writes a dispatch from the world
of liberal women bewildered by men 'previously, pleasantly,
progressive – rising up with unprecedented hostility, anger,
abandon, and resentment'. The reason for their transformation is female anger at Trump's election, his normalisation
of sexual assault and verbal degradation of women. To the
men it was too much, too strident, too shrill. It was just
'locker room talk'. The pushback began as a minimisation
of Trump's language and alleged sexual transgressions and
developed into something altogether more sinister.

'These are, make no mistake, men who wholly sought us
for our strength, our independence and education. The jobs
we held or coveted. The degrees in our name. Our passions
and pursuits and our can-do, want-it-all attitudes. They
work as medical researchers or in the arts, in teaching or
social work,' she writes. 'They queue up the *Saturday Night
Live* skits that humiliate Trump, to consume with our coffee
on Sunday mornings, but find it unpalatable and unpleasant that our resentment and our fears linger long into the
workweek.' She reported on men who burnt their wives'
Women's March and Hillary Clinton paraphernalia. Men
who left their partners because they could no longer tolerate
their anger. Men who scolded their wives for teaching their
daughters bad manners.

To some men, a woman's right to be a victim can be a
scary thing because it implies that the next stage is retri-
bution and, then simply, change. In a 1980 paper entitled
'Why Men Resist', sociologist William J. Goode ascribed
their behaviour to the natural self-preservation instinct of
any dominant group.

'Men view even small losses of deference, advantages, or
opportunities as large threats and losses,' he writes. 'Their

own gains, or their maintenance of old advantages, are not noticed as much. Since any given cohort of men knows they did not create the system that gives them their advantages, they reject any charges that they conspired to dominate women'.

If a man believes that 81 per cent of women have experienced sexual harassment since their teenage years, then it means he must examine his own behaviour and that of his male friends and colleagues. He must conduct an exercise of self-reflection on the part of his gender and take responsibility for changing a system he had no hand in creating. This is uncomfortable. And it is a lot of work to do for no material or immediate gain.

So, a woman's victimhood is rejected. Ironically, this is where denial of agency happens. It takes agency to be a victim; it takes grit, determination, confidence and honesty to stop running away from pain and perceived humiliation, to assert that you have been compromised professionally or physically for being a woman and reject the blame for that. Gritting teeth and moving on is not displaying agency.

And the good men who fail to acknowledge a woman's right to anger? Their instincts are right. They know that once a violation is validated, it paves the way for anger, for redress and for expanding the definition of a woman's right. It is a gateway to erosion of male equity. Butcher likens the sense of mission creep to a spider. It is: 'fast and without reproach. First the problem is on the porch. Then it is climbing up your bedpost. Look as it spins a web around your morning and then your month and then your marriage. Look—and please keep looking—as it grips and continues gripping everything you once held dear inside his web.'

These men, warily seeing the spider approach, will not hesitate to use the artificial division between good and bad men to preserve their status and avoid criticism by claiming that none of this is their doing because you know what, they're the good guy. So they recuse themselves from the discourse because women are just so angry all the time and it's not their fault. Call it waving the good guy card.

But it is not always about fear of status loss, it is often because 'good' men struggle with the perception of systemic bias, and even when they do not, they struggle with the notion that systemic bias can be corrected without creating a world that is unjust to men. They suffer from privilege blindness. This is not a quality that is unique to men as male, but to all who have enjoyed privilege while confusing it with fairness. There is something particularly elusive about the acknowledgement of female victimisation. It is easy to see and empathise with the troubles of the poor and disenfranchised. To a lesser extent, it is also relatively easy to acknowledge that there is a higher degree of cruelty and exclusion of immigrants, people of colour, or a specific group such as Muslims. A rational 'good' man can merely survey his own workplace and his nation's political institutions, media and elite and come to the conclusion that there is infrastructural bias against the working class or racial minorities, as so few of them are visible in numbers.

Women, on the other hand, are everywhere. They are not in purdah. They are openly competing with men for places in schools and jobs. They are interviewing men and managing them and giving them a hard time. They are jostling with them in public spaces and queues and swiping their last favourite lunch sandwiches from under their noses. Women's emotional pain is intangible, their physical pain inflicted behind closed doors – their compromised career prospects easily explained away by their childbearing and rearing responsibilities. Good men are capable of acknowledging and empathising with individual relatable pain – that of their daughters, sisters and female friends. But the connection between that and a society-wide issue is harder to make.

The good man is not the one who has sexually harassed his female colleague or hired a man instead of a woman specifically for gender reasons. As far as he is aware, he has never received overt preferential treatment for being a male. Why then must he or his son lose out on a place at school or work because it has been earmarked for a female in order to redress a diffuse gender grievance by generalising it? Why must he pay higher taxes to fund childcare from which women will earn the greatest benefit? Why must he now be more mindful of how he behaves around women in case he comes across as sexually intimidating? Why must he pay reparations for individual crimes that he did not commit?

In the eyes of good men, women have demanded group punishment for individual miscarriages – a collective land grab from the innocent. This unsympathetic position is not evidence that feminism has gone too far and alienated even progressive men, but proof of how much work there is still to do both to make the connection between the personal and the endemic and, in turn, make the case that a system that is unfair to women results in its own injustices to men. The fate of good men and women, too often separated, is intertwined on both a practical and cultural level. Yet the framing of women's rights causes in popular mythology as shrill, entitled and unnatural hides the organic and spon-taneous advantages to men who, on the most basic level, stand to benefit.

In 2015, Pew-funded research in the US revealed that fathers were as likely as mothers to say that parenting was extremely important to their identity (57 per cent of men and 58 per of women). It also emerged that around 48 per cent of fathers felt they were not doing enough childcare. Similar research, two years before, found that working fathers were as likely as working mothers to say they preferred to be at home with their children but failed to do so because of financial burdens. These are burdens that women cannot share equally because of compromised career prospects and expensive unsubsidised childcare.

Despite this obvious weight that men wish they could share with women, feminism is perpetually presented as misandry, further alienating the 'good men'. This is one of the evergreen responses to calls for female empowerment, along with the claim that feminism is some sort of grievance gravy train. But it has been given new life with a politicisation of feminism as part of a reassertion of hierarchical patriarchal order. In early 2018, a *Washington Post* survey by Ishaan Tharoor traced the centring of anti-feminist views in political rhetoric in Turkey, the United States, Russia and the Philippines. There was a pattern: 'right-wing governments all wielding anti-feminism as a political cudgel. The enduring reality of the moment is that it remains a profoundly effective tactic.'

Women against women

Anti-feminism is not only effective with men. Another barrier to gender equality is erected – by women themselves. The gender equality myth is part sustained by a hierarchy that pits women against each other in what is known as 'horizontal hostility', where the inaccessibility of the real oppressing force turns the victims on to the closest targets of their frustration – each other.

The high percentage of white women who voted for Trump and the Republican senatorial candidate Roy

Moore, despite the allegations of sexual misconduct levelled at both men, cannot merely be explained through the lens of political partisanship. It is a manifestation of systemic oppression. In all societies in which women are oppressed, they are acculturated to participate in that oppression. For the women in Saudi Arabia to emerge from an educational system that sets them up for second-class citizenship, the work they have to do to fight against it involves not only defying their families and the authorities, but undoing a lifetime of wiring. Give women privilege over another group and the impulse to be complicit in their own oppression will be even stronger because they can reach for the comfort of relative status.

In the influential book *The Second Sex*, this process of acculturation and participation in one's own oppression is laid out by Simone de Beauvoir. Women's oppression differs from other such forms insofar as there appears to be no historical starting point for it. There is no solidarity of economic interest, or even any 'social location' for this oppressed group. Women are subjugated, but remain separated from each other, often having more in common with men of their social class than they do with other women from different classes.

De Beauvoir uses the concepts of 'immanence' and 'transcendence'. Immanence is stagnation within a situation, while transcendence is reaching out into the future, through projects that open up freedom. Insofar as they work on meaningful projects that reach into the future, men occupy the sphere of transcendence, while women's oppression relegates them to the sphere of immanence, until they may no longer be aware that they have free choice.

This is the philosophical underpinning to counter-intuitive behaviour by women that not only harms other women, but themselves and their own loved ones. It may surprise you to know that in my Sudanese family, it is the women who are the strongest advocates for female genital mutilation, so invested are they in maintaining a system where a woman's sexual pleasure is dangerous. Having gone through FGM themselves, they believe that they have been spared the temptations of sex and thus maintained their virginity and reputations. They married well and had children. They want the same for their daughters.

In *Down Girl: The Logic of Misogyny*, Kate Manne expands on how this solidarity with men's interests, rather than each other's and by extension, their own, explains why white women voted for Trump over Clinton. In one 2007 New York University study, 'Motivated to Penalize: Women's Strategic Rejection of Successful Women', this premise is further refined. The study concluded that female subordination to men results in a sort of self-loathing brought into relief by successful, powerful women, who then become objects of scorn. It also found that women's choices politically have a more 'ego protective' function than those of men, and so they align themselves with men, the dominant group, as a self-preservation strategy.

Kate Manne's reading of the study concluded that: 'it is wrong but natural to protect oneself from the prospect of threatening others who challenge one's extant sense that one couldn't have been the president (say), notwithstanding one's best efforts. A way to do this is to hold that these women are different and in some way inferior or objectionable or otherwise suspect. They are, say, ruthless, callous, or uncaring. Or their success makes them witches; their power is black magic.'

In an extensive investigation into the women of the US alt-right (the movement's 'Valkyries'), *Harper's Magazine* also

uncovered a fixation on complementarity. Just like my father
with his analogy of bowls and axes, these women believe
that the sexes are different but not unequal. Women are not
weak, they are *complementary*. It was a logical contortion
that was necessary for the Valkyries if they were to rational-
ise alignment with a movement so hostile to their freedom.
It is this fear that grievance is victimhood, is lack of agency,
that drives a wedge between women across the political
divide. Sometimes it is generational, where older women
resist the younger generation's activism because it brings
into question their own life choices. To them, the younger
generation's gender activism is frivolous, indulgent and precious, focusing on the superficial rather than the structural
and on the fripperies of bourgeois feminism. This impres-
sion is strengthened by the commodification of 'girl power'
and the co-option of feminism into a capitalist popular culture, flogging jumpers and jewellery with feminist slogans
emblazoned on them. This marketplace feminism – which
turns gender activism into a lifestyle bauble, a sort of glossy
magazine feature – can be alienating. And the rift has been
deepened by social media and what could be seen as the
trivialising of feminist causes, collapsing them into the an-
ecdotal and into 'everyday sexism'. The Australian feminist
Germaine Greer is emblematic of this older generation of
feminists who have much scorn for a new breed of fourth
wave pop-feminism and how 'simply coughing up outrage
into a blog will get us nowhere'. Marketplace feminism is
also less threatening and more palatable to men. It provides
the 'woke' among them, the extremely self-identifying 'feminists' on social media, with basic tokens of feminist support
that they can then wave in women's faces as evidence of
their virtue, while not making a dent in any systemic structures. It hands them the good guy card.

There are also those women who are put off by feminism as misandry propaganda. Those who do not see the men in their lives as villains and link standing by feminist causes as allying with other women they do not know against men they do. They are the female analogues of the good men, who cannot move beyond the individual and connect the dots to the structural. And just as the good men except themselves from the whole and see that as the end of the matter, so do ostensibly liberal progressive women distance themselves from what they consider to be whiny, weak female victim culture. As if somehow if we all just collectively kicked men in the groin when they groped us, sexual harassment would be vanquished. As if somehow if we all decisively asked for pay rises, the gender gap would close. Or as if the impact of male-on-female unpleasantness can be minimised if women just chose to interpret it in a different way. This thinking, the writer Moira Donegan explains:

> partakes in a long moral tradition – one that's highly compatible with capitalism – in which personal responsibility, independence, and willingness to withstand hardship are revered as particularly valuable virtues. It's an ethos of pulling yourself up by your own bootstraps – from poverty into prosperity, or, in the anti-MeToo feminists' logic, from 'feminine' victimhood into 'masculine' strength. They believe that the pervasiveness of sexual harassment suggests that it is inevitable, and that the best response is not anger, but resolve. Theirs is a feminism that posits that individual women have the power to make choices to diminish the negative impact of sexism, and to endure any sexist unpleasantness that can't be avoided – if only they have the grit to handle it.

This 'grit' feminism focuses for example on those incidents or stories where women have expressed frustration with unpleasant sexual encounters in terms that take liberties with the definition of sexual assault. *New York Times* opinion writer Bari Weiss, when appraising #MeToo, chose to centre it on a reported sexual encounter between an anonymous woman and the actor Aziz Ansari, one during which his date alleges he was overly insistent and did not pick up on her cues. Bari generalises it to become all that is wrong with consent culture, one that returns women to 'smelling salts' and the 'fainting couch'.

This is a familiar manoeuvre – the set up. To suggest that incidents where women have been too passive or not assertive enough in the face of the aggressiveness of men during sexualised encounters proves that sexual assault is confected is like suggesting that the UK has levelled the professional playing field for women because it has had two female prime ministers. There are always exceptions to the rule. Myth-making draws its lifeblood from making rules out of exceptions.

A tell-tale sign of a myth is how deeply its tentacles stretch throughout history, how often its stories of resistance to change are rehashed and retooled. The myth of gender equality has deployed the critique of contemporary 'victim culture' at least since the early 1990s, when it was directed at 'victim feminism'. The truth is that women's responses to a profound but also diffuse problem cannot always be perfectly calibrated. But the tools of mythology focus on those responses that discredit the cause.

A new orthodoxy

The women's bargain is not just a quotidian feature of a woman's life. It is a fundamental structural fault that is hardwired into the patriarchy. What is required is, indeed, a new orthodoxy. What is required is, yes, even more policing of cultures that do not stigmatise bad male behaviour. What is required is, in fact, narrowing down consent to its most unequivocal. These are not radical notions. The fear that they are radical has been instilled by all the arguments that come together to drain the present situation of its urgency.

This urgency is underscored by a resurgence in biological determinism and a backlash against attempts to widen the definition of gender jeopardy to include the wielding of male sexual power against subordinate women. But I started with the myth of gender equality because out of all the pervasive complacencies, it is the one that has, at the time of writing in 2019, despite a cultural backlash, witnessed a moment where reality caught up. It was brief. But action was taken to seek protection and redress for women who had been sexually compromised in the workplace by powerful men. The move towards justice happened slowly and cumulatively, via the compounded effort of women who refused to believe that the sanctity of their bodies should be traded for their professional success, those who refused to be grateful and those who did not accept the stale logic of biology.

CHAPTER 2

The myth of a political correctness crisis

'The phrase "politically correct", like a will o' the wisp on the murky path to history, has glimmered and vanished again as successive movements for political change have stumbled across uncertain terrain. Its erratic appearance has always brought consternation as well as relief, resistance as well as consent. Like a recurring refrain in a song, or an incantatory line in a poem, its meaning changes each time it happens.'

Ruth Perry

Following a series of freedom of information requests, the *Independent* newspaper revealed in 2018 that racist incidents at UK universities had gone up by 60 per cent in two years. According to student body heads, this is the tip of the iceberg as most of the reported incidents only receive attention when they are circulated on social media. Ayo Olatunji, black and minority ethnic students' officer for University College London, told the *Guardian* in 2018: 'We would hear about a case a day in the media if everything that happened went online.' The situation became so dire that the Equality and Human Rights Commission, a public body in England and Wales which promotes and enforces equality and non-discrimination laws in the UK, launched an official inquiry into what seemed to be an epidemic of race or sexism related incidents. In one case, a student from Nottingham Trent University chanted 'We hate the blacks'. He said it was just 'banter' between friends. This is not a crisis that receives much attention, that is reserved for another, largely imaginary one – that of a political correctness allegedly rendering everyone hesitant to express views that could be misconstrued as prejudiced.

Take the case of Lola Olufemi. All she and her fellow Cambridge students wanted to do was introduce some new writers into their syllabus. In June 2017, they wrote an open letter to the post-colonial literature faculty, requesting that non-white authors be added to the curriculum. Four months later, after precisely zero complaints from fellow students or members of the faculty, who were considering its response, the *Telegraph* newspaper published Lola's picture on its front page with the headline 'STUDENT FORCES CAMBRIDGE TO DROP WHITE AUTHORS'.

This was a lie. Not only had Cambridge not dropped any white authors, the open letter did not make any such request in the first place. A day after the story ran, the paper issued an apology in small print. But the damage was done. The frame was frozen. Other headlines included 'FEMINIST KILLJOY BEHIND THE CAMPAIGN'. The backlash was violent. Reputable opinion makers weighed into the controversy, speaking witheringly about the new orthodoxy encroaching upon Britain's universities. Lola was subjected to a volley of abuse, as were academics who supported her. When interviewed by the BBC, she pointed out the danger of the media's fabrication and how it extends far beyond her own victimisation.

'They get to create a narrative about me that is a matter of public record, the [*Telegraph*] clarification is tiny. How many people will see it? How many people will take it seriously? It's more about who gets to create the narrative about who I am and the work that I do and what I stand for.'

The very reasonable recommendations, made by the group of which she was the media-appointed emblem, were not only misrepresented, lies about them were quite deliberately made up. A very specific academic (and ongoing) discussion about post-colonial literature, which had been proceeding in a sophisticated and well-intentioned manner between the students and university staff, had been successfully repackaged and introduced into the public discourse as another exhibit in the case against political correctness. Two images were powerfully juxtaposed – the hallowed sacred ground of Cambridge University in all its history, wisdom and contribution to humankind, and a black arriviste, with a foreign name and a foreign complexion, here to trample all over what was good and rooted. It was clear why the media chose Lola as the figurehead. She exemplified entitlement based on nothing more than her race and gender, indulged by a liberal establishment cowed into ceding space for fear of offence.

When I spoke to Lola in the summer of 2018, she was still incandescent with the injustice of how the media framed the story. 'For me,' she said 'the most frustrating thing was just being called upon to address the lies as if they were legitimate. It calls people to defend themselves and this immediately signals to people that implicitly this [allegation] is right. You don't even get to address the ideas you were suggesting because you're just denying. In the letter we specifically said that this isn't a call to replace white men but place them in their post-colonial contexts'. The most insidious element of the political correctness angle of the story, she said, was that 'it obscured things that were happening on the ground'.

The myth of a political correctness that is sacrificing free thought for the uniformity of oversensitivity to gender, race and sexual orientation is the oldest and most pedigreed of contemporary political myths, taking on the 'political correctness' terminology in the mid-twentieth century. The purpose of this myth is to undermine efforts for change by presenting them as sabotage, as attacks on a society that is fundamentally good and not in need of reform. If Lola and her fellow students feel that their syllabus needs updating because something as innocent as the passage of time has rendered it in need of a refresh, this stab at reform is presented as vandalism.

In the US, similar efforts receive the same response. One conservative commentator, Roger Kimball, identified the problem as university administrators 'falling over themselves in their rush to replace the "white Western" curriculum of traditional humanistic studies with a smorgasbord of courses designed to appeal to various ethnic and radical sensitivities'.

Like all good and effective myths, the political correctness crisis is a moral panic that appears to be a response to a current and aggressive assault on a variety of shibboleths, but is in fact a rehashing of themes that are decades old. The themes all frame a challenge of male, white and heteronormative power as a subversion of the natural order of things. (Later, in Chapter 4, we examine how default identities absolve themselves from having identity-based agendas.) While researching this chapter, I was astonished to discover how far back the leveraging of political correctness against progressive causes stretched and how identical the tools of this assault were in any given example. It is doubly astonishing that the myth was allowed to develop in plain sight. Its objectives were not very well-hidden, and we have had years to contend with the sleight of hand. The fact that today, a young woman like Lola can be savaged by the media and the public under the banner of political correctness, demonstrates both the mainstreaming of the myth and the failure in challenging it.

The origin of the term political correctness is benign. In the US Supreme Court in the late eighteenth century, it implied a social convention of language, of elite propriety in expression both for accuracy and good manners. What started as protocol became a cudgel with which to beat back basic advances towards equality.

The term lay dormant, evolving yet relatively uncontested until the post-civil rights era in the United States. Up to that point, it was deployed by the right and the left, both using it to describe what was considered to be the 'correct' political position, which made it a term open to interpretation. Anti-Vietnam riots, for example, were to the Republicans politically incorrect. On the left, supporting and upholding civil rights legislation was the politically correct position to hold. By the 1980s, the term was beginning to become perverted and take on the shape familiar today – a right-wing labelling of the left as totalitarian in its patrolling of language, thought and by extension ideology. In its current form, the political correctness crisis myth has leapfrogged from the right to the mainstream.

As far back as 1991, the right in the United States had already elevated the concern of political correctness as a crisis of orthodoxy in thought, to the presidency. In a commencement speech at the University of Michigan, then president George H.W. Bush declared: 'the notion of political correctness has ignited controversy across the land. And although the movement arises from the laudable desire to sweep away the debris of racism and sexism and hatred, it replaces old prejudice with new ones.'

These 'new' prejudices, those that flip the hierarchy in favour of women, people of colour and those who are 'other' in general, are in fact old and not prejudices at all. They are merely attempts at forging a new social order, one which cannot coexist with the old, with all its inbuilt inequalities. One of the difficulties of addressing political correctness concerns is that its definition has been hijacked by those who now use the term to mean anything they want, as long as it denotes something negative. For the purposes of this chapter, political correctness, or being 'PC', is defined as the attempt (just the attempt) to create a framework of equality of treatment, of opportunity and of respect to all, to challenge 'default settings'. Pejoratively, it is used by those who have a vested interest in maintaining a system that needs reform, while refusing to acknowledge that it does not serve everyone well. According to the journalist Amanda Taub, writing in *Vox* in 2016, 'political correctness is a catch-all term we apply to people who ask for more sensitivity to a particular cause than we are willing to give – a way to dismiss issues as frivolous in order to justify ignoring them'.

The moment these requests for sensitivity are made, they are, according to the establishment, immediately too much. Whether it was the civil rights movement in the United States in the 1960s or the request that new non-white authors be included in British university syllabuses in 2018, the most tentative of steps towards redressing imbalance are always seen as going over the top. It is always the way with myths, the fear of the pendulum swinging too far the other way, towards a matriarchy that persecutes men, towards a tyranny of people of colour over white people, towards gay over straight, immigrant over native. Dominant groups have only maintained their power via oppression, so cannot countenance a world where more rights for others just means more equality, and not a new system of oppression.

George H.W Bush's 'new' prejudices are, to their critics, always shifting and expanding. They have come to encompass everything from demanding that people be polite in their speech and manner towards others, to accommodating the sensitivities and needs of those for whom mainstream society had not been designed to cater. The myth – that there is such a thing as 'going too far' – has displayed remarkable velocity, morphing from an esoteric guide to manners, to an accusation of dishonesty and even conspiracy. Its danger is in not only creating resistance to change, but in fortifying the status quo against change.

The PC myth has a lifecycle that starts with *grievance* creation, moves on to *fabrication* and ends in *diversion*. First, it feeds an imaginary injustice, a siege mentality and fosters intolerance. Once this fear of a purge of an old order sets in, once it is mainstreamed, it creates a regressive backlash. Once the backlash becomes widespread enough, it subsumes genuine problems, such as unequal rights for women or ethnic minorities, diverting attention to the phantom 'legitimate concerns' of those who have been convinced that there is an assault on their values, culture, livelihoods and even lives. When that view takes hold, it is sustained by an industry and a political establishment that thrives off feeding false narratives about the goals of political correctness, and fabricating stories to fit that narrative.

Grievance creation – the Trump bump

The role of political correctness as oppressor of thought and behaviour was a pillar of Donald Trump's 2016 US election campaign. His elevation as some sort of truth teller, the embodier of free speech (we will come to that in Chapter 3), breaking free from the shackles of mind control, is a master class in how myths are leveraged in order to maintain power structures or, in some cases, reinstate them.

Research published by the *Journal of Social and Political Psychology* in May 2017 found a strong correlation between a perception of politically correct language orthodoxy and support for Trump. After conducting a poll of his supporters, this belief, rather than ideology as such, was a more reliable predictor of Trump's support.

'At a general level' the report observes, 'evidence suggests that Trump's grandiose rhetorical style was one of the reasons he won the Republican primary. Further and more specifically, polls from the election cycle suggested that people liked his provocative language and that feeling voiceless better predicted Trump support than multiple other variables, some of which include age, race, and attitudes towards Muslims, illegal immigrants, and Hispanics.'

The research further showed the extent of the problem by coming to an interesting conclusion – it was not in fact Trump voters' fault that they had issues with political correctness, what they displayed was a natural reaction to the 'norms of restrictive communication'. This is the deeply buried seed of grievance creation, that managing speech or behaviour, something humans do organically all the time in order for society to function, is somehow unnatural when it comes to PC. The question that needs to be asked is why did Trump voters feel like those norms were so oppressive to them? Who decided that those norms were 'restrictive'? And if indeed these norms are oppressive, what is it that lies beneath, and which we must allow to be expressed if we are to prevent this reportedly inevitable backlash?

It might look something like this. During the first debate of the Republican primaries, Fox News host Megyn Kelly asked Trump how he would answer the charge that he was 'part of the war on women': 'You've called women you don't like "fat pigs," "dogs," "slobs," and "disgusting animals",' Kelly pointed out. 'You once told a contestant on *Celebrity Apprentice* it would be a pretty picture to see her on her knees . . .'

'I think the big problem this country has is being politically correct,' Trump answered, to audience applause. 'I've been challenged by so many people, I don't frankly have time for total political correctness. And to be honest with you, this country doesn't have time either.'

In mocking a man with disabilities to raucous laughter from his crowd, calling Mexican immigrants rapists and sneering at the pain of Gold Star parents grieving for their dead son, Trump was communicating to his voters not simply a liberation from unreasonable 'restrictive norms', but a sense of grievance, of suffocation and victimisation. He was telling them that political correctness was, in fact, a danger to their lives.

'They have put political correctness above common sense, above your safety, and above all else,' Trump goaded after a Muslim gunman killed forty-nine people at a gay nightclub in Orlando, Florida. 'I refuse to be politically correct.'

'Having elevated the powers of PC to mythic status,' wrote academic Moira Weigel, 'the draft-dodging billionaire, son of a slumlord, taunted the parents of a fallen soldier and claimed that his cruelty and malice was, in fact, courage.'

Courage for speaking truths when no one else dared to.

But this 'mythic status' did not come about by accident. There has been a concerted attempt over the past fifty years or so to turn political correctness into a culture war weapon. Unlike other myths that develop in more organic ways, the political correctness myth came to be in a much more deliberate manner. It is a sort of prototype myth, in that it clearly shows how forces come together and marshal resources to fight back against progress.

The beginning can be traced to 1960s' America, during a time when rapid social change had its activist and ideological centre around university campuses.

A nascent movement of students and academics began to question things. The profile of those who traditionally studied and taught at such elite institutions was beginning to change and become less white, middle class, straight and male and so campus politics became restive. Civil rights, the Vietnam War and reproductive rights were all part of a hotbed of issues that exercised students on campuses such as Berkeley on the west coast and Cornell on the east. The American academic Nancy Baker Jones summarised that historical moment: 'The appearance of a critical mass of people representing viewpoints that disagreed significantly with established views was, from the point of view of the right, a dangerous turn of events, representing an incursion of "special interests" on a commonly accepted educational tradition of such long standing that it had come to be considered apolitical, neutral, and universal.'

The opposition to these movements from both the political establishment and the media are eerily familiar. Those campaigning for political equality among the races, the respect of human rights universally and the sanctity of human life outside of the United States were seen as elitist, out of touch, effete snobs who were getting in the way of serious governance. It played (and still plays) very well with the voting public.

In his 1966 campaign for governor of California, Ronald Reagan attacked Berkeley, claiming that 'a small minority of beatniks, radicals, and filthy speech advocates have brought such shame to a great university'. A year later, Nixon attacked university activism as 'elitist' and 'morally relativist'. The year after, presidential nominee George Wallace said on the campaign trail that he was speaking on behalf of the 'workin' folk fed up with bureaucrats in Washington, pointy-headed intellectuals, swaydo intellectual morons tellin' 'em how to live their lives'. These addresses were the progenitors of today's sneers about 'safe spaces', 'trigger warnings' and 'microaggressions'.

Similarly, more recently, in 2017 and 2018, US attorney general Jeff Sessions made two speeches in which he said that colleges were creating a generation of 'sanctimonious, sensitive, supercilious snowflakes' and that campuses were an 'echo chamber of political correctness and homogenous thought, a shelter for fragile egos'. During one of those speeches, the crowd began to chant 'lock her up', in reference to Hillary Clinton – presumably to demonstrate that there were no 'snowflakes' among them.

Sessions's and Trump's predecessors were all saying what Trump said in 2016, they had no time for political correctness, and neither did the country – they just did not have a name for it yet. There is a direct line that runs from these politicians through George H.W. Bush to Donald Trump.

The agitation against some amorphous elitist enemy imposing their ways on 'workin' folk' waxes and wanes according to what sort of consensus conservative forces need to create. When first Gulf War-era George H.W. Bush invoked PC, it was not a coincidence that the last time there was a need to mention 'new prejudices' that were not aligned with the needs of the government of the day, was during the Vietnam War. The undesirable political correctness of the early 1990s was one that would not accept the old way of doing things, where patrician white men with a penchant for foreign wars could count on the jingoism of American exceptionalism to cheer them on. A lack of uniformity breeds dissent, and so it is logical that diversity of thought becomes a threat.

By 2016, in the United States and the United Kingdom, the myth of political correctness had so taken hold that the grievance boil it had been nourishing for years finally burst.

Grievance creation – Brexit: a referendum on PC culture

If the United States' large fault line is race, in the UK it is immigration. The myth of a PC crisis was successful in toxifying an immigration debate that had been gathering momentum since the late 1970s, when Margaret Thatcher stated that British people 'might be rather swamped by people with a different culture' before introducing a tougher immigration act in 1981. It became increasingly fashionable for politicians to declare that immigration was a threat to livelihoods, but that it was verboten to say so because of political correctness. This sense that immigration was never discussed was successfully mainstreamed even though vilification of immigrants in political discourse and their persecution in the legislation of the country was commonplace. In campaigning for Brexit, the Conservative Party and the United Kingdom Independence Party (UKIP) invoked the familiar themes of an out-of-touch elite sacrificing the safety of the country's citizens because of its commitment to a liberal ideology that went weak at the knees at the sight of a grown man pretending to be a child so that he could seek asylum in the country.

What followed was the culmination of years of right-wing politicians and the media telling the British public that Islamic extremism, high immigration, diminishing access to social welfare and the failures of the National Health Service were down to the evils of political correctness. PC created an orthodoxy which had led to the indulgence of Muslims, refugees and fraudulent asylum seekers who did not have legitimate grounds for refuge.

It is an imperfect exercise to try to trace the reasons for the Brexit vote down to a specific source – the referendum posed a binary question, yes or no, to a multifaceted issue that few voters had grappled with in detail and which referendum campaigners had reduced to emotive sound bites. The vote has been linked to nativism, economic frustration, imperialist nostalgia and just plain old racism. All these correlations may be true, but there is a larger ecology to these disparate grievances. The reason the vote exercised so many to reject an institution whose myriad economic, social and cultural benefits they had little knowledge of, is precisely because it was posed as a binary question – it was a referendum on the culture in which the British people wanted to live. Mild to strong discontents, from the personal to the political, could be projected on to the scapegoat of the EU and its liberal supporters in the UK. Even though these discontents could be traced to specific British political and economic failures, from regional marginalisation to the biting effects of Conservative fiscal austerity.

The EU is but a symbol of a political culture that had been successfully smeared by what can broadly be described

as the right, but what is more accurately an establishment
of political and media interests for whom the issue of EU
membership could be leveraged as a convenient culture war
and political tool. The EU represents an imposed freedom
of movement, a stifling economic trade union, enforced
cultural cooperation, human rights collaboration, climate
change prevention legislation and most importantly, a cen-
tralised standardisation of things, be they banana shapes or
the rights afforded to criminals under the European Court
of Justice.

The EU is, as far as the grievance industry – a collection
of politicians, journalists and lobbyists – was concerned,
the epitome of political correctness. This view became so
popular that some began to associate the EU with all sorts
of rights and legislation in the UK that had nothing to do
with Brussels. In a column published in 2018 in the *Telegraph*, Colonel Richard Kemp wrote that 'after Brexit, we
can give Isil [ISIS] terrorists the justice they deserve – and
that means the death penalty'. Punishment by execution
was abolished in Great Britain in 1965, eight years before
the country joined the EU. Yet that did not stop the colonel
from making the point that if Britain wanted to reintroduce
the death penalty it would be prevented from doing so by its
membership in the EU. Even though the country had made
an autonomous decision that predated its membership, it
was still seen as somehow under the EU's control.

According to polling by *Prospect* magazine and YouGov
in 2018, there is a direct correlation between antipathy towards the EU, and perceptions of PC muzzling. By 49 to
39 per cent, those who voted Remain are convinced that
people are free to say what they think, but Leavers believe
– by 'a crushing 60 to 26 margin' – that there are important
things that Britain can't talk about.

This was one of several similarities between the Brexit and Trump campaigns. British MP Michael Gove, when challenged on expert advice that was warning that Brexit would be damaging to Britain's prospects, said: 'I think the people of this country have had enough of experts from organisations with acronyms saying that they know what is best because these people are the same ones who [have] got [things] consistently wrong.'

'Making America great again' was the US version of Brexit's 'taking back control'. Both campaigns heavily employed anti-elite and anti-intellectual rhetoric. There is a reason why that was necessary. In order to properly nurture a grievance culture, to foment a sense of paranoia and suspicion towards a counter narrative, all sources of counter narrative, those that bring with them inconvenient facts and figures, must be discredited.

In 'The Dynamics and Political Implications of Anti-Intellectualism in the United States', published in July 2017 by Matthew Motta at the University of Minnesota, research shows that there is a link between appealing to anti-intellectualism and electoral outcomes that rest on the absence of facts. Grievance is about gut and cannot be fact-checked, everything else that can stand up to scrutiny must become open to doubt. Motta concludes: 'anti-intellectualism is strongly associated with support for politicians and political movements who made the distrust of experts prominent components of their campaigns; including voting for George Wallace in 1968, holding positive views and voting for Donald Trump in 2016, and supporting the United Kingdom's decision to leave the EU. These results hold even when controlling for factors that may also predict support for the same outcomes (e.g., negative racial and gender attitudes, authoritarianism) and panel analyses suggest that they are robust to reverse-causal accounts.'

To bash academics, experts, politicians, bureaucrats and members of the left-wing media as elitist, bleeding heart, out of touch, these are all sublimated ways of saying political correctness as a whole is the enemy, that it is the cautious calculation of the mind attempting to take over the authentic feeling of the heart.

Funding the grievance industry

Funding grievance is a costly business. In the US, the successful smearing of PC was the culmination of an intellectual arms race. Since the 1970s, think tanks, books, pamphlets and strategically placed stories in the media pumped the idea of political correctness as a scourge into the public consciousness. MIT professor Ruth Perry, who was a student and activist in the 1960s and 1970s, told me that the majority of these stories were simply 'a pack of lies'. But these lies were disseminated by a machine that had considerable funding and therefore, profound reach.

Perry, who presciently wrote about how political correctness was being weaponised in the early 1990s, recalls when she first noticed that such a machine existed.

'It was in the early Eighties,' she said, still clearly indignant at the underhand methods that were used almost forty years ago. 'The right started to wage a culture war where they funded a lot of people to develop ideas. When TV or radio hosts discussed a topic such as feminism for example, they would ask a normal academic type and a funded guest, who was only there to promote policy in line with their funders.' She told me stories of campaigns on campus to discredit her and her female colleagues, libellous articles in the press and intimidation tactics. Strange things began to happen. A right-wing newspaper appeared on campus overnight. When Perry started lecturing, someone who was not a student began to appear at her classes and take notes.

Instrumental to this campaign was funding. The 'libertarian' Cato Institute, effectively a conservative lobby group that pushed research papers and books into the hands of national editors, and placed guests on to the panels of national media, is funded by the Koch brothers – billionaires and majority owners of Koch Industries, the second largest privately held company in the United States. The network of conservative promotion lobbies and organisations they have created is so well-funded and sophisticated that it serves almost as a shadow Republican Party. Over the past decades, the Koch brothers have, via their funds, campaigned against expanding the government's role in healthcare and against climate change.

According to a 2010 *New Yorker* profile, the Kochs were 'longtime libertarians who believe in drastically lower personal and corporate taxes, minimal social services for the needy, and much less oversight of industry – especially environmental regulation'. The brothers funded so many campaigns against Obama administration policies that their ideological network came to be known as the 'Kochtopus'.

Right-wing think tanks and lobbyists are slick organisations. There is no shouting, no undignified displays of anger in televised debates or at meetings, no spectacle. The purpose is not to disrupt but to disseminate. Their premises are usually bland and faceless, with elaborate logos and generic names. The job titles of those they employ are both pompous and neutral, the kind of titles that children would come up with in a game of office make-believe. Take one of the Cato Institute's symposia on the subject of political correctness, held in November 2017. The institute put together a policy forum entitled 'Marxist Origins of Hate-Speech Legislation and Political Correctness'. Speakers included Christina Sommers, 'Resident Scholar', American Enterprise Institute; Flemming Rose, 'Senior Fellow', Cato Institute; and a moderator, Marian L. Tupy, 'Senior Policy Analyst, Center for Global Liberty and Prosperity', Cato Institute. None of these individuals is unaffiliated with a policy/ideology-promoting organisation, but their elaborate titles make the event seem like a detached academic exercise and more crucially, perfectly legitimate.

There are several other such think tanks. The Heritage Foundation was founded during the Nixon period of panic about a potential liberal consensus. Its stated mission is to 'formulate and promote conservative public policies based on the principles of free enterprise, limited government, individual freedom, traditional American values, and a strong national defense'. It is particularly obsessed with political correctness and has been since its inception. In 1991, the foundation published a report entitled 'Political Correctness and the Suicide of the Intellect' which criticises affirmative action because 'two wrongs don't make a right'. 'We mustn't let things get by that we know are wrong,' it concludes, 'we must start to raise a little hell.' Searching the foundation's site for articles containing the phrase 'political correctness' throws up 13,839 results. That's an average of 512 posts a year, or 1.4 a day. The foundation is churning out anti-PC propaganda on a daily basis.

Other organisations practically sponsored public 'intellectuals' into being. Dinesh D'Souza, one of the most successful far-right conservative commentators in the US, was positively incubated by them. He started his career as editor of the *Dartmouth Review* in the early 1980s. At the time, the paper harassed an African-American faculty member and published a criticism of affirmative action that was so racist in tone that it pierced the niche academic discourse to capture nationwide attention. The *Review* was receiving thousands of dollars from the rightist Olin Foundation, which also sponsored D'Souza during a stint at the American Enterprise Institute, the end result of which was a book about illiberalism.

The point of rehearsing this history is to demonstrate that political correctness has been overestimated from the moment of inception. Ruth Perry wrote as far back as 1991 that 'no sooner was it invoked as a genuine standard for sociopolitical practice – so that we might live as if the revolution has already happened – than it was mocked as purist, ideologically rigid and authoritarian'. Immediately too much.

Fabrication – the grievance industry and the media

In the UK, there was less coordination than in the US when it came to grievance creation. The war against political correctness in Britain, as opposed to the United States, was less partisan. The country did not go through a similar civil rights/foreign policy activism era which set off a tussle between left and right. But a culture war was brewing around immigration, identity and class, one that deepened during the near decade of economic austerity preceding the UK's Brexit referendum. The cracks became clear when the country split along the lines of EU membership. Now, the British public seems even more averse to such things as political correctness than Americans are. To the naked eye, what took five decades to develop in the US, took only about five years to come about in the UK.

According to the 2018 poll by *Prospect* magazine and

YouGov, in the UK, two out of three people believe others are too offended by language, while nearly half say they're not allowed to say what they think about key issues. The expectation of the researchers was that there would be less concern around PC in the UK than in the US, but in fact the opposite was true. The research found that 67 per cent of Britons believe 'too many people are too easily offended these days over the language that others use,' as opposed to the view that care with language is needed 'to avoid offending people with different backgrounds'. In the US, Pew research in 2016 found that 59 per cent of Americans felt the same way about PC. More revealingly, the research found that PC in the UK was less of a partisan issue than in the US. That is, concern over political correctness was no longer a right-wing issue. It was now mainstream.

How did this view take hold in a country in what appears to be such a short time, where there was no long legacy of culture war? Simply, it was home bred – and over a much longer time than its post-Brexit history suggests. When PC controversies could not be found to occur in nature, they were created. Not only by politicians for whom pressing these buttons will reap huge rewards and votes, but by the press, too.

The PC media fabrication arm of myth-making depends on three strands – branding minor updates to language/public discourse as political correctness, taking true fragments of a story and spinning them into a larger fake one, and then simply making stuff up.

It is a lucrative business. Whipping up outrage based on fake or loosely researched stories is convenient for some media outlets for two reasons. The first is that well-researched, accurate stories are more costly to produce. The second is that there is no payoff, no 'hit' to the news consumer if the story does not somehow tickle a reactionary buzz. The reason these consumers return to media outlets, such as Fox News in the US or the *Daily Mail* in the UK, is to have their world view validated. Or to feel some frisson of something – jealousy, schadenfreude, anger. It is a business model.

Think of PC fabrications as tabloid journalism, but instead of bikinis and celebrity gossip, the stories are about immigrants on the dole and lesbians getting IVF at the taxpayers' expense. At the *Daily Mail* and its online subsidiary Mailonline.com, in the last ten years, there has been an entire genre of PC stories, covering a wide range of topics, written in heavily editorialised outrage speak. According to this publication, the website of which is the most read in the English-speaking world, political correctness is responsible for, among other horrors, the clandestine leaking of halal meat into British schools, the incubation of Islamic terrorism and the watering down of criminal penal law to a state of near anarchy.

In 2017, the *Mail* helpfully published an 'A to Z of politically correct madness'. The list is a mish-mash of unverified reports, one-off incidents and simply quite sensible suggestions that bring harm to no one. One of the items on the list, 'X is for *X-Factor*', claimed that on the ITV talent show, competitor Saara Aalto from Finland 'was accused of cultural appropriation for dressing in a Japanese kimono and a long wig, like a geisha'. The claim was based on a tweet by a viewer who wrote: 'I found Saara's performance very offensive. A culture is not a dress up costume.' This tweet demonstrated that, according to the *Mail*, 'a self-appointed priesthood now ruthlessly polices language and behaviour for any signs of heresy that their diktats state are unacceptable'.

Other items on the list, such as abandoning the description 'lame' when referring to the disabled, using the term 'undocumented' as opposed to 'illegal' migrant, not referring to grown women as 'girls' and replacing the term 'forefathers' with the gender neutral 'forebears' or 'ancestors', seem like rather harmless accommodations.

The 'A to Z' guideline is a popular gimmick. Both the UK's *Daily Telegraph* and *Spectator* also ran such lists. The *Telegraph*'s includes the item 'N IS FOR . . . NIGGER', a term that is 'perfectly acceptable, nay, compulsory if you are a rapper; no longer so if you are Guy Gibson in *The Dam Busters* (when the 1955 film is shown now, his faithful black dog's unfortunate name is often bleeped out). Nor even if you are Huckleberry Finn: in a new version of his *Adventures*, the offending word – used in Mark Twain's 1884 classic 217 times – was replaced by "slave".' Other items include unproven reports that Christmas is now 'Winterval' and that A-level exams aren't as hard as they used to be.

There are generally two types of media coverage that have successfully created a false sense of grievance and pinned it on political correctness. There is the drip-feed kind – the daily, mostly fake updates on how the country (and therefore you, dear embattled reader) has succumbed to a new PC police state. A Muslim bus driver emboldened by a PC transport authority is allowed to 'throw passengers off the bus' so that he could pray, according to the British paper the *Sun*. It transpires that the driver was praying on his statutory break and that there had been no interaction with any passengers regarding the matter. The bus driver won £30,000 in compensation. A female journalist egged on by the #MeToo movement accuses a British MP of inappropriate behaviour, following which he resigned. Screenshots of her texts to the MP are acquired, manipulated to make it look like she had solicited his interest and published by the *Daily Mail*. The paper also lied about pictures that she had sent him. She won £11,000 in compensation. Alongside these stories were the regular false reports about how Christmas and Easter were being rebranded, how healthy competition was under threat because schools were cancelling sports days as it would hurt children's feelings to lose and how local councils were banning England flags.

Then there are the big flagship anti-PC campaigns and themes which recur. Human rights legislation is one of them. A classic case is a *Daily Mail* front-page story from December 2017: 'ANOTHER HUMAN RIGHTS FIASCO – Iraqi caught "red-handed with bomb" wins £33,000 – because our soldiers kept him in custody for too long'. The Independent Press Standards Organisation (IPSO) ruled: 'Neither on the front page, nor in the main body of the article, was it explained that the claim that Mr Al-Waheed had been caught with a bomb had been discredited shortly after his detention or that the judgment recorded the judge's finding that the claim he had been caught with a bomb was "pure fiction".' It was also found that the headline was misleading, as Mr Al-Waheed had in fact only been awarded £3,300 for unlawful detention; the rest of the amount was for ill treatment.

Other stories along this theme bang on the drum of the European Court of Human Rights – PC central. According to the *Mail*, the court's purpose has been thwarted: it was based on a European Convention of Human Rights that was 'designed to prevent a repeat of the horrors of the Nazi concentration camps', but 'has instead become a charter for criminals and politically correct special interest groups'.

Some things are not entirely made up. It is true, for example, that the *Daily Mail*'s 'J is for jazz hands' did happen, where a university union urged people not to clap or whoop because it might be triggering for those with any psychological condition or trauma that might be set off by the sounds, and out of sensitivity for the hearing impaired. But they are not in themselves phenomenal (and in the case of the jazz hands, it was a one-off suggestion that was not implemented). These stories are often recycled. The 'jazz hands' story has had at least three incarnations since 2015. It came around once again as I was writing this book, this time picked up by the BBC. It is true that there are indeed cultural appropriation hysterias that stretch the limit of the reasonable. Even the most 'woke', the most politically aware, can recognise that there are excesses.

To Ruth Perry, by no means an absolutist, 'we all have our limits'. Hers, she told me, is teaching video games and comic books in college, 'that's my resistance to change'. For me, a lover of English literature, it is the attempts to cordon off experiences that a fiction author has not lived because they belong to people of different races or sexual orientation, demanding that white writers refrain from writing black characters for example. But these are not overflows of a system saturated with PC, they are peripheral and uncoordinated events. They are attempts at negotiating the parameters of respect in a diverse society. The picture of a coherent creep is painted to stigmatise reform and to monetise fear.

And so readers return to buy and to click in order to have their fear and prejudices watered and reaffirmed. It is the Fox News model of indoctrination, where PC is now such an established genre of moral panic that it has been deployed to cover everything from defending antisemitic tweets by entertainers ('it makes no sense ever giving up your own taste in art to meet the expectations of your fellow partisans' says a Fox News op-ed by Chris Stirewalt) to suggesting that gay marriage paves the way for bestiality.

Corrections and clarifications are sought in only a small number of cases and, even then, they are not given the prominence of the original offending news item. In many cases the stories do not target a particular person or organisation. With that in mind, if one takes into account that as a whole, the *Daily Mail* is the UK's most complained about newspaper, the lie's dimensions become clear. The *Sun*, the *Express* and the *Daily Mail* have issued upwards of twenty corrections and apologies over the past two years to stories such as schools in the UK being banned from singing Christmas songs and the new £5 note potentially being banned as it is not 'halal'. The scale of the PC-crisis fabrication is inestimable.

The tool – diversion and frequency scrambling

The most effective myths tend to come with a clever technical tool that not only denies reality, but prevents a discussion about reality. In Chapter 1, the myth of gender equality's tool was the set up, where comparison to other cultures with worse problems is used to prevent discussion of issues in our culture. In the case of political correctness, it is Frequency Scrambling, a technique which uses the concept of political correctness for diversion, to distort the conversation and move it away from what it is people are fundamentally disagreeing about.

In a debate about whether halal slaughter should be banned in the UK because it is cruel to animals, the pro-ban arguments are often framed around political correctness rather than animal welfare. This signals to the target audience that it is not just about cruelty, it is about other people being accommodated to do things *their* way in *your* culture.

A British far-right and white nationalist movement called Generation Identity launched a petition in 2018 to ban halal slaughter in the UK, a country according to the group, which refuses a ban 'because our government remains pacified by political correctness and the food industry also panders to a minority group because of the big money involved'. People who had hitherto little to say about the battery farming of chickens, pigs being enclosed in quarters so narrow that they could not lie down to sleep and the industrial slaughter of young calves in the milk industry for being non-milk-producing 'waste products', suddenly developed a very sensitive conscience with regard to halal slaughter. Not only that, they also developed a high level of technical sophisti-cation about the cruelty of halal slaughter to the exclusion of knowledge about any other forms of animal murder, such as stunning cows and pigs and running chickens through an electrified water current before dismembering. The conversation became about the entitlement of a foreign and uniquely cruel practice that must be cleansed off our shores, rather than about animal cruelty. It has become about the status that the minority, in this case Muslims, presume they should have in a society in which they don't belong. This in turn challenges the legitimate, legal and regulated right of Muslims to follow religious practice, under the pretence that it is Muslims who are robbing the native majority's right to protect animals. Or more accurately, the native majority's right to have a random, inconsistent and prejudicial attitude towards perceived cruelty to animals whenever it feels like it.

These debates also stress exceptionalism by claiming that there is disproportionate attention paid to minority issues at the expense of the white working class. But just like the fake pearl clutch of animal cruelty, the concern for white working classes by PC critics seems only to arise when it can be used as a cudgel with which to beat others. The 2018 *Prospect* magazine research stated: 'Some have suggested political correctness shoots itself in the foot by privileging concern about the slights shown to minorities over that shown by other groups, such as poor whites. But among the voters [who perceive PC as an issue], there was little concern about class snobbery. Only 6 per cent named working-class people as a group that gets treated with disdain, and only 2 per cent saw people who hadn't been to university as being prone to contempt. And even among less-educated and working-class voters, these figures weren't much higher.'

This is Frequency Scrambling. What this technique achieves effectively is to divert us away from a genuine grievance by raising a false one. So much time is consequently spent on rebutting the false grievance, for example that curricula in elite British universities are being forcibly changed to include more black or female writers, that no time at all is then spent on the original grievance, which is that some elite universities' syllabuses are out of date, ethnocentric and not sufficiently inclusive. The time that I have spent writing these words is, ironically, a triumph of Frequency Scrambling, in that this chapter is dedicated to rebutting false allegations of political correctness, but the myth is so deeply ingrained that first it must be dispelled, before the facts can be argued.

Every time an issue is presented as one of PC, the air is sucked out of it and it cannot catch fire. If minorities demand some form of affirmative action, we end up discussing the non-minorities who might be victimised as a result, as opposed to why affirmative action is needed in the first place. If women demand that there be a new way of speaking to and about them in the workplace, we end up discussing the men who will be bewildered and prone to victimisation, rather than why women have made the demand in the first place. It is a diversion tool that depends on couching demands in terms of their impact on others, rather than their inherent merit. It is a technique that stresses excess (PC is unnatural and is asking for too much, just like feminism) and purloins victimhood from its rightful owners.

This is necessary to provide cover for the next component of the myth and why it is so durable.

PC as sanction

Political correctness serves many purposes, but the most valuable is its moral shield, a get-out-of-jail card, for those who hold intolerant views, but do not wish to be held accountable for them, or even at least to feel bad for them. The PC myth does not only work to dampen efforts for change by repackaging these efforts as assaults, it also works to absolve people for their prejudices.

This is why 'you can't say anything anymore' is such a frequently deployed defence by those who make prejudiced statements. The issue is not that their opinions are bigoted, it's that they have been wrongly stigmatised.

In 2017, while reporting on Trump's supporters' unconditional loyalty, the *Atlantic*'s Adam Serwer came across a frequent excuse for Trump's racism. 'I believe that everybody has a right to be in the United States no matter what your colour, no matter what your race, your religion, what sex you prefer to be with, so I'm not against that at all, but I think that some of us just say racial statements without even thinking about it,' a Pennsylvania woman told him. But when pressed on Trump's comments on race and Islam she said, 'I think the other party likes to blow it out of proportion and kind of twist his words, but what he says is what he means, and it's what a lot of us are thinking.'

This is the most common response to any queries about Trump's sexism, racism or Islamophobia. Members of a large second-generation Irish-American Jersey family of Trump supporters I interviewed in 2018 rattled off variations on the same theme – it was how Trump's comments and behaviour were received that was the problem.

Trump's sexist comments were 'locker room talk'; his racist comments were not racist at all, he was just stating facts; his abuse of, and aggression towards, the media and political opponents was 'straight talk'. Hillary Clinton came up often as the sinister politically correct analogue to Trump. 'You don't know what she's thinking,' the matriarch of the family said, 'You can't trust her, because she's trying to be politically correct all the time'. When it came to Islam, they were taking no prisoners. When I put it to them that I, as a Sudanese citizen would be banned from visiting the US under Trump's Muslim ban, they did not even try to pretend that it wasn't a Muslim ban (a common fig leaf is that if it were a Muslim ban if would cover all Muslim countries, not just the few that it does). 'If you want to keep the bad ones out you've got to keep the good ones out as well,' came the answer. They felt it was, indeed, brave of Trump to go against what they perceived to be the pressure of political correctness.

This is the final stage of PC as sanction, to make those who are anti-PC feel not only that they have been victimised, but that they are, in fact, courageous to go against this imaginary tide. It's an impressive mental contortion that is only possible because there is so much invested in it – the preservation of status, the need for impunity, the projection of collective grievance on to a single convenient source, the flattering of the self.

A model of this thought pattern, one which ends inevitably in the sanction and normalisation of extremely problematic views, is Sam Harris's reanimation of IQ race wars that began with the publication of *The Bell Curve* in 1994. The book's authors, political scientist Charles Murray and psychologist Richard J. Herrnstein, argue that intelligence is a mixture of social and genetic factors, making assertions about racial differences in IQ that critics say irresponsibly discount environmental factors.

Harris later came to an epiphany, believing that his dismissal of Charles Murray's views that genetic IQ difference between races was merely a fact was born out of group-think, and decided to rectify his error by hosting Murray on his podcast. 'Unfortunately,' Harris concluded, 'the controversy over *The Bell Curve* did not result from legitimate, good-faith criticisms of its major claims. Rather, it was the product of a politically correct moral panic that totally engulfed Murray's career and has yet to release him.'

Once Harris summoned political correctness, he immediately cast himself as a lone crusader pursuing a pioneering and taboo subject, 'forbidden knowledge' he calls it. But in fact, as Ezra Klein of the *Vox* news website observed: 'this isn't "forbidden knowledge." It's ancient prejudice. For two white men to spend a few hours discussing why black Americans are, as a group, less intelligent than whites isn't a courageous stand in the context of American history; it's a common one.'

And of course, the timing is also important to note. A work that for decades had been consigned to the fringes of respectable debate just happens to be enjoying a renaissance at a time where false equivalence and the notion of PC as cover for regressive views is in the ascendance. This is no co-incidence. Harris does not just happen to be fitting in with the zeitgeist – one where if a thing has not been entertained (racial differences, biological differences between men and women), then it must be entertained, regardless of why it was dismissed or marginalised in the first place. Anything else, to borrow Harris's words, is 'moral cowardice'.

Harris often refers to 'bad faith' when discussing his critics. That they approach his positions with prior assumptions about his intentions and therefore will not engage in honest discussions about what he is arguing. So in good faith, I would suggest that Harris is not in fact a racist who would like to establish that there are genetic differences between races that cannot be accounted for by anything other than genetics. I would suggest that he is a narcissist. The allure of the PC warrior is sometimes too strong to resist for those who view themselves as brave arbiters of truth. PC knights are having a moment in popular discourse. They make up an entire cohort, feted in the *New York Times* as members of an 'intellectual dark web' that is making 'an end run around the mainstream conversation'. They are also joined by liberals who have succumbed to the grandiosity of defending liberal values. *New York Magazine*'s Jonathan Chait obsesses about US free speech campus controversies, even when he reluctantly admits they might be small fry and have been occurring for some time now without somehow bringing about fascism. But this will not stop him from presenting them as part of a great threat to liberalism.

There is something unavoidably macho about it. Much of the language around political correctness is expressed in terms of strength and weakness. Those who care about abusive language, racial and sexist slurs and so on, are weak,

thin-skinned, demanding that we go against nature by over
legislating and policing innocent and inevitable human
behaviour. The implication is that to indulge political correctness is to create a sort of artificial state of oppression,
where humans cannot exercise discretion or shrug things
off. A learnt victimhood has made us forget that 'facts don't
care about your feelings'. At the heart of this is the kind of
biological determinism that assumes that just because some
things occur in nature, e.g. suspicion of other races due
to group self-preservation instincts, that means that they
should be accepted. This argument, strangely, is rarely made
about violent crime or child abuse, both things that have
occurred in nature since record keeping began.

Related to that, there is also something unavoidably free
market capitalist about the anti-PC animus. Just as the invisible hand regulates the market, so shall it regulate human
interaction. The unintended accrued social benefits of an individual's self-interested actions, with no intervention, will
not just create the fairest economy, but the fairest society.

When I spoke to Lola Olufemi, she had in her brief
experience of PC scam media culture already developed a
jaundiced attitude towards such quarters of the left. 'There
are always these voices that have access to mainstream
media outlets, that grass roots organisers do not have access
to. They genuinely believe in the PC trope and it betrays an
astounding lack of knowledge. Their liberal ideas have no
solid basis, they do no meaningful political work and are
not exposed to the real-world effects of anything. So you're
going to get caught up in the manufactured outrage.'

Such liberals have succumbed to Frequency Scrambling,
in that they dedicate their time to hyperventilating about
trivial or made up PC issues, rather than the context in
which they occur. The branding of PC as a rarefied thing

has been so successful, that it has meant that defending it is toxic for the left because it suggests elitism and inauthenticity. Particularly at a time when right-wing populism is on the rise, the left cannot afford to play into any of the stereotypes populists have painted; enriched and out of touch. It is why, when Hillary Clinton was interviewed by the *Guardian* newspaper in November 2018 on the topic of how to combat populism, her first suggestion was to curb immigration, because that is what 'lit the flame'. Her view was not that immigration was bad, rather that it was helping the right and must be jettisoned if the left is to be seen as on the side of the man on the street. Clinton's frequency was well and truly scrambled if her solution to populism is playing into the hands of the right by mimicking its tactics, rather than challenging it because they are objectively wrong. Frequency Scrambling makes values negotiable.

Clinton and her political tribe have succumbed to a kind of crisis of confidence – caught out on the wrong side of history and power they contemplate, maybe things really have gone too far? Ironically, they ally with the right in bringing about a new orthodoxy, a sort of double bluff political correctness. The journalist Arwa Mahdawi calls this 'populist correctness', which she describes as 'the smearing and silencing of points of view by labelling them "elitist" – and therefore at odds with the will of the people and the good of the country'. She cites as examples the rhetoric around 'remoaners' (British people who voted to remain in the EU and 'moan' about the result), which can be summed up as 'the people have spoken, so the rest of you should shut up'.

This has led to anti-PC muscle beauty parades. In the United States, being politically incorrect on the right has ironically enforced its own sort of orthodoxy. In 2018, Georgia Republican gubernatorial candidate Brian Kemp's campaign ad was simply entitled 'Offends'. In it, he issues a series of dog whistles while wrapped in the cloak of plain talking.

'I'm Brian Kemp,' he says, 'and I believe in God, family and country – in that order. I say Merry Christmas, and God bless you. I strongly support President Trump, our troops and ironclad borders. I stand for our national anthem. If any of this offends you, then I'm not your guy. If you're ready for a politically incorrect conservative who will end corrupt pay-to-play politics, I'm Brian Kemp, and I'm asking for your vote.'

The man he was running against, a hardcore conservative by any standards, was caught on tape complaining that the gubernatorial nomination process had turned into a competition to show 'who had the biggest gun, who had the biggest truck, and who could be the craziest'. Two days after the 'Offends' ad ran, Trump endorsed Brian Kemp. A few days later, Kemp won the GOP nomination for Georgia governor.

A week before, Ed Kilgore observed on the Daily Intelligencer blog that, 'If Kemp wins his runoff on July 24 with this strategy, it is going to reinforce the already powerful Trumpian impulse to treat conservative "base" voters as motivated above all by the desire to go back to the wonderful days when a white man could without repercussions tell a racist joke, "tease" women about their physical appearance or sexual morals, and mock people who in some way (say, a disability) differ from one's own self.' He wrote, 'At some point we may all come to understand that it's not (except in some scattered college campuses) the politically correct who are imposing speech norms on the rest of us, but the politically incorrect who won't be happy until offending the less powerful is again recognized as among the principal Rights of Man.' Or as the British writer Polly Toynbee put it, political correctness crisis mythology is used as 'coded cover' for those who 'still want to say Paki, spastic, or queer.'

Perpetuation via paranoia

The maintenance stage of a myth is achieved when those who believe in it have so much invested, that reality is actively resisted without much encouragement from politicians or the media. This is clearly demonstrated by the continued paranoia on the part of some American and British voters who actually got what they wanted in electing Trump and bringing about the Brexit vote. Rather than enjoy the triumph of the huge upset they have managed to pull off by exercising their democratic will, they fixate on how their victory is constantly at threat of being usurped. The *Prospect* magazine–YouGov 2018 poll notes: 'Despite Brexit voters winning the referendum and having a government committed to Brexit, they are more likely to think that people are not free to speak their mind on important issues. Their views have the political upper hand at the moment, yet it seems they still feel culturally embattled.'

This is the cornerstone of myth perpetuation, to convince those at the top of the totem pole, enabled and empowered, that they are weak and threatened by those with far less political capital. And so Trump voters must continue to fear Mexicans and Muslims, and the (in reality weak and inchoate) forces of the left. Brexit voters must continue to worry about the 'saboteurs' that the *Daily Mail* believes include Members of Parliament, and the British Supreme Court. The entire industrial complex of myth-making is in the business of creating sore winners.

The forces that gave Brexit and Trump momentum

coalesced around grievance rather than vision. There was no agenda, no genuinely thought-out project that the winners could soberly set about executing, just resentment. The grievance narrative must be continued even in success.

Growing pains

Edward Said described the origins of political correctness as not 'a matter of replacing one set of authorities and dogmas with another, nor of substituting one centre for another. It was always a matter of opening and participating in a central strand of intellectual and cultural effort and of showing what had always been, though indiscernibly, a part of it, like the work of women, or of blacks, and servants—but which had been either denied or derogated.'

In this most basic form, as respect for others, as integrating the voices of the marginalised, political correctness has been hugely successful in regulating how we interact peacefully. From the 1980s onwards in the United Kingdom, political correctness banished antisemitic and racial slurs such as 'Paki' from the public space and the mainstream media. It stigmatised homophobic language, and went some distance in limiting language that demeaned or objectified women. The knock-on effect of this is an informing of behaviour at best, and the creation of a safe and inclusive society for all. But this effort needed to be sustained by constant vigilance and structural reform, a sincere adoption of these norms into the political culture of a country. It is the absence of that which has created an almost universal resignation to the fact that PC is a bad thing, even if its goals are noble. Nobody likes to be told what to think or how to behave is the argument, and look at the frustration that it sowed? This is not a failure of PC, it is a failure in arguing for the value of PC and enthusiastically promoting it with as much force as it was stigmatised. Political correctness is not wrong, it is merely unfashionable. As the British broadcaster James O'Brien put it to those who resent not being able to be offensive, where would you like your sewage? In the pipes underground or flowing in the streets?

The reason PC was resisted in the first place was because it pointed out that the existing state of affairs was artificially imposed via coercive political, racial, social and economic forces, rather than a natural blossom that just found its level. In the 1990s, PC quickly became defined as an incursion by 'special interests' because the establishment viewed itself as apolitical, natural and promoting universal values.

The problem with dismissing political correctness (and here I am using the term in its pre-1990s, non-pejorative form) is that doing so reinforces cultural entitlement. Only people who are not transgender or do not care about a transgender person can afford to dismiss Trump's recent military ban on transgender soldiers as a mere distraction. Only people who are not afraid that a person of colour will be shot by the police on a whim can afford to dismiss Trump's racism as a 'side issue'. In a moral universe, political correctness would not exist at all. Until we achieve that moral universe, political correctness is a must. Likewise, in a homogenous universe, political correctness would not exist. In a diverse world, political correctness is the stretching, expansion and often the growing pains of a society enlarging to accommodate all its members.

The most effective way to counter political correctness crisis myth is not succumbing to Frequency Scrambling, and recognising the scale and history of confection. The way to dispel the myth is by sticking with a forceful presentation of reality and avoiding hesitation when making the case for respect and social cohesion. Political correctness is not the problem, it is part of the answer. The solution is not less political correctness, it is more.

Because instead of a halal creep there is rising Islamophobia, instead of university campuses full of privileged snowflakes, British universities have recorded a rise in racism. In the US, instead of a salving of the wounds of slavery, on the back of the free-for-all language of Trump, the non-PC president, there are white nationalist marches and an escalation of antisemitic violence. The threat to social cohesion is not that there is too much political correctness, it is that there is not enough.

CHAPTER 3

The myth of a free speech crisis

'The claim that free speech is under attack is often a mask for other political frustrations and fears.'

Will Davies

I began writing in an online age. My first column was published in 2008 and I remember well how unprepared I was for the comments that began appearing underneath. From the beginning, there was no space between me and the reader, no intermediary, just an online 'moderator' whose job it was to delete comments that violated the terms of the newspaper. I remember walking away from the screen and taking a stroll around the corner to breathe through the nausea that my stomach had knotted itself into, then going back to read comments that questioned my intelligence, honesty and sneered at my writing capabilities.

I got over it quickly. A few columns later, it seemed a futile exercise to worry about what an audience would think. Instinctively, being from a generation that straddled the real and virtual worlds, I had a sense of what was worth engaging with and what was a sort of online compulsion to say something because you could; to make a noise because you know someone, ideally even the writer, might hear it. But at the same time, having never written in the age when

95

there was no way to receive immediate feedback, the writing process to me was always two-fold, as action and reaction. I would engage with the commenters who made valid points and urge those who I sensed had something interesting to say, but emotion had got the better of, to reread the piece and return. Sometimes I would react to those who were abusive in a calculatedly dismissive tone. It was like being a teacher in front of a difficult class, trying to encourage the good students while striking a balance with the disruptive ones, asserting authority but not dropping to their level.

In those days, comments were open for seventy-two hours. Coming up for air at the end of a thread felt like mooring a ship after a few days on choppy waters, like an achievement, something that I and the readers had gone through together. We had discussed sensitive, complicated ideas about politics, race, gender and sexuality and, at the end, via a rolling conversation, we had got somewhere.

In the decade since, the tenor of those comments became so personalised and abusive that the ship often drowned before making it to shore – the moderators would simply shut the thread down. When it first started happening, I took it as a personal failure – perhaps I had not struck the right tone or not sufficiently hedged all my points, provoking readers into thinking I was being dishonest or incendiary. In time, it dawned on me that my writing was the same. It was the commenters who had changed. It was becoming harder to discuss almost anything without a virtual snarl in response. And it was becoming harder to do so if one were not white or male.

As a result, the *Guardian* overhauled its policy and decided that it would not open comment threads on pieces that were certain to derail. Where some other columnists were relieved, to me it felt like giving up. I still feel a little stab of disappointment when I see that an article of mine is not open to comments. A couple of times, I even remonstrated with the moderators to change their minds, but they knew better than me. They had a duty of care to the writers, some of whom struggled with the abuse, and a duty of care to new writers who might succumb to a chilling effect if they knew that to embark on a journalism career nowadays comes inevitably with no protection from online thuggery. Alongside these moral concerns there were also practical, commercial ones. There were simply not enough resources to manage all the open threads at the same time with the increased level of attention that was now required. These were all fair and sensible reasons. The ship was now not even leaving shore. The commenters and I were grounded.

I go through this history to demonstrate how in the past ten years, many platforms in the press and social media have had to grapple with the challenges of managing users with increasingly sharp and offensive tones, while maintaining enough space for maximum expression, feedback and interaction. Speech has never been more free or less intermediated. Anyone with internet access can create a profile and write, tweet, blog or comment, with little vetting and no hurdle of technological skill. But the targets of this growth in the means of expression have been primarily women, minorities and LGBTQ+ people. A 2017 Pew Research Center survey revealed that a 'wide cross section' of Americans experience online abuse, but that the majority was directed towards minorities, with a quarter of black Americans saying they have been attacked online due to race or ethnicity. Ten per cent of Hispanics and 3 per cent of whites reported the same. The picture is not much different in the UK. A 2017 Amnesty report analysed tweets sent to 177 women British Members of Parliament. The twenty

of them who were from a black and ethnic minority background received almost half the total number of abusive
tweets. I participated in a *Guardian* survey that crunched
my beloved comments on the site, and was shocked to find
out that I had the dubious honour of receiving the third
highest number of abusive comments under my articles. The
second and the first most abused were a gay black man and
a white feminist, respectively.

The vast majority of this abuse goes unpunished. And
yet it is somehow conventional wisdom that free speech is
under assault, that university campuses have succumbed
to an epidemic of no-platforming, that social media mobs
are ready to raise their pitchforks at the most innocent slip
of the tongue or joke, and that Enlightenment values that
protected the right to free expression and individual liberty
are under threat. The cause of this, it is claimed, is a liberal
totalitarianism that is attributable simultaneously to intolerance and thin skin. The impulse is allegedly at once both
fascist in its brutal inclinations to silence the individual, and
protective of the weak, easily wounded and coddled.

This is the myth of the free speech crisis. It is an extension
of the political correctness myth but is a recent mutation
more specifically linked to efforts or impulses to normalise
hate speech or shut down legitimate responses to it. The
purpose of the myth is not to secure freedom of speech,
that is, the right to express one's opinions without censorship, restraint or legal penalty. The purpose is to secure
the licence to speak with impunity; not freedom of expression, but rather freedom from the consequences of that
expression.

The myth has two components: the first is that all speech
should be free; the second is that freedom of speech means
freedom from objection.

The first part of the myth is one of the more challenging to push back against, because instinctively it feels wrong to do so. With the previously covered myths in Chapters 1 and 2, it seems a worthy cause to demand more political correctness, politeness and good manners in language convention as a bulwark against society's drift into marginalising groups with less capital or to argue for a fuller definition of female emancipation. These are good things even if you disagree with how they are to be achieved. But to ask that we have less freedom of speech, to be unbothered when people with views you disagree with are silenced or banned, smacks of illiberalism. It just does not sit well. And it is hard to argue for less freedom in a society in which you live, because is it not the logical conclusion that limiting rights of expression will catch up with you at some point? Will it not be you one day, on the wrong side of free speech?

There is a kernel of something that makes all myths stick, something that speaks to a sense of justice and liberty, due process, and openness that allows them to be cynically manipulated to appeal to the good and well-intentioned. But what this chapter is arguing is that challenging the myth of a free speech crisis does not mean enabling the state even further to police and censor, it is arguing that there is no crisis. If anything, speech has never been more free and unregulated. The freedom of speech crisis myth's purpose is to guilt people into giving up their right of response to attack and to destigmatise racism and prejudice. It aims to blackmail good people into ceding space to bad ideas, even though they have a legitimate right to refuse. And it is a myth that demands in turn, its own silencing and undermining of individual freedom. To accept the freedom of speech crisis myth is to give up your own right to turn off the comments.

The myth and its promoters thrive on cognitive dissonances and good intentions, feeding them with *false equivalence*, *fabrication* and *'slippery slope' fallacies*. The first, false equivalence, is based on the notion that free speech is absolute which, both on a customary and legal level, is false.

False equivalence

At the same time as a proliferation in platform, a right-wing counter push was taking place online. It claimed that all speech must be allowed without consequence or moderation, and that liberals were assaulting the premise of free speech. I began to notice it around the time of the fashionable atheism that started in the late noughties following the publication of Richard Dawkins' *The God Delusion*. These new atheists were the first users I spotted using argumentative technicalities (e.g. Islam is not a race) to hide what was rank prejudice and Islamophobia. Their tribe expanded to include the free speech what-abouters. If a column of mine was published but the thread was not opened, readers would find me on social media and cry censorship, then unleash whatever invective they were prevented from spewing below the line on Twitter or Facebook which had a, shall we say, much more commercial attitude to moderation. The company's duty of care was to its bottom line. As platforms multiplied, there were more and more ways for me to receive feedback from readers. I could be sworn at and told to go back to where I came from via at least three mediums. Or I could just read about how I should go back to where I came from in the pages of print publications, or on any number of websites. The comment thread seemed redundant. The whole internet was now a comment thread. As a result,

mainstream media establishments began to struggle with
this glut of opinion, failing to curate the public discussion
by giving into false equivalence. Now every opinion must
have a counter opinion.

I began to see it in my own media engagements. I would
be called upon by more neutral outlets, such as the BBC,
to discuss increasingly more absurd arguments with other
journalists or political activists with extreme views. Conversations around race, immigration, Islam and climate change
became increasingly binary and polarised when there were
no binaries to be contemplated. Climate change deniers
were allowed to broadcast falsehoods about a reversal in
climate change. Racial minorities were called upon to counter thinly veiled racist or xenophobic views. I found myself,
along with other journalists in the media industry, regularly
ambushed. Appearing on BBC's *Newsnight* to discuss an
incident where a far-right racist had mounted a mosque
pavement with his car and killed one of the congregation,
and after I tried to make the point that there was insufficient
focus on a growing far-right terror threat, the presenter
asked me: 'Have you had abuse? Give us an example.' This
became a frequent line of inquiry, the personalisation and
provocation of personal debate, when what was needed was
analysis.

It became common for me and like-minded colleagues to
query, when invited on the TV or radio to discuss such topics
as immigration or Islamophobia, who was appearing on the
other side, because the interlocutors were increasingly just
garden variety racists dressed up with the titles of columnists
or authors. One British Asian writer was ambushed a few
hours before going on air by the BBC because they had set
him up to discuss populist anger with the British columnist
Melanie Phillips, a woman who referred to immigrants as

'convulsing Europe' and stated that they were wiping out the continent's cultural identity by 'refusing to assimilate'. When he refused, because he believed the topic did not warrant such a polarised set-up, the editor said: 'this will be good for your book, surely you want to sell more copies?' The writer replied that if he never sold another book in his life because he would not debate Melanie Phillips, he could live with that. This was now the discourse; presenting bigotry and then the defence of bigotry as a 'debate' from which everyone can benefit, like a boxing match where even the loser is paid along with the promoters, coaches and whole cast behind arranging the fight. The writer Reni Eddo-Lodge has called it 'performing rage'.

Two things began to happen. The first was that views that had previously been consigned to the political fringes made their way into the mainstream via social and traditional media organisations that previously would never have contemplated their airing. The expansion of media outlets meant that it was not only marginalised voices that secured access to the public, but also those with more extreme and fringe views. In 2009, Nick Griffin, head of the British National Party (BNP), a far-right neo-fascist (and at times self-described neo-Nazi) party was invited on to *Question Time*, the BBC's most popular current affairs debating programme. The outrage that followed – public protests, appeals on the part of government ministers to the BBC Trust and the BBC director general – would be hard to fathom today. This is simply because seeing or hearing someone like Griffin would be treated as a much more prosaic affair. He would be on social media with hundreds of thousands of followers, on a YouTube channel and hosted on podcasts and live broadcasts in the UK and the US. In a world where traditional and broadly centrist media organisations no longer curate the public discussion, there is no longer a 'fringe' view. Nick Griffin would simply be mainstream.

This inevitably expanded what was considered acceptable speech. The Overton window, the range of ideas deemed to be acceptable by the public at any one time, shifted as more views made their way from the peripheries to the centre of the conversation. Any objection to the airing of those views would often be considered an attempt to curtail freedom of speech. In my own journalism, it became clear that whenever I attempted to push back against what amounted to incitement against racial or religious minorities, opponents fixated on the free speech argument, rather than the harmful ramifications of hate speech.

In early 2018, four extreme-right figures were turned away at the UK border. Their presence was deemed 'not conducive to the public good'. When I wrote in defence of the Home Office's position, my email and social media were flooded with abuse for days. Right-wing media blogs as well as mainstream publications such as the *Economist* published pieces on how my position was an illiberal misunderstanding of free speech. No one discussed the four figures who were banned, their neo-Nazi views, or the hate speech implications on community relations in the UK had they been allowed in or just the risk of violence.

What has increased is not intolerance of speech. There is simply more speech. And because the influx was from the extremes, there is also simply more objectionable speech, and in turn more opposition to it. This is what free speech crisis myth believers are picking up, this pushback against the increase in intolerant or bigoted speech, but they are misreading it as a change in free speech attitudes.

This increase in objectionable speech came with an

entitlement, a demand that it be heard and not challenged, and the freedom of speech fig leaf became a convenient tool. Not only do free speech warriors demand all opinions be heard on all platforms they choose, whether it be college campuses or Twitter, they demand that there be no objection or reaction. It became farcical and extremely psychologically taxing for anyone who could see the dangers of hate speech and the connection between a sharpening tenor on immigration, for example, and how this could be used to make the lives of immigrants and minorities harder.

When the ex-UK British foreign secretary Boris Johnson compared women who wear the burqa to 'letter boxes' and 'bank robbers', it led to a spike in racist incidents against women who wear the niqab according to the organisation Tell Mama, a national project which records and measures anti-Muslim incidents in the United Kingdom. Pointing this out and making the link between mockery of minorities and racist provocation against them was, according to Johnson's supporters, assailing his freedom of speech. The British journalist Isabel Oakeshott tweeted that if he were disciplined by his party for 'perfectly reasonable exercise of free speech, something has gone terribly wrong with the party leadership,' saying that it was 'Deplorable to see [the Tory leadership] pandering to the whinings of the professionally offended in this craven way.'

Free speech, according to this definition, came to mean that no one had any right to object to what anyone ever said. Which not only meant that no one should object to Johnson's comments but, in turn, that no one should object to their objection. Free speech logic, rather than the pursuit of a lofty Enlightenment value, became a race to the bottom where the alternative to being 'professionally offended' is never to be offended at all. This logic today demands silence from those who are defending themselves from abuse or hate speech. It is, according to the drector of the Institute of Race Relations, 'the privileging of freedom of speech over freedom to life'.

Our alleged free speech crisis was never really about free speech. The backdrop to the myth is rising anti-immigration sentiment and Islamophobia. Free speech crisis advocates always seem to have an agenda. They overwhelmingly wanted to exercise their freedom of speech in order to agitate against minorities, women, immigrants and Muslims. But they dress these base impulses up in the language of concern or anti-establishment conspiracism. Similar to the triggers of political correctness hysteria, there is a direct correlation between the rise in free speech panic and the rise in far-right or hard-right political energy, as evidenced by anti-immigration right-wing electoral successes in the US, the UK and across continental Europe. As the space for these views expanded, so the concept of free speech became frayed and tattered. It began to mean many things, to lose its grounding caveats. And it began to become muddled by false equivalence, caught between fact and opinion, between action and reaction. The discourse became mired in a misunderstanding of free speech as absolute.

Free but not absolute

There are many things that people do and can say in public, with little fear of legal intervention from the state. But there are always limits and always should be. This applies to almost all human behaviour in secular, democratic societies. The most straightforward example is how we dress. Broadly we can wear what we want, but most will stay within the confines of social custom because otherwise a

judgement may be made about their character or they may
offend others. Men will generally wear a tie to a funeral;
women will limit more revealing clothes to their social,
rather than professional lives. Where social custom fails,
the state intervenes. There are legal limits in even the most
permissive societies on public nudity, and legislation against
the wearing of the burqa and the niqab are gathering momentum in Europe. In France, both the burqa and revealing
private parts is banned. And in countries where there are
few explicit laws on dress, people still tend to fall back on
customary behaviour even when there is no legal threat of
punishment. In Germany, nudity is legal, as is the burqa, but
there is no preponderance of either.

What free speech crisis advocates do, in terms of offence,
is equate those who walk into a public area nude and those
who enter it clothed. In terms of harm, they equate those who
expose their genitalia at the public and those who object to
that behaviour. Free speech is not an abstract notion, it has
a purpose; it is a regulator of interaction, rather than an end
in itself. It sets specific parameters.

As a value in its most pure form freedom of speech
serves two purposes: protection from state persecution,
when challenging the authority of power or orthodoxy;
and the protection of fellow citizens from the damaging
consequences of absolute (completely legally unregulated)
speech such as slander. According to Francis Canavan in
Freedom of Expression: Purpose as Limit, his analysis of
the most permissive free speech law, the US First Amendment, free speech must have a rational end, which is to
facilitate communication between citizens. Where it does
not serve that end, it is limited. Like all freedoms, it ends
when it infringes upon the freedoms of others. A summary
of his position on the US Supreme Court itself 'has never

accepted an absolutist interpretation of freedom of speech. It has not protected, for example, libel, slander, perjury, false advertising, obscenity and profanity, solicitation of a crime, or "fighting" words. The reason for their exclusion from First Amendment protection is that they have minimal or no values as ideas, communication of information, appeal to reason, step towards truth etc.; in short no value in regard to the ends of the Amendment.'

Those who believe in the free speech crisis myth fail to make the distinction between 'fighting' words and speech that facilitates communication, between free speech and absolute speech.

Using this litmus test, the first hint the free speech crisis is actually an absolute speech crisis is the issues it focuses on. On university campuses, it is overwhelmingly around race and gender. On social media, the free speech axe is wielded by trolls, Islamophobes and misogynists, leading to an abuse epidemic that platforms have failed to curb. This free speech crisis movement has managed to stigmatise reasonable protest, which has existed for years without being branded as 'silencing', in itself an assault on free expression.

What is considered speech worthy of protection is broadly subjective and depends on the consensual limits a society has drawn. Western societies like to think of their version of freedom of speech as exceptionally pristine, but it is also tainted (or tempered, depending on where you're coming from) by convention. A good example of how there are, in fact, agreed upon limits to freedom of speech, outside the limits of the law, and how they are in fact arbitrary, is the case of Milo Yiannopoulous.

Popularly known simply as 'Milo', a British university dropout and lapsed journalist, he emerged into the public sphere in 2015 after joining Breitbart News and styling himself into a lightning rod for online campaigns against women and minorities. He believes that 'feminism is a cancer' and that 'rape culture is a myth'. In 2016, he was permanently banned from Twitter for conducting a coordinated abuse campaign against US actor Leslie Jones.

'With the cowardly suspension of my account,' Milo stated, 'Twitter has confirmed itself as a safe space for Muslim terrorists and Black Lives Matter extremists, but a no-go zone for conservatives.'

In 2017, Milo was offered $250,000 to write a book for the publisher Simon & Schuster. When faced with public outcry, the publisher defended its decision by releasing a statement in which it described Milo as simply someone with 'controversial' opinions, who will take his place among their stable of other authors, many of whom are also 'controversial', who appeal to 'many audiences of readers'.

Calls for a boycott sent liberal free speech campaigners into an indignation of chivalry. Like the political correctness gone too far hysteria, free speech crisis concerns appeal to a certain type of liberal, one who is oblivious to how these moral panics are fabricated and manipulated by those with an agenda. This liberal is blinded by the eagerness to land generally on the right side of freedom and individual liberty. Led by the National Coalition Against Censorship, free speech advocates issued a statement in opposition to a nascent boycott of Milo Yiannopoulos's publisher, claiming that it will have 'a chilling effect' on authors and publishers and will not prevent the spread of 'noxious ideas'. The statement, signed by, among others Index on Censorship, the Authors Guild and the National Council of Teachers of English, said: 'The suppression of noxious ideas does not defeat them; only vigorous disagreement can counter toxic speech effectively.'

This chimed with Simon & Schuster's defence of the book deal. All ideas good or bad should be heard (if someone will buy them of course, is the unspoken rule), Milo was just another flower in the flourishing garden of opinion. But it was not enough that Milo just be, it was also important than he have an audience that was willing to purchase his book. Who were Simon & Schuster to dictate what should be published and what should not? The company was just an intermediary between opinion maker and audience, that's all.

It turns out that it was a little bit more than that. Most unfortunately for his publisher, later in the same year that he secured his book, footage emerged in which he endorsed pederasty. In a podcast called *The Drunken Peasants*, which aired in 2016, Yiannopoulos commented 'we get hung up on this child abuse stuff'. He said he believed the current legal age of consent was 'probably about right' before saying that some teenagers are 'capable' of consenting to sexual activity at a younger age.

It gets worse: 'There are certainly people who are capable of giving consent at a younger age. I certainly consider myself to be one of them, people who were sexually active younger.' This 'particularly happens in the gay world', he added. Relationships between 13-year-olds and 25- or 28-year-olds were fine, he specified. Consent was an 'arbitrary and oppressive' idea he said, 'people are messy and complex, and in the homosexual world particularly, some of those relationships between younger boys and older men, the coming of age relationships' are places in which 'those older men help those young boys to discover who they are and give them security and safety and provide them with love and a reliable rock where they can't speak to their parents'.

This was too much even for one of the presenters of the podcast, who said in response: 'This sounds like priest molestation to me.' Milo replied: 'And do you know what? I'm, grateful to Father Michael, I wouldn't give nearly as good head if it wasn't for him.'

If I were narrating this, here there would be a dramatic pause.

Reader, the free speech winds turned. Milo was dropped by Simon & Schuster. The free speech campaigners fell silent. Condemnations and distancings and disavowals followed. He resigned from his position at Breitbart News.

Once Milo's book deal with the prestigious publishing house was rescinded, the writer Roxane Gay wrote:

> When his comments about pedophilia/pederasty came to light, Simon & Schuster realised it would cost them more money to do business with Milo than he could earn for them. They did not finally 'do the right thing' and now we know where their threshold, pun intended, lies. They were fine with his racist and xenophobic and sexist ideologies. They were fine with his transphobia, anti-Semitism and Islamophobia. They were fine with how he encourages his followers to harass women and people of color and transgender people online. Certainly, Simon & Schuster was not alone in what they were willing to tolerate. A great many people were perfectly comfortable with the targets of Milo's hateful attention until that attention hit too close to home.

This is the dirty secret about freedom of speech, rather than being an ideal, it is a litmus test of a society's prejudices. Milo's case proves that very bluntly, many saw the harassment of women and people of colour as inoffensive, as an opinion that can be tolerated and, where his publisher was concerned, an opinion that could be sold. When Gay says the red line was breached when it 'hit too close to home', this is not just a turn of phrase. 'Home' in this scenario is anything that the powerful forces in a society consider to be their own. The sexual exploitation of children is something anyone can abhor, but other races, religions, sexual orientations are just that, 'other', not 'home', and so are fair game. That is the honest appraisal of why people like Milo are indulged, and not because of any cant about freedom of speech.

You hear a lot about 'the marketplace of ideas' as justification for the defence and embrace of Milo by publishers and free speech advocates. This is a myth-sustaining notion. Its promoters fail to see the inherent imbalances of a society in which not all have equal access to means of speech.

The oligarchy of ideas

It is clear that Milo was also indulged because trolling has become an industry. It is now a sort of lucrative contact sport, where insults and lies are hurled on television, radio, online outlets and in the press. CNN's coverage of the 'Trump transition', after Donald Trump was elected as US president, was a modern version of a medieval freak show. Step right up and gawk at Richard Spencer, the Trump supporter and head of far-right think tank the National Policy Institute, as he questions whether Jews 'are people at all, or instead soulless golem'. And at the black Trump surrogate who thinks Hillary Clinton started the war in Syria. And at Corey Lewandowski, a man who appeared on CNN as a political commentator, who appears to make a living from lying in the media and who alleged that the Trump birther story, where Trump claimed that Barack Obama was not born on US soil, was in fact started by Hillary Clinton. In pursuit of ratings – from behind a 'freedom of speech' fig leaf, and perhaps the good intention of balance on the part of some – many media platforms have detoxified radical and untruthful behaviour that was until recently confined to the darker corners of Reddit and Breitbart. And that radical and untruthful behaviour has a direct impact on how safe the world is for those smeared by these performances. Trump himself is the main act in this lucrative show. Initially seen as an entertaining side act during his election campaign, his offensive, untruthful and pugnacious online presence became instantly more threatening and dangerous once he was elected. Inevitably, his incontinence, bitterness, rage and hatemongering, by sheer dint of constant exposure, became less and less shocking, and in turn less and less beyond the pale.

A world where all opinions and lies are presented to the public as a sort of take it or leave it buffet, is often described as 'the marketplace of ideas', a rationalisation for freedom of expression based on comparing ideas to products in a free market economy. The marketplace of ideas model of free speech holds that what is true factually, and what is good morally, will emerge after a competition of ideas in a free, unmoderated and transparent public discourse, a healthy debate where the truth will prevail. Bad ideas and ideologies will lose out and wither away as they are vanquished by superior ones. The problem with the marketplace of ideas theory (as with all 'invisible hand' type theories) is that it does not account for a world in which the market is skewed and not all ideas receive equal representation, because the market has monopolies and cartels.

David Uberti, a contributor to *Columbia Journalism Review* who has written on false equivalence in the media since Donald Trump's election, spoke to me about inherent imbalances in the American media, which render it less a marketplace of ideas and more a sort of prison tuck shop or commissary that provides few and overpriced goods to captive consumers. He cites the example of support for the Iraq War as a failure of media judgement for which there was no censure.

'Most of the people in the upper echelons of the American media today are the same people who were there during the Iraq War,' he said. 'They have not been punished. And these are the people who are now responsible for framing the dangers of Trumpism.' If it were a real market, their stalls would have been shut down long ago.

The analogy is further stretched by the fact that real marketplaces actually require a lot of regulation. There are anti-monopoly rules, there are interest rate fixes and, in many markets, artificial currency pegs. In the press, publishing and the business of ideas dispersal in general, there are players that are deeply entrenched and networked, and so the supply of ideas reflects their power.

In a world where funding and lobbying groups can sponsor public opinion makers from university all the way through to publication of their first book, where lazy or time-stressed TV producers keep returning to the same voices for their commentary, and where publishers and top media executives tend to come broadly from the same pool, social class and universities, it is inevitable that there is a failure of curation. This is not deliberate. There is no actual oligarchy sitting in a glass tower, conspiring to keep other voices out, but there is a cumulative tipping of the scales and unevening of the ground, which means freedom of speech becomes concentrated in a few stalls. Even though there are more platforms and speech has never been less regulated, the views that are projected are skewed.

In the UK Nigel Farage, the former head of the Eurosceptic right-wing populist United Kingdom Independence Party (UKIP), is an example of this lopsided marketplace of ideas. An elected member of the European parliament, Farage headed up a party that at its peak held only two seats in the British Parliament. Farage himself has run for a British parliamentary seat a total of seven times. He lost every single election. But when one looks at his media profile, it is vastly disproportionate to his modest success. By February 2018, the BBC's most prestigious political debate programme *Question Time* had invited Nigel Farage on the show thirty-two times, making him the joint most invited guest in the history of the show. The other was Kenneth Clarke, a sitting Member of Parliament and former Chancellor of the Exchequer. At the time Farage achieved that status, he had not been the head of UKIP for almost two years and the party's electoral share was hovering around 2 per cent.

Farage was networked, available and sufficiently controversial with hardline views on immigration. That was sufficient for him to be handed a platform to broadcast his ideas on a scale that did not reflect his support or relevance. This has never stopped him from claiming that he was silenced and shunned by the 'establishment'. This is an era when there has never been more airtime given to extremist views, while constantly having to listen to the purveyors of those fringe views complain about their lack of platform.

It's not only an entitlement, it's also a tactic. Claiming to be silenced plays an important part in both sexing up views that have become dulled by mainstreaming, while at the same time conferring a sort of underdog legitimacy on to plain old bigotry. When there is no evidence that prejudice is being silenced by a cabal of liberals, as ever, it must be fabricated.

Fabrication – free speech grifting

Stephen Yaxley-Lennon (known by the pseudonym Tommy Robinson) is a British far-right activist. A garden variety racist, Robinson started his career as leader and spokesman for the English Defence League (EDL), an anti-Muslim far-right extremist organisation that believes in the repatriation of Muslims and immigrants from the UK. He and the EDL had mixed success in gathering momentum and, after two spells in prison for travelling to the US on a fake passport and mortgage fraud, Robinson's profile diminished. He then tried to refashion himself as born again, 'deradicalised' at the hands of the counter-extremism organisation The Quilliam Foundation. But that did not last long, presumably due to the lack of media attention and associated money-making opportunities that he expected he would receive. By 2017, he was reduced to ambulance-chasing journalism, where he appeared on the scene of Islamic terror or attempted terror attacks with rudimentary filming equipment, to report on the dangers of Islamic extremism. At one point, an Uber driver lost control of his car and mounted the pavement near London's Natural History Museum. Robinson appeared on the scene not long after to declare a 'jihadi attack'. One could almost have felt sorry for him – he had failed to make a going concern out of the business of hate.

This was not the end of Robinson. Unfortunately, he discovered a trick that would renew his fortunes. Within months, Donald Trump's ambassador to the UK would be lobbying the British government on Robinson's behalf. That trick was to relaunch himself as a free speech martyr. He stalked a trial of British Muslims accused of child abuse and broadcast an hour-long video over Facebook from outside the court. In the video, he made comments that risked the trial's collapse. The year before, Robinson was given a suspended sentence for committing contempt during a rape trial in Canterbury, after he attempted to film the defendants. He was aware that he would go to prison if he broke the law again. It was suicide by contempt of court.

What ensued was a campaign for his release that was based on the lie that his freedom of speech had been violated. A petition drew half a million signatures and far-right European leaders came to his support. Steve Bannon, former Trump strategist and alt-right publisher, almost came to blows with a London radio journalist who challenged him on his support for Robinson. 'Fuck you,' Bannon barked. 'Don't you fucking say you're calling me out. You fucking liberal elite. Tommy Robinson is the backbone of this country.' Within a little over a year, Robinson had gone from a has-been, to the locus of an international far-right free speech crusade, to being the 'backbone' of Great Britain.

Rob Ford, professor of politics at the University of Manchester told the *Observer* newspaper that Robinson's 'true ingenuity' in striking a chord with an international far-right movement was marrying his street vigilante credentials with the motif of a censoring establishment. 'This is exactly the argument they like,' said Ford, 'because it means they can say, "we're the truly brave liberals". The degree to which it has gone viral as an argument shows this is a winner for the radical right. It strongly motivates their core electorate.'

The freedom of speech crisis myth brought Tommy Robinson back from the dead. By legitimising his Islamophobic agenda as conspiracy resistance, Robinson managed to re-fashion himself from a convicted street thug to a principled crusader. By doing so, Robinson disempowered his critics, because to attack him now was not to critique his politics, but his right to freedom of speech. He also empowered his supporters, they were no longer racists, they were moral warriors in a fight against a state that wished to prevent them from exposing the truth. They were disciples of the freedom of speech crisis myth according to Tommy Robinson.

Both Robinson and Milo trade in a sort of insurance scam politics, where an individual throws themselves at a sensitive area and then claims they are victimised by political correctness or the left or women (or all of the above), before cashing in on the attention. The scams range from Robinson's contempt of court and his YouTube shenanigans to Milo threatening to name undocumented students from his speaker podium at Berkeley and getting exactly the response he might have hoped for. Protestors prompted police to evacuate him before he could even speak. If there were no internet, most of these people, and their attendant free speech controversies, would not exist. Milo refers to himself as an 'internet supervillain'.

Free speech calibration in a digital context is something we have not even begun to grapple with, choosing still to litigate it as if it were simply a matter of competing views. There have been moves to ban or demonetise the social media accounts of people who have made free speech a commercial success. In 2019 Tommy Robinson and a number of white supremacist accounts were either suspended or blocked from receiving donations, a move which Robinson blamed for his loss when he ran for a seat in the European parliament. But these measures are random, inchoate and not linked to any solid hate speech policy as smaller less high-profile users continue the work of the banned celebrities. The companies that host such self-styled internet villains have competing interests, and so it's extremely hard to make responsible calls on the harm these characters are inflicting. They have to balance out their bottom line, one which is fed by the traffic abuse and hate speech creates, with their responsibilities as platform providers. Twitter in particular demonstrates the mess that is online free speech policy. Abuse on the platform is ubiquitous and reluctantly policed because to block every vile user is either prohibitive or at some point harms the business model, which is built on user growth. And so the internet supervillains thrive, and if they are finally banned from online platforms, become free speech martyrs.

The writer Mari Uyehara calls this group 'free speech grifters'. They come from a broad church, one that encompasses cynical bottom-feeders such as Milo, Robinson and various other digital con artists, but also a more rarefied bunch – the pin-striped grifters, who use free speech as a tool to score points against progressive causes. These are gentrified, suited, slick grifters such as Bill Maher, a popular HBO talk show host whose show *Real Time With Bill Maher* has run for seventeen years. Maher dedicates far more time alleging that he is persecuted for criticising Islam, than he does addressing an epidemic of Islamophobia.

'Given the myopic focus on liberals' Uyehara pointed out in *GQ* magazine, 'it would seem that Free Speech Grifters are not actually interested in the free exchange of ideas, per se; they are interested in liberal caricature for clicks, social-media followings, and monetisation.' They are interested in goading people into performing rage, so that rage can be recycled as censoriousness, which in turn enhances their stature as liberal inquisition martyrs. Grifting fabricates free speech crisis news and events, the same way the grievance industry fabricates PC crisis reports. The final stage is where the scam really pays off, in that with every alleged silencing incident, the censored views receive even more attention.

The fabrication of the 'no-platforming' epidemic

Much of free speech moral panic stems from incidents of 'no-platforming', where guests are prevented from speaking, mainly on university campuses. Both in the US and the UK, 'no-platforming' is regarded by both those on the right and the left as an epidemic. In 2015, the libertarian website *Spiked* published a Free Speech University Ranking. The only conclusion to be drawn from the data it harvested was that there was a plague of free speech suppression.

This conclusion was a result of massaging the data. *Times Higher Education* (*THE*) called it 'misleading, ill-informed and worryingly influential'. Upon closer analysis the *THE* found that: 'about 85 per cent to 90 per cent of Spiked's evidence each year amounts merely to human resources policies and codes of conduct, of a sort now standard in most large organisations and often required by law. Spiked offers no evidence that these policies have ever been applied in a fashion that repressed free speech, or that they have generated discontent among staff, students or the wider public.'

This did not stop the *Spiked* research from being widely quoted. The *Telegraph* newspaper republished the results without question, as well as running an op-ed entitled 'The poshos pushing campus censorship' which was written by the 'neutral' pen of *Spiked* assistant editor Tom Slater. 'You'd have to have been living under a rock' he writes, 'not to know that British universities have in recent years turned into a cross between Stalinist Russia and a soft-play area.' During a British parliamentary select committee looking into free speech issues in higher education, three of the four witnesses called upon were connected with the *Spiked* network. Unfortunately, Tom Slater is correct – you would have to have been living under a rock not to think that there is a left-wing crèche patrolled by Marxists on British campuses. But the data simply does not hold up. What the *Spiked* research does is come to the issue with a clear agenda, which is to torture the data as much as possible in order to produce an alarming result. It collapsed HR codes of conduct, measures against hate speech and incitement (to be found in the majority of professional establishments, academic or otherwise) and general decisions made in the interest of protecting the student body into censorious activity. One university was given a 'red' ranking, indicating that the institution 'has banned and actively censored ideas on campus', because its student union banned advertising by payday loan companies on campus. The university said it was 'simply a common sense effort to prevent exploitation of students.' In 2018, it emerged that *Spiked* received six-figure donations from the Charles Koch Foundation – the Kochtopus was extending its tentacles to the UK.

Manipulating of data to come up with free speech campus hysteria headlines is a common practice. Research by *Vox* published in 2018 takes issue with what has become an entire genre of US college campus free speech panic, one that includes books, online magazines and is the theme of regular columns in the American press. The research looked at both alleged incidents of free speech violations on college campuses and at the overall trends regarding freedom of expression among college students in particular and liberals in general. The conclusion was that overall public support for free speech has in fact risen over time, not fallen, and that those on the political right are less supportive of free speech than those on the left. The research also concluded that college graduates are on the whole more supportive than non-graduates and that college students are less likely than the overall population to support restrictions on speech on campus.

The academic Jeffrey Sachs came to the same conclusion after sifting through data on attitudes among US college students towards freedom of speech and also incidents of free speech terminations or withdrawal of platform based on political ideology. The most compelling data comes from a 'disinvitation database', created by the Foundation for Individual Rights in Education (FIRE), a watchdog group that promotes free expression on campus and tracks attempts by students to disinvite or prevent campus speakers. It showed just thirty-five attempts at disinvitation in 2017, down from forty-three in 2016. Sachs makes the point that out of a pool of almost five thousand colleges, disinvitation attempts, and by extension attempts that have actually succeeded, are quite rare. According to FIRE, in 2018, there were nine attempts at disinvitation. Among them was the political commentator Dave Rubin, invited to debate at the University of New Hampshire. His invite was opposed for racial and anti-immigration views that the student body found objectionable. They were not successful. Nigel Farage makes an appearance on the 2018 list as well, when a request was brought to stand him down from a debate at the University of Maryland for race and immigration related concerns. It was also not successful. BBC *Question Time* would approve.

'There is no campus free speech crisis,' Sachs concluded, 'the right's new moral panic is largely imaginary.'

There are also indications that there is insurance scam politics at play here as well. In the United States, well-funded right-wing groups are increasingly funnelling controversial

speakers into campuses, in some instances paying and train-
ing them, with the purpose of provoking a protest that can
then be used as evidence of left-wing campus illiberalism.
In 2017, the University of Buffalo hosted Robert Spencer,
an anti-Muslim author and blogger who was quoted by
the Norwegian mass-murderer Anders Breivik in his man-
ifesto sixty-four times, along with other Western writers
who shared his view that Muslim immigrants pose a grave
danger to Western culture. This was not an invite that arose
organically out of the normal course of events at the college. He was invited by the Young America's Foundation,
a well-funded conservative lobbying group that engages
in 'gotcha' tactics to promote its right-wing culture wins.
On social media, the organisation's tone is pugilistic and
seems less concerned with promoting conservative values
than it is scoring points against the left and 'triggering the
libs'. In 2018, it promoted videos and content with captions
such as: '✹ SHOTS FIRED ✹ @DLoesch completely EX-
POSES the Left's gun control agenda! You can't fool her'
and '🖐 THERE 🖐 ARE 🖐 ONLY 🖐 TWO 🖐 GENDERS
🖐 WHEN WILL THE LEFT LEARN??? @BenShapiro has
had enough'.

The foundation paid Robert Spencer a $2,000 fee, and
trained a student leader to organise both the event and the
distribution of literature beforehand. They then waited for
the money shot. And they got it. Members of the college's
Muslim population and non-Muslim sympathisers staged a
sit-in, although Spencer's talk was allowed to proceed. Inevitably it became about the protest, something that Spencer
himself appeared to be briefed on, as he concluded his talk
by saying: 'The forces you are enabling are going to come
back to haunt you.'

On the group's website, it boasted of 'dispatching'

thirty-one speakers to colleges in one month in 2017. Among them was Ann Coulter. After Spencer's talk, the *New York Times* reported on this suicide by boycott tactic, pointing out that the foundation's invitees seemed to be getting edgier and more controversial. The report gave voice to protesters who questioned 'whether such events are cynically intended to provoke reactions'. A student quoted by the paper said that regular speaker controversies were 'part of a larger systematic and extremely well-funded effort to disrupt public universities and create tension among student groups on campus'.

It is often the case, when following the breadcrumbs of a myth, to find that not only is it not true, but that its *opposite* is true. What *Vox*'s research did find, was that even though data indicates a trend towards more willingness to hear from disagreeable people, the exception to that was speech from disagreeable Muslims.

The same exception applies in the UK. In the exact way that political correctness concerns divert attention from actual crises such as incidents of racism or rape culture on university campuses, so does the free speech crisis myth conceal actual persecution based on arbitrary judgements of what is considered problematic speech. The British government's anti-terror strategy Prevent, introduced in 2006 and expanded in 2011, has had implications on free speech that has not exercised any of the usual free speech advocates. Prevent places responsibility on schools, universities and colleges to challenge any unusual or potentially dangerous behaviour that could be a sign of radicalisation or underlying terrorism. In 2018, SOAS director and former leader of the House of Lords Baroness Amos said that the policy is responsible for a perceived 'chilling' of free speech on university campuses.

'Given the nature of our student body, and given the

concerns about an overall political environment in which –
certainly our students and a lot of our faculty feel – there is
a squeezing of the ability to be open, diverse and inclusive,
for example, how we treat refugees, our visa policy, how
Prevent is being implemented. All these things are having an
impact on how young people, particularly young people of
colour, or who are Muslim, actually feel in terms of being
under additional scrutiny.'

Patrick Kilduff, president of Edinburgh University Students' Association, echoed Amos. 'The real threats [to free
speech] are coming from government legislation like Prevent', he said.

So not only does the data show that there is no free
speech crisis as such, it also illustrates that, as myths tend
to do, there is a mobilisation against progressive causes that
outstrips any activity on the allegedly censorious left. An
analysis of the FIRE disinvitation data by Heterodox Academy, shows that the most successful attempts to shut down
speakers have come from right-leaning groups. The analysis
concluded that 'speaker disinvitation attempts have a higher
success rate when they come from the right of the speaker
(54.64 per cent) than when they come from the left of the
speaker (32.89 per cent).'

All these conclusions do not seem to be making a dent in
the overall conventional wisdom about a freedom of speech
crisis. And attention is being diverted from what is essentially a growing resistance movement. There was only one
type of speech that Jeffrey Sachs found to be tolerated less –
racist speech. I spoke to him a few weeks after he published
this research and he pointed out that an important point
that is often missed among the smoke and mirrors of free
speech crisis mythology is the degree of polarisation that is
often present in these debates.

'Nothing new is happening,' he says, 'The emergence on the right of things like Campus Reform is what constituted a turning point.' These organisations, according to Sachs, have made it their job to bring attention to campus skirmishes. Campus Reform he said: 'are very well funded by the Mercer family, and have a very successful infrastructure that has no corollary on the left. Nothing new is happening. But they have been very effective in drumming up hysteria in a way that we didn't have five years ago.'

Funding always seems to be the smoking gun. Where there is polarisation, before there was funding. Little of this is organic.

The rise in intolerance of racist speech and the rise in the scale of racist provocations are intersecting and we are drawing the wrong conclusion – that there is a free speech crisis. In fact, it is a polarisation crisis. What is really on the cards with this misdiagnosis is a chilling effect and the quieting of voices that are protesting harmful speech. This objection is being delegitimised by dismissing it as a rejection of free speech, and deploying 'what next' fallacies. What next fallacy promoters claim that curbing free speech, even if it is harmful, is a 'slippery slope'.

The tool – the 'slippery slope'

The logic of the 'slippery slope' is the technical tool that the freedom of speech crisis myth deploys to either end the argument or divert attention away from the inconvenient distinctions and nuances that conflate freedom of speech and right to platform with freedom from consequence. It goes something like this: if you enable censorship or the silencing of views you do not like that exposes the views you do like to censorship as well. You will be next. University of

Amsterdam academic Magdalena Jozwiak summarises the slippery slope argument as: 'Today this speech restriction, tomorrow the Inquisition.'

It is a compelling argument that has achieved almost canonical status. It just sounds like it makes sense. It seems neat and logical and the imagery, that of an evil nourished by our shortsightedness, is vivid. Its essence is in Martin Niemöller's famous poem 'First they came . . .', which ends with the chilling line: 'Then they came for me – and there was no one left to speak for me.'

It is also a flattering conviction. To believe in defending views with which you disagree implies a moral robustness and intellectual largesse. But the slippery slope argument is based on two wrong assumptions. The first is false equivalence. The second is that there is simply no evidence that the slippery slope exists.

On an abstract level, slippery slope logic doesn't hold. Everything turns on the fact that the initial premise, the first step on the slope, is not false or implausible. The starting point of slippery slope logic, that which equates speech which is incendiary, demeaning, threatening or stigmatising with all other possible forms of speech, is implausible. It is less, 'First they came for the socialists, and I did nothing, then they came for me' and more, 'First they came for the Holocaust deniers, and then they did not come for me or anyone else, because none of us were Holocaust deniers'.

In a 2015 paper entitled 'Internet, Freedom of Speech and Slippery Slope Argument – The Case of the "Right to Be Forgotten"', Jozwiak wrote that 'slippery slope arguments are slippery themselves: if any limits of freedom of speech are simply too dangerous to be accepted, why not call for tearing down the copyrights, or law prohibiting deceptive commercial speech?'

The slippery slope fallacy is a relation of the 'where do you draw the line?' fallacy. Another tool used against those who try to argue that there is a way to challenge hate speech without that having implications on freedom of speech as a whole. Where do you draw the line? Well, where myriad other lines are drawn all the time as part of society's customary and legal boundaries.

The line drawing fallacy argues that just because a precise line cannot be drawn between two things, then no other distinctions can be made. So, for example, if neo-Nazi groups are restricted, then other unpopular but not actual Nazi groups will also be silenced on the basis that they are advancing some sort of racially divisive idea. Policing hate is not always very straightforward, and sometimes it might get messy and mistakes may even be made, but on the whole, it is clearly possible to make this and other distinctions. When one considers the binary way in which this argument is made, it becomes even more clear that distinctions can be drawn because it is essentially saying 'your opinion, Y, one you believe is moral and antithetical to opinion X, which you want to restrict, will inevitably also be indistinguishable from X'. So the draw the line fallacy is in fact making the case that diametrically opposed ideas will become impossible to tell apart.

Lines are drawn to limit drinking, sexual activity and voting by age, abortion by foetal growth stage, prison sentences by severity of crime. The entire existence of a functioning society is predicated on the business of drawing lines and distinctions between things where there are only shades of difference, often in extremely complicated and emotive areas. But somehow, according to the freedom of speech crisis logic, our ability to do so will collapse when trying to draw a line between the KKK and Black Lives Matter.

The slippery slope is also often presented as a 'what if' hypothetical, as opposed to pointing out something that has already happened (which would be helpful in validating the premise). If so many freedom of speech transgressions are already being made (and according to some, this has been happening for decades), then surely a very clear slippery slope example should be evident? I managed to find some-one who had made an effort – the author Kenan Malik. Two examples he produces fall apart at the most cursory scrutiny. In March 2018, Malik wrote in his *Observer* news-paper column in defence of three white nationalist activists who were barred from entering the UK. 'Who next?' asked the subheading of the piece.

'Anti-racists in particular should be wary of such bans,' he says, in a classic example of how the tool is used to prove that, when it comes to racism in particular, defend-ing yourself against hate speech is equivalent to inciting it because censorship is blind to even such stark differences. He goes on to state that: 'Censorious laws that some ap-plaud when applied to the far-right *inevitably* [emphasis mine] get turned on to the left and anti-racists. The 1965 Race Relations Act introduced Britain's first legal ban on the incitement of racial hatred. Among the first people convicted under its provisions was the black power activist Michael X.'

This seems pretty damning and a clear case of how one thing did really lead to another, to an unintended conse-quence. But the conviction of Michael X was not because he made anti-racist statements that the Race Relations Act misread as incitement (the point that Malik was making), it was because he advocated for the immediate killing of any white man seen 'laying hands' on a black woman. He was later also arrested for extortion and then convicted of murder in his native Trinidad. His sentence was execution. Now, one could argue that Michael X's conviction was too loose an application of the act (although I am not sure how), but it would still not fit Malik's definition of 'anti-racism'.

The second example he raises is that 'the 1936 Public Order Act, brought into control Oswald Mosley's fascists, became used after the war to target trade unionists – most notoriously during the miners' strike of 1984–85 – and anti-fascist demonstrations in the 1970s and 1980s'. The year-long miners' strike saw violent confrontations between flying pickets and the police, who used the act on the grounds of preventing a breach of the peace. Anti-fascist demonstrations and the Public Order Act are a much messier affair. There is a specific British antipathy to acts of public protest, which authorities prefer to be tightly curated and to follow a strict definition of peaceful. That is the problem, not the legal act.

This is a point made by the left-wing activist Aaron Bastani in a 2013 *Guardian* column in which he analyses the heavy-handed police response to public protest and states that the UK 'increasingly accepts protest only overseen by official administrators of dissent, such as the TUC (Trade Union Congress), whose lives more closely resemble those with whom they are supposedly in contestation'. With this as context, Malik's Public Order Act point seems a stretching of the slippery slope argument.

None of the above context stopped Malik from concluding that 'if we allow the state to define the limits of acceptable speech, it will not just be speech to which we object that gets curtailed'.

It seems if there is a failure to make a distinction, it is on the part of such slippery slope advocates. Being left-wing or anti-racist does not mean that one cannot also succumb to lower impulses of violence or incitement. It is possible to be broadly on the side of a black activist such as Michael X and yet still find his speech objectionable and support that it be curtailed. And so it is by no means proven, let alone 'inevitable', that a free speech slippery slope does exist. The limits of free speech are by all means debatable, but there is no evidence that continuum logic should be part of that debate.

'Next the inquisition' arguments are popular because they appeal to both the right and the left. To the right because they are useful in securing licence and to the left because they chime with liberal positions on individual liberty and right to express dissent. The origin of free speech advocacy is in anti-authoritarianism, intended to protect the right to oppose and criticise power, be it the Church or secular state, without fear of punishment. The left continued this tradition by trying to maintain the widest possible definition of protected speech. In the United States, the three seminal Supreme Court decisions on free speech in the twentieth century were successfully brought by the left in order to prevent a chilling of dissent. The decisions made for a higher burden of proof to show 'clear and present danger' before blocking speech, the allowance for false statements of fact when criticising public officials, and the objection to 'prior restraints', such as injunctions and licensing laws to forbid speech. The way in which free speech principles are now being used by the powerful to attack the weak is a difficult development to come to terms with for some parts of the left – and so they argue technicalities, while those they set out to protect, the dissenters, the vulnerable and excluded, are savaged.

Freedom to respond

Freedom of speech is not a neutral, fixed concept, un-coloured by societal prejudice. The belief that it is some absolute untainted hallmark of civilisation is linked to self-serving exceptionalism, a delusion that there is a basic template around which there is a consensus uninformed by biases. The recent history of fighting for freedom of speech has gone from noble, striving for the right to publish works that offend people's sexual or religious prudery and speaking up against the values leveraged by the powerful to maintain control, to attacking the weak and persecuted. The effort has evolved from challenging upwards, to punching downwards.

It has become bogged down in false equivalence and extending the sanctity of fact to opinion by a media that has an interest in creating as much heat and no light from the discourse. Central in this process is an establishment of curators, publishers and editors for whom controversy is a product to be pushed. That is the marketplace of ideas now, not a free and organic exchange of intellectual goods.

The myth of the free speech crisis has been pushed by right-wing funding and activism, but it has also been in-dulged by those on the left who are prone to commitment to abstract ideals that are virtuous in essence, but sometimes unfit for application without modulation. Enlightenment prophets and their aphorisms are rolled out, but with little accounting for nuance or adjustment for a modern context (it is no wonder that the US constitution, extended from Enlightenment values, is often critiqued as fossilised). Voltaire's misattributed 'I disapprove of what you say, but I will defend to the death your right to say it' is thrown like a single blanket over a house fire.

The truth is that freedom of speech, even to some of its most passionate founding philosophers, always comes with brake mechanisms, and those mechanisms usually reflect cultural bias. John Milton advocated the destruction of works that are blasphemous or libellous: 'Those which otherwise come forth, if they be found mischievous and libellous, the fire and the executioner will be the timeliest and the most effectual remedy, that mans [*sic*] prevention can use.' Today, our brake mechanisms still do not include curbing the promotion of hate towards those at the bottom end of the social hierarchy because their protection is not a valued and integral part of our popular culture, despite what the PC and freedom of speech myth peddlers say.

Free speech as an abstract value is now directly at odds with the sanctity of life, it's not merely a matter of 'offence'. Judith Butler, a cultural theorist and Berkeley professor, speaking at a 2017 forum sponsored by the Berkeley Academic Senate, said: 'If free speech does take precedence over every other constitutional principle and every other community principle, then perhaps we should no longer claim to be weighing or balancing competing principles or values. We should perhaps frankly admit that we have agreed in advance to have our community sundered, racial and sexual minorities demeaned, the dignity of trans people denied, that we are, in effect, willing to be wrecked by this principle of free speech.'

We challenge this instrumentalisation by reclaiming the true meaning of freedom of speech (which is freedom to speak rather than a right to speak without consequence), challenging hate speech more forcefully without getting caught up in liberal preciousness, being unfraid to contemplate banning or no-platforming those we think are harmful to the public good, and being tolerant of objection to them when they do speak. Like the political correctness myth, the free speech myth is a call for orthodoxy, for passiveness in the face of assault.

A moral right to express unpopular opinions is not a moral right to express those opinions in a way that silences the voices of others, or puts them in danger of violence. There are those who abuse freedom of speech, who wish others harm, and who roll back efforts to ensure that all citizens are treated with respect. This is just a fact. One can be a Voltairian without being a Panglossian.

CHAPTER 4

The myth of damaging identity politics

'*What makes identity politics a significant departure from earlier [movements] is its demand for recognition on the basis of the very grounds on which recognition has previously been denied: it is qua women, qua blacks, qua lesbians that groups demand recognition. . . . The demand is not for inclusion within the fold of "universal humankind" . . . nor is it for respect "in spite of" one's differences. Rather, what is demanded is respect for oneself as different.*'

Sonia Kruks

On the morning of 16 June 2016, a man carrying a black holdall and a Tesco carrier bag, ate a bar of chocolate in the market square at Birstall, a village in West Yorkshire. He loitered there for a while and then at some point made his way towards the library just off the square. At 12.50 p.m. Jo Cox, a Labour MP, and her two aides pulled up in a car in front of the library where she was scheduled to meet some of her constituents.

As Cox and her two companions stepped from the car on to the pavement, the man ran towards her and shot her in the head with a sawn-off .22 rifle. When she fell to the ground, he dragged her by the hair into the road and stabbed her repeatedly with an army dagger. Her aides tried to come to help, but he pushed them back with his knife. An elderly bystander attempted to intervene. He was stabbed in the stomach.

Believing Cox was dead, the man began to walk away, but then she spoke, possibly sealing her fate. 'Get away you two,' she said to her aides, 'let him hurt me, don't let him hurt you.' Alerted to the fact that she might survive, he returned and shot Cox two more times, once in the head, another in the chest. Then he stabbed her again. At various points during the attack, he said, 'This is for Britain', 'keep Britain independent' and 'Britain first'. Jo Cox was pronounced dead at the scene within an hour of the attack.

The killer was found a short while later, walking aimlessly in the town. When he was arrested, he told police 'I'm a political activist.'

What looked like a random act of violence, perhaps by someone who was unwell, against a widely loved MP, quickly began to take on a more sinister shape. In his house, the police found an entire library of neo-Nazi literature, neatly categorised in a bookcase on top of which sat a swastika-etched gold eagle. It was biblio-evidence of a motive for the killing. Some form of white supremacy merged with Nazi cultural fetishisation and underscored by a hatred of not only those of other races, but those seen to enable them. It would have made sense if the assassin had murdered a black or Jewish person, but his politics soured him towards those of his own ethnic group who had frittered his and, by extension, the country's, capital away by handing it over to others of inferior races. Without the enablers, to his way of thinking, there would have been no contamination. When he was asked to give his name in court once his trial began, Cox's killer replied: 'Death to traitors, freedom for Britain.'

His was not a recent conversion. A long history of identitarian politics unfolded. He had links to right-wing political
groups such as the National Front and the English Defence
League. In addition to the Nazi insignia and literature, information on the construction of bombs was found in his
home. He had been plotting – or at least fantasising about –
killing a 'collaborator', someone he perceived was complicit
in compromising white ethnic superiority, for the better part
of twenty years. To him, Jo Cox was that collaborator. She
was a supporter of the European Union at a time of frenzied
EU referendum campaigning in which dog whistles came in
chorus from the right. She extended welcome to refugees
and asylum seekers, particularly to those from Syria, and
had spoken passionately upon her election in her maiden
address in Parliament, about what grounded her politics.
'We are far more united and have far more in common with
each other than things that divide us,' she said.

It was the first assassination of a serving politician on
British soil since the death of Conservative MP Ian Gow,
who was killed by the Provisional Irish Republican Army
in 1990. The country was in shock. The face of Jo Cox,
a mother of two and an idealistic newly elected politician,
smiled beatifically on television screens across the country as
Britons tried to absorb the obvious but also unthinkable. It
was the Brexit campaign, in all its ugliness and toxicity, that
had done this. Nigel Farage, then head of UKIP, had only a
few hours before the murder unveiled what was to become
the low watermark of the campaign – a poster of a queuing
throng of brown male migrants with the tag line 'BREAKING
POINT'. Cox was a passionate Remain advocate and, a few
days before her murder, had argued in a column in a local
newspaper for a vote to stay in the European Union.

'I know for many people that this is a tough decision, that

the debate has been highly charged and the facts difficult to pin down,' she said. 'But I believe that the patriotic choice is to vote for Britain to remain inside the EU where we are stronger, safer and better off than we would be on our own.' Police found a copy of this column in her murderer's house, printed out and neatly filed along with other press cuttings.

Apart from this printout, there was nothing that he had said or done that specifically referenced Brexit, but the timing, his choice of target, the very air we were breathing in the UK at the time was polluted. Something new had been released into the political atmosphere.

The episode to me can only be remembered in two halves, the significance of the moment – and then its almost immediate diminishment as things went back to the toxic normal. Brexit campaigning was suspended out of respect but it barely held for twenty-four hours. Rather than ushering in a moment that gave the country pause to think about what it was that had been unleashed, the assassination seemed to make some more determined not to let it arrest the momentum of a Brexit vote. It worked. The country was not ready for reflection. Britain voted out.

Since Brexit, Jo Cox's murder has been reduced to charges of cynical politicising from both ends of the political divide. In November 2016, the Equality and Human Rights Commission advised Westminster party leaders to 'tone down' campaigning rhetoric that, it argued, has 'legitimised hate'. Those on the pro-Brexit right saw moves like this as using Cox's killing to smear the movement. Dominic Lawson in the *Daily Mail* accused the commission of instrumentalising her 'horrific murder' in 'a contemptible campaign to smear Brexit supporters'.

*

Rather than alerting the country that behind some of the right-wing, anti-immigration rhetoric something darker was lurking, it only helped sharpen it. Cox's murder has since been reduced to a political football, kicked around in the muddy gutter of the post-Brexit culture wars.

It was a lost opportunity. The Labour MP's killing has become the kind of event that the public is accustomed to dismissing when it comes to race-related violence committed by white perpetrators. The murderer was unemployed, a misfit, a classic one-off 'lone wolf'. But he was not deranged; he was not acting out of passion, on the spur of the moment; he was not temporarily agitated by political events. He was declared fit by court experts and launched no defence on the basis of mental impairment. And he was not a 'lone wolf', he had his people, having been radicalised by years of exposure to both historical formulations of white supremacist politics, such as Nazism, and contemporary white grievance mythologies. The former advanced the ideology that the world should be organised around racial hierarchy, demanding more power for white people, especially men, and the latter demanded the restoration of power to white people. To stand at the intersection of these two currents is to feel powerful, dispossessed and dangerously entitled.

Since Cox's murder, another man, Jack Renshaw, has been sentenced to life in prison for plotting the murder of the Labour MP Rosie Cooper. As he left the court Renshaw made a Nazi salute to his supporters, one of whom shouted 'We are with you, Jack.' Another not-so-lone wolf. The patterns are clear. In 2018, far-right terror convictions in the UK surpassed those of Islamic terror organisations for the first time. In the US, white-orchestrated terrorism has claimed more lives on US soil than any other identity-based terrorism since 9/11.

But somehow, the idea of a white identity politics which is hostile and aggressive is not an established part of the modern political discourse unless it is manifested in coordinated violent acts, and even then the threat is minimised. A strange oversight, considering that exclusionary white identity politics has been a cornerstone of domestic and overseas American and European politics for the last two centuries. The threat such white identity politics poses is often trivialised, and the impact of other individual or group behaviour that can be seen as rooted in a similarly exclusionary view of the world, such as gender segregated Muslim schools, is dramatised and pathologised.

This double standard is applied to all political activity that is based on racial identity. There is a lacuna, a colour blindness so to speak, to acts of politics committed in the name of white power and those committed in reaction to the wielding of that white power. This is the myth of a damaging identity politics; that group behaviour to secure rights denied on racial grounds is corrosive, restricted to non-majority white groups and is offensive, rather than defensive. The myth is helped along by constant denial that race is relevant to how white populations behave politically. Their race-based mobilisation is minimised, it's just 'white self-interest', or a number of other euphemisms. In fact, it is others who are obsessed with race.

The damaging identity politics myth creates an *exception* for whiteness, promotes *racial entitlement* via dog whistling ('*the wink*') and *grievance flipping* and is sustained by appeals to '*universalism*'.

For the purposes of this chapter, there are two definitions of identity politics. The first is the effort to secure the rights denied to some on the basis of their identity (defensive identity politics). The second is that which seeks domination on the basis of identity (aggressive identity politics). This chapter will focus on identity politics on ethnic or racial lines and the different standards and definitions applied in order to render white identity politics natural and benign, and identity politics as practised by others as dangerous, indulgent and damaging. But it is only due to absence of space that I cannot flesh out all the other ways 'default' identities, those vested with so much power that they do not see themselves as identities at all – maleness, heterosexuality, heteronormativity – also conspire to dismiss the concerns of others marginal to them.

An exception for whiteness

History repeats itself not because humans fail to learn from their mistakes, but rather because the mistakes that come from within a society are harder to identify until it is too late. There is a discount applied to behaviour by those we see as our own. In Saudi Arabia, it was official policy never to use the word 'terrorist' or 'terrorism' when referring to religious insurgents waging war against the royal family for the past forty years. Perpetrators were referred to as 'those who have lost their path' – or 'the lost ones'. Terrorist groups came to be known as 'The Lost Front' or 'The Lost Category'. In the 1990s, the country even set up a Betty Ford-style deradicalisation clinic, offering amnesty once its graduates had completed a full terror detox programme. When that was unsuccessful, the Saudi government decided to claim that any internal opposition to it was funded and stoked by external enemies such as Iran and Qatar.

A similar moral amnesty is extended to white people who continue to behave and vote along racial lines harmful to minorities, while condemning other political movements that are based on identity as self-indulgent and damaging to the achievement of universal goals. To the left, those goals are anti-capitalist, first and foremost; healthcare, housing and unionisation. To the right, universal goals that defensive identity politics undermines are mostly to do with community and national cohesion. These cannot be achieved if everyone is playing 'oppression Olympics' all the time.

Defensive identity politics is mistakenly seen as a disruptive influence that divides the electorate and has pushed white voters into the embrace of populists. But it is merely a reflexive movement that is responding to both the constant subordination of the non-mainstream identity, and a push-back against equality. It is a response against the dominance and ubiquity of a white identity. As Hannah Arendt said, 'if one is attacked as a Jew, one must defend oneself as a Jew'. When you are attacked and threatened because of your identity, you respond in terms of your identity. When the Republican gubernatorial candidate Roy Moore ran his 2017 campaign, his history of racist positions came to light. This was a candidate who said that America was better during the slavery era, that the Quran was comparable to Hitler's *Mein Kampf*, and who endorsed Trump's Obama birther conspiracy. Black voters turned out and voted against him in their racial interest, regardless of ideology. When they were threatened as blacks, they voted in one racial block.

The American political researcher Asad Haider summarised the problem with this disparity in how demands from different racial groups are viewed. At a 2018 talk, he stated: 'By coding demands that come from marginal or subordinate groups as identity politics the white male identity is enshrined with the status of the neutral, general and universal.' He continued: 'We know that this is false, we know that there is a white identity politics, a white nationalism, and in fact whiteness is the prototypical form of racial ideology itself.'

But 'we' do not know this is false. The danger of the myth is in the smearing of legitimate campaigns for dignity and equal treatment as obsessed with victimhood, and the empowering of 'backlash' political behaviour (such as whites across classes voting for Trump in the election). There's an almost satisfying identical engineering to how these political myths are structured. In their DNA, somewhere there is always a coding that, when reproduced into the world, functions to deny victimhood to the subjugated and then blame them for the bad behaviour of their oppressors. Women are trying to get more than they deserve or have rightfully earned. The victims of hate speech are in fact the intolerant party. Those who ask for respect and accommodation of difference are using political correctness to bully others. In the case of the damaging identity politics myth, this strain is most evolved.

To look at defensive identity politics as a phenomenon that has fractured common national causes because minority groups are obsessed with securing recognition is to look at the issue back to front. In the 1960s, the struggles for black rights, women's rights and gay rights were closely linked to the wider project of social transformation and the wider struggle against white supremacism and heteronormativity. The damaging identity politics myth is based on the belief that things have reverted to some benign mean – that slavery and racial segregation have ended (and for those particularly committed to the myth, ended by white people) and so now we must all stop asking for special dispensation (the 'politics of recognition' is what the writer Amy Chua calls it) as fundamentally, there are no serious problems anymore that are not universal.

Since Trump's election and the Brexit referendum, the euphemisms for votes motivated by racial grievance or anti-immigration sentiment rapidly have become a part of the political lexicon; these people are not racist, they are the 'left-behind', acting out because of 'economic anxiety'. Even when they are not the meek of the earth, they appear to be legitimately acting out of 'white interest'. The British journalist and writer David Goodhart in his book, *The Road to Somewhere*, adds to the by-another-name genteelisms with the term 'Somewheres', as distinct from 'Anywheres'. The Somewheres are rooted in a specific place or community, such as a small town or in the countryside. They are socially conservative, less educated and less mobile than their metropolitan counterparts. The Anywheres are, well, anywhere; unrooted to a particular place or community and able to relocate easily for work, education or love. Goodhart had written less euphemistically a decade before this book was published, in *Prospect*, when he stated, 'To put it bluntly – most of us prefer our own kind.' This sentiment is echoed by Derek Black, the son of a grand wizard in the Ku Klux Klan, in a 2018 NPR interview: 'The fundamental belief that drove my dad, drove my parents and my family, over decades,' he says, 'was that race was the defining feature of humanity . . . and that people were only happy if they could live in a society that was only this one biologically defined racial group.'

This direct honesty about white racial loyalty is helpful in understanding how minorities are blamed for white tribal behaviour, just by existing. Alas it is rare. The conviction that white people behave in a distinct political unit because other identities absolutely force them to produce some fine pretzel logic.

In a 2016 op-ed for the *New York Times*, American academic Mark Lilla manages to blame the Trump 'whitelash' on liberals, in general, and Hillary Clinton, in particular. He calls it 'identity liberalism'. Liberals, he claims, do not recognise 'how their own obsession with diversity has encouraged white, rural, religious Americans to think of themselves as a disadvantaged group whose identity is being threatened or ignored'. He does not follow that revealing thought through – in other terms, whiteness is an identity. He then goes on to assert: 'liberals should bear in mind that the first identity movement in American politics was the Ku Klux Klan, which still exists. Those who play the identity game should be prepared to lose it.'

Even though Lilla thought he was producing a knockout punch, proving the damaging effects of identity politics with his reference to the KKK, what he was doing was in fact exposing the very heart of the myth. He refuses to believe that white identity politics came first and is aggressive, while identity politics by non-whites came second and is defensive.

White 'Somewheres' and left-behinders in economic anxiety are all demonstrating the same thing – aggressive identity politics. But the view that defensive identity politics (its most basic the drive to secure equal rights for historically disenfranchised groups) has fractured political solidarity and created white anger fails to account for the fact that whiteness itself *is* an identity. In fact, not only is it an identity, it is such a clear and potent one that it has behaved as such quite consistently, erecting high barriers to entry via slavery, colonialism, segregation and institutional discrimination. These barriers created the need for defensive identity politics in the first place.

Crucial to this misperception is the belief that whiteness

is the default. So much of mythology is down to this defaulting of certain identities – being white, a certain sort of masculine, hailing from a certain class and being a specific form of straight – as base case, neutral, unmotivated by anything as vulgar as colour or gender. The assumption that these identities are simply standard and correct, rather than merely powerful, underpins the need to create myths. These myths then continue to approach resistance to this defaulting as a revolt against the natural order of things, rather than an attempt at correction.

What the damaging identity politics myth is based on is the perception that political motivations of the powerful are rational and untinged by anything as base as furthering an identity agenda. This kind of thinking is a cousin of that which holds that free speech is a neutral concept. It is similarly silencing, in that it demands that responses to the aggressive disenfranchisement should be to sit still and root for universal values. It demands when, for example, some American Muslims cannot have their non-American relatives visit them because of Trump's Muslim ban, that they be zen. Perhaps reaching for some abstract notion of American citizenship for comfort would be helpful in their acceptance of this group punishment as 'patriotism', rather than a violation of their rights based on their identity.

Racial entitlement

Since 2016, there has been a lot said about 'economic anxiety' in the United States and how it motivated white voters to elect Trump. During the campaign, the dust-streaked image of the Appalachian coal miner stalked the pages of the American press. He was losing his living, his extended family support network and community falling apart, alienated and angry. 'I kind of feel that people are looking down on us,' Neil Hanshew, a miner told the *New York Times* in August of that year. He was voicing a 'common sentiment' the report said. 'They're looking at us like we're a bunch of dumb hillbillies who can't do anything else.'

It was lapped up. The *Atlantic* reported that 'the billionaire developer is building a blue-collar foundation.' The Associated Press pointed out 'Trump's success in attracting white, working-class voters'. On 9 November 2016, the *New York Times* ran a front-page article saying that Trump's support was 'a decisive demonstration of power by a largely overlooked coalition of mostly blue-collar white and working-class voters'.

There was a fixation on this most sympathetic of figures. The spectre of Hanshew angered the right and shamed the left. But two things were missed. There were other disenfranchised working-class voters who didn't flock to Trump. They were not white. And there were affluent people who were not alienated or looked down upon who voted for Trump. The common denominator was not economics, but race. It took about a year for the narrative to catch up.

Research published in the *Washington Post* in late 2017 determined that the economic anxiety claim was, broadly, nonsense. 'Contrary to what some have suggested,' the authors Matthew Fowler, Vladimir E. Medenica and Cathy J. Cohen concluded that 'white millennial Trump voters were not in more economically precarious situations than non-Trump voters. Fully 86 per cent of them reported being employed, a rate similar to non-Trump voters; and they were 14 per cent less likely to be low income than white voters who did not support Trump. Employment and income were not significantly related to that sense of white vulnerability. So what was it? Racial resentment.'

'White vulnerability' and 'racial resentment' are in themselves euphemisms (political correctness is sometimes not a myth, you see, when it comes to refusing to call prejudices what they actually are). Both terms imply that Trump voters' motivation was legitimate and understandable – they were just vulnerable and resentful. 'Racial entitlement' would be a more accurate and less unnecessarily forgiving descriptor. Racial entitlement, rather than economic concerns, made Trump a more attractive proposition for white voters who, in the millennial category, were in fact less likely to be economically deprived than voters who did not support Trump. White non-Hispanics without college degrees making below the median US household income made up only 25 per cent of Trump voters. On the whole, Hillary Clinton lost to Trump among white voters in every single income category, across classes, educations and incomes. He won among poor working-class voters and their wealthy overlords. This was not an economic revolution; it was a white nationalist one.

And those who genuinely felt that they were worse off may have imagined it. There is evidence to suggest that feelings of economic anxiety are correlated to racial entitlement. In his book *Post-Racial or Most-Racial? Race and Politics in the Obama Era*, the political scientist Michael Tesler found that perceptions of the American economy were influenced by the colour of the president at the time. The unemployment rate in particular during election years varied significantly between the times when Barack Obama was running for re-election, and when George W. Bush ran. By 2012, those voters who registered higher levels of 'racial resentment' were less likely to perceive that in reality the unemployment rate, for example, had improved under Obama. Real changes in economic performance did not affect levels of racial resentment. When the economy really was doing badly or when voters themselves were worse off, this did not make them more predisposed to feeling racial grievances. But no matter what the economy was doing, where Obama was concerned, white voters felt things were worse than they really were.

'The evidence is pretty clear,' concludes Telser, 'economic concerns are not driving racial resentment in the Obama Era.' It was the other way around. Racial resentment was driving economic anxiety. The *Washington Post* polls found that feelings of entitlement based on race were the single most dependable predictor of 'white vulnerability'. Everything else, all other variables such as education and economic status, did not make a difference.

This is aggressive identity politics that is constantly legitimised by reaching for false economic analysis. The evidence, both from academic research papers and media polls, that prejudices about race, gender and immigration animated support for Trump, has been mounting since the election. Trump's tenure has been characterised by even more racist and sexist dog whistling, without impacting his popularity among his base. Some called it fear of 'losing status' or concerns about 'cultural displacement'. There were also indications that Trump voters had stronger feelings about the ostensibly declining status of America globally. Dominance at home and abroad meant sitting on top of the totem pole racially. On the whole, the votes for Trump were not just conservative, they were regressive – in that they were strongly motivated by a need to freeze the status quo, or ideally return to a much more hierarchical time just before things get a bit too blurry (the time of Obama's re-election

would not be too wild an estimation for when status pres-
ervationists felt the scales tip further than they would have
liked).

When surveys assessed 'social dominance orientation', a
psychological measure of a person's belief in hierarchy as
necessary and inherent to a society, those who displayed a
belief in the importance of this sort of vertical order were
more likely to be Trump supporters. They saw in him a pro-
tector of their positions. Those positions fell along the lines
of race, gender and culture. In 2018, an author of one such
study told the *New York Times* that 'it used to be a pretty
good deal to be a white, Christian male in America, but
things have changed and I think they do feel threatened'.

This is not only aggressive identity politics, in the sense
that it is political activity along the lines of race, it is one
that is based on paranoia. It is politics that does not even
have the excuse or justification of grievance. It is an exercise
in power maintenance or reclamation, rather than real injustices. It is shadow-boxing.

There is a very high bar for what some are ready to
call racist or racially motivated behaviour when it comes
to white entitlement. I was in the United States during the
summer of the 2016 election campaign and remember
noticing how absent the race question was from the interrogation of Trump voters' motivations. One New York
journalist told me (in what became a heated discussion)
that coal miners had not mentioned race once when he
interviewed them. When he brought up race, they did not
seem overly exercised by it. What was missing from his
absolving of his subjects was the fact that they were not
bothered or disturbed by the fact that nominee Trump had
already made racist statements about Muslims, Mexicans
and immigrants. This ambivalence towards his racism was

interpreted as neutrality, rather than endorsement. This element was heavily discounted during the electoral race.

There are broadly two responses when confronted with proof that white people acted in racial concert: the first is that it is a reaction to changing demographics and the encroachment of other races – 'the browning of America', the demographer William Frey called it; the second is that it is benign tribalism – 'people preferring their own'. The phrases 'legitimate concerns', in the UK, and 'economic anxiety', in the US, are now memes, jokes, ironic comments to be appended to viral videos of hate crimes and racial and religious abuse targeting Muslims and ethnic minorities. A lot of economic anxiety seems to take place on public transport.

But it is nothing new. The dominant identity has been articulating politics in terms of imaginary grievance for as long as there have been minorities demanding anything; from freedom from slavery to freedom from police persecution. While it is non-whites who are accused of overstating their victimhood and triggering that in others, in classic myth fashion, the opposite is true.

In the 1990 US Senate election in Louisiana, David Duke, the former grand wizard of the Ku Klux Klan, ran against incumbent Democratic senator J. Bennett Johnston and, while Johnston was re-elected, Duke earned 43 per cent of the vote. One could cut and paste the justifications for voting for him today and not be able to distinguish them from the reasons white people allegedly voted for Donald Trump. Even though he was David Duke, a man whose name is synonymous with the KKK, the logic cited for him losing the election by a nose was along the same lines as in 2016: a working-class post-recession revolt, an angry message from the disenfranchised to the elites of Washington.

No one seems to ask why this anger can only be expressed by voting for a KKK grand wizard or a man who wants to ban Muslims or build a wall around Mexico, as opposed to, say, Bernie Sanders. This is the excepting of group white behaviour from its obvious animus – racial entitlement – and ascribing benign, even sympathetic, qualities to it.

And the left-behind story again is, simply, not true. Duke picked up the majority of the white vote, and the middle class was split evenly between him and his opponent. He lost only because blacks voted overwhelmingly against him. The same thing happened almost thirty years later when Roy Moore, Alabama's Republican candidate for the US Senate, ran what the *Washington Post* called a 'white populist' campaign. Moore romanticised the era of slavery, referred to Native Americans and Asian Americans as 'reds and yellows', questioned whether former president Barack Obama had been born in the US and argued that Muslims should not be allowed to serve in Congress. Who can tell those black voters, going to the ballot to vote against a KKK leader and a slavery-era nostalgic that it was not about race and so they should stop with the identity politics card?

The wink – it's not race

The damaging identity politics myths is sustained by constant denials that race is an element in white politics, while dog whistling that it is. It is a wink, a secret sign that is flashed at white voters to signify that there are two messages: one for them and one for us. The way to go about it is to absolutely deny, in fact abhor and object in the strongest terms, that race has anything to do with a political position. It is a trick that has a long and successful history. Even David Duke, a KKK grand wizard (I repeat this point because it bears repeating) was scandalised by the suggestion that race had anything to do with his campaign. Allegations of racism were a 'smear', he responded to his supporters. 'Remember,' he told them at rallies, 'when they smear me, they are really smearing you.'

There's an uncanny echo of that in a speech by Steve Bannon, Trump's former strategist, to a crowd at a French National Front rally in Lille almost thirty years later: 'Let them call you racists,' he said. 'Let them call you xenophobes. Let them call you nativists. Wear it as a badge of honour.' Allegations of racism, according to Bannon, speaking to supporters of a far-right party that had proposed that jobs be first offered to 'native' French people before immigrants (a measure that is thought by constitutional experts to be unconstitutional and has been judged by French law to be unlawful), were just bad faith slurs. It is patriotism, some- thing which liberals with their 'anywhere' unrootedness, do not understand.

In the UK, white entitlement arguments hide behind criticising 'multiculturalism'. By making demands for the return of white spaces as legitimate critiques of the failure of multiculturalism, the issue is removed from race, its edges softened. It becomes about how the new arrivals have not integrated and how there needs to be some common ground for a society to function without friction. 'Multiculturalism has failed' is the wink.

The language of the wink contains a whole lexicon of terms and postures. One of them is to insist and aggres- sively deny labels such as 'far-right', while adopting and promoting far-right policies. Sometimes it is a pre-emptive wink. On the website of Generation Identity, a pan- European identitarian movement (we met them in Chapter 2 when they were very concerned about halal slaughter), the party aims are set out using 'wink' language:

'Generation Identity (in some countries, "Identitarian Movement") is a Europe-wide patriotic youth movement that promotes the values of homeland, freedom and tradition through peaceful activism, political education, and community & cultural activities. We want to create an awareness for a meta political patriotic value base.'

These are all good things – homeland, freedom and patriotism (meta-political or otherwise). But as the ruse unravels, the more specific the aims become. The three core aims are to 'stop the Islamisation of Europe, oppose globalisation and reverse the Great Replacement'. That would be the 'Great Replacement' of the white indigenous population, one of the founding myths of far-right, neo-Nazi and white nationalist political movements. But not according to Generation Identity. A disclaimer runs at the bottom of their political statement. The group 'does not provide a platform for any kind of national-socialist or fascist groups or views'. It continues: 'We also do not get involved with conflicts outside of Europe.' Just a peaceful, non-fascist, non-Nazi, patriotic group, but one that campaigns to repatriate immigrants.

The group's leader, the Austrian Martin Sellner, stretches the plausibility of this stance even further. When interviewed, in 2018, by the BBC, he insisted that he was not racist despite associating with neo-Nazis in his youth. 'There was no alternative' to neo-Nazis, he claimed, if one was on the right. 'There was no right-wing patriotic movement'. When asked bluntly if he was racist, he said: 'I don't think so. I wouldn't say I was. It was a very ambiguous thing. I would say I was like a conservative, patriot.' Earlier in 2018, he and his fiancée were banned from entering the UK as it was decided that they were intending to spread hate speech. In a video filmed in the same year he was caught using the word 'Paki', but denied that he had any idea that it had an offensive connotation, saying that he really thought that '"Paki" was a completely normal term.' He added, 'If I would have known it, that it was considered a racial slur, I would have definitely not used it.' At this point even the BBC interviewers were exasperated.

'Come off it,' they told him. 'You come to the UK a lot – the idea you wouldn't know it was offensive isn't believable.' But he would not budge. The *Guardian* writer Gary Younge calls it 'the art of deniable racism', where we have plenty of racism, 'but apparently very few racists'.

This is not just a strategy of white identitarians or the far right. Politicians deploy it effectively. Congo-born Cécile Kyenge, the first black politician to serve in Italy's government and the first black minister in Italian history, was regularly the target of racial abuse from the country's far-right League Party during her ministerial tenure in 2013–14. She was accused of wanting to impose her 'tribal traditions' on Italy and of running a 'bonga bonga' government. After an Italian woman was allegedly attacked by an African migrant, a League councillor wrote on Facebook that Kyenge should be raped so she would 'know what it feels like'. In an interview during which she was showed images of her comparison to an orangutan, she called the League Party racist. Four years later, Matteo Salvini, Italy's interior minister and the leader of the League, sued her for defamation. The case is still ongoing.

This method of gaslighting was continued in America, when Donald Trump, a man with a long record of racist statements which he continued while on the campaign trail, was asked about his history of clear and explicit prejudice, from blocking black tenants from his buildings to fanning the flames of the Obama birther myth. Not only was he not racist, he replied, he was 'the least racist person you have ever met'.

And it works. White aggressive identity politics is maintained by nailing this implausibility. Its political agenda is to glorify national and racial purity and sell a guarantee of social status based on that racial purity, without making it so obvious that it turns off everyone apart from the most extreme ethno-nationalists. It is the only way it can achieve mainstream traction, to maintain deniability about fundamentally racist agendas. The goal, the sweet spot of this identity politics, is to achieve a state where a white person can believe that they are good, while also believing that discriminatory policies against non-white people are either necessary or are simply being made up. This is a duality that exists at the heart of Anglo-American history. From the seventeenth century, Great Britain invaded, starved and plundered millions of Africans and Asians, while maintaining that barbarity was a necessary civilising mission. Similarly, the United States built its nation on the backs of black slaves, then, in the nineteenth century, ratified a constitution which declared that all men were equal before God.

This demand for status softened by self-delusion applies across the board of dominant identities. Trump's misogyny is welcomed, or at least not abhorred, by his male supporters. His targeting of transgender soldiers in the US military is welcomed, or at least not abhorred, by his cis supporters. His banning of gay partners of diplomats unless they are married, with the full knowledge that many of them will hail from countries where they cannot be, is welcome, or at least not abhorred, by his straight supporters. Trump's pact with his base is a promise of coronation based on identity. A pledge that he will restore the old ways, the old hierarchy of race, gender, nationality and sexuality. White elites are susceptible to wink logic because it gives them an easy way out, a disclaimer.

Wink logic broadly has two schools. The first innocently invokes patriotism, love for one's country and the virtues of tradition. The language here paints a picture of an ideal snapshot in a country's history. In the United States, it would be a suburban scene from the 1950s, an advertorial from before the civil rights movement encroached on the public peace, when blacks were commendably free and yet conveniently separate. It evokes a time of post-war reconstruction, growing affluence and consumerist plenty. The image is of a white man in a suit and a hat, carrying a briefcase, with a trench coat casually hanging over one arm. He is walking towards his Chevrolet, presumably to go to work, but is half turning towards his bungalow to wave goodbye to his wife and child.

In the UK, it would be a black and white image from the Swinging Sixties, a few years after the end of wartime rationing and before the strikes, power cuts, pickets and inflation of the 1970s. Two young white women in mini dresses, sharp bobs and heavily made-up eyes walk on each side of a swaggering man in a fur coat. He is smoking a cigar and feigning shock at the camera as he walks down a cobbled London street.

The second school appeals not to a glorified national zenith past, but a disgraced present. This is where the economy comes in very handy, it is shorthand for something else – the diminishment of the native in their own home, neglected by a metropolitan elite that is preoccupied with women and minorities. Again, Steve Bannon gives us a clear exposition of this strategy:

'The Democrats – the longer they talk about identity

politics, I got 'em . . . I want them to talk about racism every day. If the left is focused on race and identity, and we go with economic nationalism, we can crush the Democrats.'

Grievance flipping

The flip side of this coddling of white entitlement is a denigration of other groups' expressions of (real) political grievances and accusing them of racism. In 2016, the *Guardian* writer Sir Simon Jenkins declared that 'pale, male, stales' such as him were the only remaining group that it is 'OK to vilify'. When interviewed about the column, he said that the way he feels now, white, male and above a certain age is sometimes 'like what it must have been like to be a black person 20 or 30 years ago'. There were no black women (or men for that matter) with two columns in mainstream newspapers, the *Guardian* and the *Evening Standard*, twenty or thirty years ago. In fact, at the time that Sir Simon Jenkins made his comments, there was not a single black woman columnist writing full-time for any mainstream British newspaper. He added that black women 'slide' into important jobs these days, that he generally feels like him and his cohort are being 'squeezed' out of the commentariat and that there are things that he used to be invited to that he is no longer invited to. At the time of writing, Jenkins remains in his column at the *Guardian*, his tenure still unthreatened by a 'sliding' in of black women.

He ended his column by contradicting all that went before it. 'The stales, like the pale males, will have their revenge. They have the spending power, the pensions, the houses; above all, they vote. Call us hideous and disgusting if you want, they will say, and we shall honour your right to offend

us. But prick us and we still bleed. We have our pride. We
are going to be around for longer and longer – and we are
going to cost you dear.'

This switching between pathos and menace, between
plaintiveness and threat, between claiming dispossession
and then bringing revenge to bear on those you allege are
oppressing you with all the might of your vastly superior
resources, is the doublethink that lies at the heart of the
identity politics myth.

The writer Lionel Shriver manages an even more impressive contortion of logic by accusing non-whites both of
racism and of triggering it in others. In a 2018 article in the
British magazine the *Spectator*, she argued that a newfound
attachment to race by white people was the responsibility
of other racial minorities – 'which have whipped up racial
antagonism, encouraged nakedly anti-white bombast and
ushered in a glaring double standard that's unsustainable.
You cannot have black identity politics, and Latino identity politics, without conjuring the pastel version.' This is a
myth. The reversal of that sentence, with the pastel version
conjuring up the others, is the reality. 'The sleeping giant
of white identity politics?' she asks, 'thanks to misguided
hard-left activism, it's *woke*.'

What Shriver and her compatriots do not realise is that
it is them who have been sleeping. Blaming identity politics
for triggering white people has been, as mythical tales usually are, deployed for a long time. Like political correctness,
the moment identity politics came to be, it was seen as a
revolution before it had made any inroads. Surveying the
media and publishing landscape after the 2016 election, one
would not be blamed for thinking that Hillary Clinton and
Barack Obama had invented identity politics, as opposed to
it being a foundational feature of American politics.

Ashley Jardina, assistant professor of political science at Duke University and author of the book *White Identity Politics*, agrees that a short-term lens has been applied to the topic of identity politics. 'Social scientists have been studying it since at least the 1950s,' she says. 'Since public opinion polling isolated the union vote, the Catholic vote. It just so happens that race is a major cleavage in the US. But identity politics as far as the civil rights and women's movements, was politically effective. Black political activity is equal to or surpasses white.' Identity politics she stresses, is not an 'incidental and unfortunate outcome' of politics. It is central to it. The roundabout logic that beholds the clear animation of whites electorally and then concerns itself with how other identities have forced them to behave that way is myth thinking.

White liberal elites have been forced to pay attention because for the first time in a long time, white identity politics has not worked in their favour by ushering in a Republican president with which they share no establishment interests, intellectual synergy or networks. But white elite guilt could also not countenance that their own were part of this nationalist movement; it had to be the other whites, the poor ones, those going through some terrible crisis, and so the economic deprivation reasoning again won. Adam Serwer of the *Atlantic* calls this 'the Calamity Thesis', the belief that 'Trump's election was the direct result of some great, unacknowledged social catastrophe – the opioid crisis, free trade, a decline in white Americans' life expectancy – heretofore ignored by cloistered elites in their coastal bubbles.' 'The irony', he points out, is that 'the Calamity Thesis is by far the preferred white-elite explanation for Trumpism, and is frequently invoked in arguments among elites as a way of accusing other elites of being out of touch.'

The only thing white elites are out of touch with is the pervasiveness of white identity politics. There are many expressions of it. At its most basic, it is a yearning for and a covetousness of status based on race. At its most sophisticated, it is the means by which a complicated infrastructure ensures the spoils of whiteness are maintained.

It is nothing as crude as racism, of course, although, by definition to pursue political goals that will come at the expense of other races is a sort of passive racism, just not the zealous, knowing kind. It is more a preservation of currency. The black studies scholar George Lipsitz calls this 'the possessive investment in whiteness'. Whiteness, he argues, has a 'cash value', because it 'accounts for advantages that come to individuals through profits made from housing secured in discriminatory markets through the unequal educational opportunities available to children of different races through insider networks that channel employment opportunities to the relatives and friends of those who have profited most from present and past racial discrimination and especially through inter-generational transfers of inherited wealth that pass on the spoils of discrimination to succeeding generations.' He adds, 'White Americans are encouraged to invest in whiteness to remain true to an identity that provides them with resources, power and opportunity.' A white identity is a trust fund, and its currency is grievance that is stolen from others.

The tool – universalism

If there was a pithy way to summarise the damaging identity politics myth, it would be with the anti-Black Lives Matter slogan, 'All Lives Matter'. Like the heavily memed 'economic anxiety' trope, 'All Lives Matter' has become facetious shorthand, an eye-roll, calling out logic that swerves the issue by using whataboutery.

This is the tool of universalism. It sidesteps specific concerns by dismissing them as special treatment tantrums, thus avoiding engaging with, or invalidating them. 'All Lives Matter' does not only suggest that black lives are not lost more brutally and more frequently than white lives, it suggests that to care about black lives is to do so at the expense and exclusion of others. And like all tools, it is not new. In 1991, the American historian C. Vann Woodward wrote: 'The cult of ethnicity and its zealots have put at stake the American tradition of a shared commitment to common ideals and its reputation for assimilation, for making a "nation" of nations.'

That is not to suggest that there are instances where defensive identity politics has not resulted in individualistic patterns of behaviour that have led to dead-end, identity-for-its-own-sake, politics. It has spawned 'as a' culture, where it is fashionable to ground one's opinion in their experience 'as a Muslim' or 'as a black man'. As a way of approaching the world, it links credibility to identity, rather than critical faculties. This is doubly damaging – it cedes and vacates space to the white experience as 'mainstream' and diminishes the authority of non-white people by painting them into a corner where they are unreliable witnesses, because everything is based on their own subjective experience. That is partly a fallout of whiteness as a default setting: white people have ideas; non-white people have experiences. It is also a result of the lack of access that people of colour have into mainstream media or publishing – and so they stay in the lane of identity.

There is a pressure that emanates from acquisitions meetings in publishing houses, newsrooms and television

commissioning huddles on people of colour to perform
rage. It is a benign pressure most of the time, arising from
unexamined good intentions, scarcity of resources and laziness. But as a whole it achieves a sinister end, which is the
sustained marginalisation of ethnic minority voices.

I continue to struggle with this tension, between the desire
to write about topics that affect me directly, especially those
involving an imminent danger (such as Islamophobia) that
is not receiving enough attention, and the fear that my voice
is then co-opted in the 'as a' discourse. It takes constant
vigilance and often a discipline that means rejecting opportunities and income. Then there is the guilt and a grappling
with the responsibilities of having a platform. These are
the tithes of playing in a game where one does not set the
rules. The representation business is riddled with risks
where ethnic minorities feel like they can only succeed if
they speak as non-natives. Commercially, white gatekeepers
leave themselves open to moral entrepreneurship schemes
where identity projects are indulged in a box-ticking fashion. An anthology of stories called *The Good Immigrant*,
a shockingly overdue series of personal stories by people
of colour, is a good example of an important work that set
something in motion in UK publishing, but which also risks
entrenching a voice ghetto. Few of the writers were in fact
immigrants – they were born and bred in the UK. The title,
deployed ironically, in its own way upholds the view that
British non-whites are immigrants, rather than what they
often are, second- and third-generation British nationals. If
there is a young black girl somewhere in the UK right now,
who dreams of writing science-fiction but sees that her most
likely route to publishing is via a personal immigrant story,
then a certain strain of identity politics, one I call representative identity politics, has failed her.

Granted, there is a gap for these stories, and there is space for all, but there is a risk that this becomes a minority pen for minority voices to write only about minority issues. In the absence of real authority, we all must come to the table with whatever currency of authenticity we do have, which is often 'otherness'.

A report published in 2015 called 'Writing the Future: Black and Asian Writers and Publishers in the UK Market Place', found that British black and Asian authors reported 'that they felt pressured into delivering a "certain kind of book", which conformed to a white trade's perception of what was "authentically" black or Asian'. This reifies power dynamics in a frustrating self-fulfilling prophecy, where 'diversity' is confused with 'representation' – and where campaigning for equal rights ends up as a demand for a seat at the table, while the structure of inequality remains unchanged and the table itself stands on jagged ground. Identity becomes an accessory, a gold 'feminist' necklace, a high-fashion hijab, a Colin Kaepernick T-shirt where his Afro curves into a black fist. Identity as territory, as 'recognition'. This makes it easier for the tool of universalism to be effective. But again, this is not the fault of representative identity politics, it is the fault of white monopoly on the means of cultural production.

The very origin of the identity politics movement was an effort to find common cause, rather than ghettoise demands for equality. The history of the term 'identity politics' and how it was first used illustrates how much it has been corrupted and deliberately misunderstood over the years as divisive and distracting from 'universal' causes. In the mid-1970s, a group of Afrocentric black feminist scholars and activists in the United States formed an organisation specifically to address the concerns of black women, concerns which they felt had been ignored by the wider feminist movement. They called themselves the Combahee River Collective, the name of the location from which the abolitionist Harriet Tubman launched a military campaign in 1863 to successfully liberate more than 750 slaves.

In 1977, the group released 'A Black Feminist Statement' in which they declared that they were 'actively committed to struggling against racial, sexual, heterosexual, and class oppression' and that black feminism was 'the logical political movement to combat the manifold and simultaneous oppressions that all women of color face'. They concluded that other groups were not up to the task of helping black women and people of colour in general, and that it was therefore incumbent upon the collective to advance independently. 'We realize that the only people who care enough about us to work consistently for our liberation is us . . . This focusing on our own oppression is embodied in the concept of identity politics. We believe that the most profound and potentially the most radical politics come directly out of our own identity, as opposed to working to end somebody else's oppression.'

If one ended the reading there, it would indeed appear that this was a splinter group, a balkanisation of resistance. And most analyses do end there. But if we read on, the statement goes on to say: 'If Black women were free, it would mean that everyone else would have to be free since our freedom would necessitate the destruction of all the systems of oppression.' These black women were not splitting off from a main movement, they were establishing an infantry in a coalition.

If there is a criticism to be made of the left and how it has pursued identity politics, it is that it has done so, in the United States at least, in a tokenistic manner since the big electoral conversions of the 1960s. The loyalty of blacks and other people of colour to the left is taken for granted and gestured towards without there being any substantive engagement. Hillary Clinton's buzzwords of 'intersectionality' and 'privilege' may have turned off some voters, but they failed to win over others. This has enabled the 'All Lives Matter' tactic of invoking universalism – which always means one thing, passiveness. And it is something which the right, the centre and the left agree on because identity is so subjective – you cannot hold on to it, you cannot achieve traction with it, it is too atomised for an ideology, whether that ideology is nationalism or socialism. You can see this frustration in the works of thinkers who have come to the identity debate. Francis Fukuyama, in 2018, pines for a time when the nation state was the unit of identity, in his book *Identity: Contemporary Identity Politics and the Struggle for Recognition*. Philosopher Kwame Appiah, in the 2018 book *The Lies That Bind*, thinks identity is 'imagined'. Unable to conceive of coalitions of inequality as the way forward, people reach for universal values that are not relevant when people are disenfranchised. How can someone achieve national patriotism and pride, if they feel that their country does not represent them?

Going back twenty years to 1998, critical theorist Nancy Fraser pointed out that identity politics is used as a derogatory term because the implication is that gender, race and sexuality are seen as ephemeral, flimsy, imagined or cultural. Class relations on the other hand, 'in the eyes of the identity politics critic, exhibit a depth, profundity and materiality that "mere identity" lacks. Furthermore, 'the alleged universalism of class is contrasted with the narrow, sectional concerns characteristic of so-called identity politics.' This is how the left falls down again and enables the right (as with the political correctness and free speech crisis myths) by remaining narrowly obsessed with the abstract principles of a fight, rather than what is actually happening on the ground.

Class fundamentally is about inequality; identity politics is about aspiring to universalism by way of vanquishing inequalities. Economic inequality and identity are inseparable. What is missed by those who are blind to this intersection is that historically, activism based on identity marginalisation has been the most successful way by which class concerns were addressed and lasting economic mobility was secured. For example, only by campaigning for the admission of black students into universities could they be promoted into white-collar jobs. The universalism argument assumes that minorities are no longer discriminated against in clear and discreet ways that can be addressed by targeted activism. And so now we must down tools and hold hands for the only remaining cause that should bind us, whatever that is. For some it is nationalism, for others it is class. It is a cousin of the 'progress' myth where women have achieved all the technical legislation wins that can be achieved. Universalism logic imagines successes that are non-existent.

Defensive identity politics is not at odds with universalism, it just changes the order, putting the horse before the cart: it is a step towards universalism, a building of coalitions. Without identity politics which addresses structural change, rather than advocates for tokenistic seats at the table or on the bookshelf, there is no common cause. All lives do matter, but the dangers they face are specific – and where those dangers fall along the lines of identity, it makes no sense to treat them in any other way apart from activism through that identity. Like the members of the Combahee River Collective found out all those years ago, no one else is going to do it for you, so push your own cause and find allies.

The call is coming from inside the house

I started this chapter with British MP Jo Cox's murder because of all the myths, the identity politics one shows the clearest path to danger. We simply miss things if we refuse to pathologise them. There is a threat to cohesion and there is a fracturing of universal causes, but it's not coming from where the myth is saying it is. In 2018, the *New York Times* reported that US law enforcement has failed to see the threat of white nationalism and is struggling to stop it as it has caught them unawares. 'In the atmosphere of wilful indifference', the report started, 'a virulent movement has grown and metastasized.'

It could be argued that the *New York Times* itself 'missed it', so busy was it with reinforcing white entitlement narratives.

The fashion of knocking identity politics poses another danger. Instead of trying to understand failed tokenism, the inclusion effort is jettisoned altogether. Instead of retreating from pursuing equal rights for all, we should understand how not making the case forcefully enough has enabled the ideological usurpation of identity, and the resurgence of white nationalism.

Yes, ideally we should strive to appeal to all and create a solidarity based on common goals. But this ideal world where an identity hierarchy does not exist is a fiction that only exists in the minds of those more preoccupied with the control aspect of universalism (which is about being able to direct people en masse and mobilise them politically) rather than the purpose of universalism. The myth that identity is something that only others do, not white people, is one that has enabled politicians to play on white racial grievance across classes while their liberal counterparts made the right noises in the direction of minorities but never genuinely engaged with their causes. And so now, even the cosmetic effort to appeal to non-whites is at risk of being abandoned. By doing so, we are doubling down on a mistake, which is to allow populists to set the terms of the debate around identity, and ultimately use it to win votes.

In an article for site The Outline, in 2018, US writer Sean McElwee summarised why if liberals do not in fact embrace identity politics, they have no future. 'There is simply no electoral benefit to be gained from abandoning identity politics because voters are increasingly sorted in such a way that those who support economically progressive policies are also supportive of racial justice and gender equity.' He concluded 'the path forward will require an understanding of how deeply liberation from patriarchy, white supremacy, and capitalism are intertwined'.

Defensive identity politics is not the problem, it is in fact, the only way forward.

CHAPTER 5

The myth of virtuous origin

'*What we choose to forget often reveals the limits of justice in our collective imaginations. What we choose to memorialise reflects what we actually value.*'

Eddie S. Glaude Jr

'*False beliefs are so integral to our culture that if they did not exist, like Voltaire's God, they would have to be invented.*'

Thomas A. Bailey

There is no mainstream account of a country's history that is not a collective delusion. The present cannot be celebrated without the past being edited. If the United Kingdom is to have a sense of pride in its contemporary self, there is no way it can be acknowledged that the country was built on global expansion, resource extraction and slavery. For the United States to believe in its American dream, in its land of opportunity, where all men are equal before God and able to achieve whatever they wish through toil and virtue, it cannot be acknowledged that it was built on the enslavement of Africans and Europe's poor. For Sudan, my country of birth, to believe that it is a unique blend of African and Arab tribes that have thrived by the River Nile for millennia, it cannot be acknowledged that it has been engaged in ethnic warfare for the better part of a century.

Every country has its airbrush. Some are universal banal fictions; others are central to a hubris that is internally corrosive and externally predatory, feeding domestic division and global aggression.

And so our historical heroes too must be edited. Everything from their human rights records and prejudices, to their minor foibles and imperfections, is cleansed. An assassinated Egyptian president is remembered as a pious Muslim, even though he had poured himself a stiff glass of Scotch whisky after every evening prayer. Barack Obama was the healthy basketball playing president, but was reportedly a chain smoker. His image was that of swaggering virtue, fist bumping janitors and channelling the conscience of the nation when he shed tears for the young victims of gun crime, all while he intensified a drone campaign in Afghanistan and kept Guantanamo Bay open. In Sudan, Al Mahdi, the glorified founder of the first Sudanese quasi-nation state and vanquisher of the Anglo-Egyptian occupation, led an army which, as well as defeating the occupying forces, plundered, murdered, raped and sold into slavery tens of thousands of its own people. Al Mahdi, a man who believed that he was the messiah, sent by Allah himself to purify his land, is revered in history books and his progeny continue to hold political sway. If he were born in current day Sudan and announced he was God's messenger, he would be tried for apostasy.

The past is rewritten in broad brush strokes, but the present is also revised in small amendments or omissions. George W. Bush, a president who, in his time, was seen as a reckless warmonger and intellectually challenged trust fund beneficiary, became the subject of a curious rebrand that began precisely at Donald Trump's inauguration. Something about seeing Bush looking like a mischievous schoolboy unselfconsciously perplexed by Trump's speech (after which he reportedly said to Michelle Obama that it was 'some crazy shit'), immediately recast him: Bush, compared to Trump, was a competent member of the political establishment. He launched one of the most disastrous wars in the Middle East with no plan or reliable intelligence – but at least he wasn't this rambling, sloppy fool.

American history is particularly prone to such fictions, so strong is its dependence on a foundational myth for its sense of identity. In *White Trash: The 400-Year Untold History of Class in America*, Nancy Isenberg repeatedly skewers America's imaginary history. It was not, contrary to conventional wisdom, founded by the pious pilgrims of England, but successive waves of Europe's destitute sent to exile and indentured servitude. The settlers did not blossom. 'Americans' sketchy understanding of the nation's colonial beginnings reflects the larger cultural impulse to forget – or at least gloss over – centuries of dodgy decisions, dubious measures, and outright failures,' Isenberg writes. 'Most settlers in the seventeenth century did not envision their forced exile as the start of a "City upon a Hill".'

Paintings of the "Founding Fathers" were changed as the lens of history shifted; they became more English and grand as time went by. This is the myth of history, that of the virtuous origin. Not successive facts and moments frozen in time, but a painting touched and retouched to reflect back to society its sense of stature and purpose. A sort of Dorian Gray reversed, where the painting remains impeccable as the real-life version grows gnarled and grotesque.

The whitewashing of the history of colonialism and slavery is integral to the belief that there is something inherently noble about ex-colonial Europe and the US. The myth of a virtuous origin is the strongest, most corrosive myth and lies at the heart of a culture's failure to self-reflect. There is a straight line that runs from this belief and another; that there is an essential moral superiority about a white race that has managed to create material wealth by virtue of its own enterprise, rather than the leveraging of poor people both in their home countries, and imported against their will. The myth feeds the assumption that there is a continuum of enlightenment, briefly interrupted by two world wars, two aberrations, that lasts to this day. The truth is that Anglo-American history (and to a similar extent, Western European history) is founded on both the cultification of whiteness in order to instil a sense of superior national identity and the pursuit of conflict abroad which confers a sense of purpose at home.

The Prussian military theorist Carl von Clausewitz coined the aphorism that war is the continuation of politics by other means. From the late 1800s, imperialist expansion into the Americas, Africa and the Indian sub-continent was war as an outsourcing of politics by other means. Take Cecil Rhodes, a man whose life is a testament to the happy marriage of expansionist white supremacy and capitalist success. In 1870, his jaunt as a teenager to South Africa for health reasons, resulted in him founding both De Beers and the South African territory of Rhodesia. He offered a clear unapologetic summary of outsourcing. In his view, imperialism was a 'solution for the social problem'. He said, 'in order to save the 40 million inhabitants of the United Kingdom from a bloody civil war, we colonial statesmen must acquire new lands to settle the surplus population, to provide new markets for the goods produced in the factories and mines'. He believed that 'if you want to avoid civil war, you must become imperialists'.

The myth of virtuous origin is nourished by what is

essentially state propaganda via academic *curricula*, popular culture *fetishisation*, calls for *contextualisation* (it was all a different time, you see) and a '*balance sheet*' analysis.

It is also a myth that is, ironically, ahistorical. The West's current day domination, even if it were secured via the industrialisation of exploitation, is merely a snapshot in time. It is a domination that has built on and benefited from the technological and intellectual efforts of preceding civilisations, that rose, ruled and then had their day.

A curricular blind spot

The way many countries curate their taught histories is little short of an exercise in mass consensual dishonesty. If a country retelling its story were a person recollecting a heavily edited and falsified view of the past, they would broadly (and accurately) be considered an unreliable witness on their own experience. There is no mention of Al Mahdi's massacres in the Sudanese school history curricula. In Saudi Arabia, one of the most significant and bloody events in its history, the storming of the holy mosque in Mecca in the 1970s by another Mahdi-type figure (such delusional political leaders pepper the modern Arab world's history), not only is absent from the public records, but any books that mention it are banned. The incident determined the shape of politics in the country in the decades that followed, where the royal family forged a pact with the religious establishment and its powerful mullahs to save its neck and stave off further threats of political religious insurrection. I lived almost my entire life in the Arab world until the age of twenty-five, some of those years in Saudi Arabia, but only learnt of the siege of Mecca when I moved to Europe. When my mother came to visit me in the UK for the first time,

I gave her a book recounting the incident and its fallout. A university professor who thought she knew a thing or two about history, she was left stunned by the extent of the suppression. My little sister, a medical doctor who grew up in Saudi Arabia and received her entire education in the Saudi state schooling system, still does not believe the siege of Mecca ever happened.

Not many are shocked to learn this, or that, for example, Chinese history books omit the Cultural Revolution's purges. But the assumption is not extended to Anglo-American history, which, in reality, is just as calculating and subjective. When I arrived in the UK, the process by which I discovered all the censored history of the Saudi state was mirrored by another, when I realised that I knew far more about British history than my peers who had grown up in Britain. This was simply by virtue of the fact that I had been educated in ex-British colonies and protectorates – Sudan, Egypt and Kenya, where there was not only a more honest appraisal of the legacy of empire, but a reality in which the shadow of empire was still long.

Just as it was impossible to understand the strange shape of the Saudi state without reckoning with the undercurrent of religiously inflected political resentment against a profligate and extractive royal family, so it is impossible to understand the modern United Kingdom without engaging with its colonial past.

In 2011, British writer Simon Akam, who studied history at Oxford, reflected in *The New Republic* on the lacuna of empire in British education. He was jolted out of his fugue by his grandparents, one born in Nairobi, the other in Hong Kong. 'They were not there on holiday' he writes. He had a typical schooling. 'In history, the industrial revolution came up, and, at 14 or 15, World War I appeared, a conflict that has enormous cultural weight in Britain, an equivalent in national significance to the Civil and Vietnam wars for the United States. Later, when I chose history as one of my four A-levels ... there were two syllabuses on offer, Early Modern and Modern. I took Early Modern. That meant sixteenth-century England. The Henrys [the Tudors]. I believe that Modern, true to form, focused on Hitler. Early Modern was fascinating, and I had an excellent teacher. But it did not explain Britain's place in the world.'

I had the opposite experience. In Sudan, my father fought and his compatriots died, in a civil war seeded by the British. Lacking the resources to cross the dense marsh-land that separated the north and south of the country, the British sealed off the lower half of Sudan, thus preventing modernisation and integration and dividing the country. In reality, South Sudan's resources were of no use to the British. It would have cost too much to extract them and the area was a landlocked grouping of so many tribes that there was no strategic benefit that would justify the cost. When they withdrew in 1956, it was without looking back at the problems that they had created. Civil war erupted the very moment Sudan declared independence. I was born only about twenty years after the British left and both my parents were born and grew into adolescence under a co-lonialism which remained in Sudan long after the end of World War II.

These are not ancient histories. But that does not mean that colonial history should be seen as a binary, as an exclu-sively good or bad period. History is a matter of record, of facts. Sudan stumbled on after independence and made its own mistakes, played badly the cards that it had been dealt, struggled with the limitations of British mismanagement, but also succumbed to an ethnically purist ruling elite.

Colonialism does not absolve Sudan of its failures, but neither do its failures mean that there is not a parallel timeline in which Sudan's path could have been an organic one, to success or catastrophe, wrought by its own hands.

The British curriculum, based on research by Professor Terry Haydn in 2016, does cover empire under the classification 'ideas, political power, industry and empire: Britain, 1745–1901'. But the research also found that there was often not enough time dedicated to the course, some schools covered it in a single day, and not enough time was given to the end of empire.

By glossing over the detail and omitting the legacy of imperialism, the British approach towards history is defensive, inevitably dishonest and ultimately delusional. It is precisely in viewing history as a source of self-definition that it is reduced to national hagiography. It is, quite literally, myth-making. And it is an era of British history that is most likely to trigger defensiveness. There is not a similar impulse to whitewash say, the policy of appeasement followed by Neville Chamberlain towards Nazi Germany. But then, World War II ended well for the British, something which allowed its imperial delusions to intensify.

There are hundreds, thousands of stories. Large fault lines struck in the soil that pitted tribes, ethnicities and religions against each other as nation states were born confined in strange unnatural borders. From partition in India, to mini-conflagrations between pastoral African tribes whose hitherto stateless land was now contested and split between new sovereigns, Europe's history is its ex-colonies' present.

Britain claims the expansionist triumph of empire without owning its detail. This cherry-picking, this confining of history committed by Britain outside of its borders as belonging to the countries which it colonised, leaves us with a heavily editorialised and truncated history – it leaves us with Henrys and Hitler. And it is, indeed, Britain's history. The fact that it took place off the British Isles seems to be the benchmark for what qualifies as British enough to be taught, and what is not. But British colonies were not administrative outposts, they were British soil, and their residents were British. Until 1948, nationals of British colonies were called 'British subjects', meaning they had de facto citizenship of the United Kingdom and the British Empire. Until 1949, everyone born or naturalised in the United Kingdom or the British empire, including independent dominions such as Canada and Australia, enjoyed that right.

But British history is still confined to the isles, and the lack of acknowledgement of the rights of offshore British subjects became eroded over the years. This culminated in the 2018 Windrush scandal, where Caribbean British subjects with the right to British nationality were treated like illegal migrants, persecuted, harassed and deported. Fixation only on past glory erases not only the memory of past crimes, but informs current ones.

In response to comments made by MP Michael Gove about how British history teaches students to be ashamed of their past, in 2016, the Secret Teacher blog noted that she had found 'an inherent bias in the curriculum that runs the other way'. She wrote: 'Pupils are brought up learning about the strength and heroism of this country and its once "grand" empire rather than about how other countries have suffered under its rule. It's as if teachers are expected to protect this image of Britain rather than facilitate real learning.' For an empire which lasted half a millennium, administered millions of citizens and resulted in large movements of people and resources around the globe, to be edited in such a simplistic way can only be down to ideology.

And it has subtle and dangerous reverberations. Curating the history of colonialism as a civilising mission that ended peacefully when British colonies were ready to make their own way, rather than one primarily rooted in financial motive and sustained by a codified racist hierarchy of exploitation, results in holes in the common consciousness of a nation. Absent are a healthy sense of doubt, a realistic appraisal of status in the world and a clear understanding of the importance of alliance with other countries. It has resulted, according to the political columnist Rafael Behr, 'in a nation that is neurotically worried about its greatness'.

Historian Alex von Tunzelmann argues that this process of fair appraisal of empire happened because of a 'brilliant PR operation' that rendered it a neatly concluded, benevolent enterprise that does not need to be studied or interrogated. The country 'hasn't really ever faced up to the embarrassing end of empire,' she told me. 'The handovers were very sophisticated, no British flags were lowered and only national flags were raised, it allowed people to feel positive about it. No one has ever really come to terms with it. Mountbatten found a way to end empire while making people feel like they had won.'

The way empire came to an end was carefully managed at home, not a humiliating ejection, but a handover, where the 'half devil and half child' people of Kipling's poem 'The White Man's Burden' had been finally rendered human enough to be masters of their own fate.

In a way, this lack of resolution meant that empire remained frozen in that moment, in the amber of delusion. 'Empire is still all around us,' von Tunzelmann observes. 'It is still so integral to everything about Britain that we don't really see it at all.' But there are moments when we do, when its rhetoric and bumptious swagger come alive in unexpected ways.

Brexit and putting the 'Great' back into 'Great' Britain

Putting the 'Great' back into Great Britain. This was the rallying cry of the Brexit vote. But what had diminished Britain's greatness? What did 'greatness' imply? What state of 'great' was to be returned to after Brexit? What mythological country had the British lost and would now regain, once free of the shackles of one of the most successful economic, political and secure unions of the twentieth century?

Suddenly history was everywhere. In 2018, the UK's then Brexit secretary, David Davis, said: 'Anyone who suggests that the United Kingdom cannot be trusted, and isn't the proven friend of every single country in Europe, needs to brush up on their history.' 'The first Eurosceptic,' said Tory Brexiteer Jacob Rees-Mogg, was the Anglo-Saxon king Alfred the Great who defeated the Norse 'great heathen army' in AD 865. UKIP leader and Brexit advocate-in-chief Nigel Farage campaigned while wearing a Bayeux Tapestry tie. Prime Minister Theresa May was compared to Boudica. Men of faith had their say, drawing similarities between Brexit and the Reformation, with one priest writing in a newspaper column that 'we survived our break from Europe then, and we'll do so again'.

MP Michael Gove said that Brexit was justified somehow because the history of Britain 'showed the world what a free people could achieve if they were allowed to govern themselves', as if Britain had only recently shaken off the yoke of occupation, rather than being itself the occupier. Spanning the ninth century to World War II (1939–45), a fevered invocation of history took hold of Britain, projecting a chimera of crowded and contradictory images. Britain was somehow simultaneously a small plucky country that managed to vanquish its larger enemies, and an empire, a

colossus that bestrode the world. British World War II fetishisation, never far from the surface in the first place, burst
its banks.

Peter Hargreaves, a businessman who donated millions to
the Leave campaign and funded a leaflet delivered to every
household in the country, welcomed any instability that
Brexit might bring; 'it will be like Dunkirk again'. Things
got a bit surreal. Liam Fox, secretary of state for international trade, supported the idea of a round-the-world flight
by a restored Spitfire plane as a PR operation to market
British exports. In the months after the referendum, when
there were some noises being made about Gibraltar's status,
former Conservative Party leader Michael Howard immediately began speaking of war. 'Thirty-five years ago this week,
another woman prime minister [Margaret Thatcher] sent a
taskforce halfway across the world to defend the freedom
of another small group of British people against another
Spanish-speaking country, and I'm absolutely certain that
our current prime minister will show the same resolve in
standing by the people of Gibraltar.' Liberal Democrat
leader Tim Farron responded to this escalation by observing
that it was 'unbelievable that within a week of triggering
Article 50 there are Conservatives already discussing potential wars with our European neighbours'.

The 1940 Dunkirk evacuation of British soldiers by the
British navy and a flotilla of private small vessels was mentioned repeatedly as an example of British bravery under
fire and of the power of the solidarity of unremarkable
people. Dunkirk was a retreat that Churchill referred to as
'a colossal military disaster', 68,000 members of the British Expeditionary Forces perished. The remaining troops
were only saved from total annihilation by, again according
to Churchill, a 'miracle of deliverance'. All this has been

conveniently lost to fabricate a story that is still pressed into service anytime Britain seems to be in trouble. Parts of the British political establishment and the public were asked to vote on a highly detailed matter of bureaucracy, of tariffs and trade and legislation, to be given a choice to leave an organisation whose membership is voluntary. But the moment the first minor complexity emerged after the Brexit vote, Leaver Britons came out swinging, ready to defend their vote by calling on the myth of virtuous origin.

What was always a quirk of British popular culture, a playful nostalgia or amusing eccentricity, began to take on more sinister dimensions, which suggests that it was never benign in the first place. It was almost as if people wanted to be at war again. Leaving the EU, itself an exercise in unpreparedness and hubris, would have no downside. If it succeeded, the vote was validated. If it failed, then the country could launch into a sort of war re-enactment video game, where rights and wrongs are absolute and Britain is heroic and everyone else is Hitler. One gets the feeling that Britain is an old soldier or imperialist officer who has been purposeless since being decommissioned at the end of a war. An ex-warrior bored and slighted by his new role as a parochial civil servant and who secretly still polishes his medals and boots and keeps his uniform starched and pressed, ready, and hoping, to be mobilised once again.

It is impossible to draw a direct link between Brexit at the ballot box and an accumulation of intense fixations on might, obsessions with status, and misconceptions about moral virtue. But the sudden outpouring of pornified pugnacious history might be somewhat of a tell.

Churchill fetishisation in particular became more fevered. Brexit turned Churchill, long the subject of attempts at historical reappraisal for his role in colonial atrocities in Africa, South Asia and his part in the Bengal famine, into a culture war figure. Any implication that Churchill was not an absolute hero is met with spluttering rage, as if the essence of Britain itself had become distilled into Churchill's image. Like a religious saint, he has been invoked as supportive of Brexit or of facing challenges that have been compared to Brexit. The former British foreign minister claimed that his dilemma over Brexit was similar to that faced by Winston Churchill at the outbreak of World War II. 'Sometimes', Boris Johnson said, 'you must take the decision which is fraught with risk.' Brave, swashbuckling, risk-taking Churchill taking on the dark forces of Europe is Brexit Britain's spirit animal.

Fundamental to the objection to EU membership is this particularly British problem, a fixation on triumphs of the past, an overestimation of status today and a refusal to acknowledge all the ways that the world has changed. Unlike its European counterparts, the nation had never been occupied, never succumbed to the trauma of fascism nor the expansive ambitions of Soviet communism. What are mostly the good fortunes of geography were taken to be the superiorities of military cunning and political resolution. Britain's self-perception, informed by its selective and contradictory recollections of history, feeds political adventurism.

In the case of Brexit, three inventions dominate – the idea that Britain 'stood alone' in the war (conveniently forgetting the allies and US intervention – they were called 'the allies' for a reason), the view that the EU is a continuum of attempts (beginning with Hitler) to subordinate the country and the perception that Britain was sort of doing the EU a favour by joining in the first place, after saving the continent from the Nazis singlehanded.

One moment at the beginning of the Brexit negotiations

demonstrated the madness that these collective delusions culminate in. The German chancellor Angela Merkel told a bizarre story about early talks. She claimed Theresa May repeatedly asked her to 'make me an offer'. Ms Merkel replied: 'But you're leaving – we don't have to make you an offer. Come on, what do you want?', Prime Minister May replied again, 'Make me an offer.' This went on and the two women found themselves trapped in a recurring loop of 'what do you want?' and 'make me an offer'. May came to the negotiations thinking that she somehow had the upper hand because Britain was such a loss to Europe, one which the EU would try to mitigate.

With Brexit, the nation seems to be replaying the hubris of the Suez Crisis, continuing to refuse to learn any lessons. It can be argued that the moment that was supposed to humble the country was missed. When empire was lost and Suez then rubbed salt into that wound, that was Britain's cue to look in the mirror, to reckon with its diminished 'greatness', its small and struggling economy, its relegation to a single country rather than an empire and its domination by the two superpowers, the United States and the USSR. This was a moment at which other European countries came to that realisation and did the rational thing – found strength in numbers.

At the peak of the Suez Crisis, French premier Guy Mollet and French minister of foreign affairs Christian Pineau were with the chancellor of West Germany, Konrad Adenauer, completing the negotiations for the formations of the European Economic Community. 'France and England will never be powers comparable to the United States and the Soviet Union,' Adenauer observed to Mollet. 'Nor will Germany. There remains then only one way of playing a decisive role in the world, which is to unite to make Europe. England is not ripe for it but the Suez affair will help to prepare her spirits. As for us, we have no time to lose: Europe will be your revenge.'

The referendum, and the constant agitation on the right of the Conservative Party to leave the European Union prove that Britain never really accepted its new status. Brexit came with a baffling Commonwealth revivalism, as if the economies and arrangements of the British Commonwealth, long since lapsed, could become resurrected because Britain chose to emerge, like the Seven Sleepers, from their slumber, into an unchanged world. This is the same Britain that showed none of this fraternal (or paternal) spirit when it threw the Commonwealth under the bus upon joining the EEC (European Economic Community) in 1973. When Britain first decided to join the West European union in the early 1960s, it was purchasing half of New Zealand's total exports. New Zealand protested that if the move were to happen, the former colony's economy would be ruined, as tariffs, particularly on butter, would devastate its exports to the UK. This was not any of Britain's concern, and so the best it could offer was a staggered system, whereby New Zealand was given the chance to sell decreasing quotas until it became less dependent on Britain and repositioned its exports elsewhere.

In 2013, Brexit agitator Boris Johnson said that in joining the EEC, Britain had 'betrayed our relationships with Commonwealth countries such as Australia and New Zealand'. That Britain should not think of itself as a nation of 'little Europeans run by Brussels'. In 2017, the ludicrous idea of an 'Empire 2.0' was floated, where Britain would rekindle its trading relationships with former colonies and thus replace potentially lost trade with the EU. But even the idea of resurrecting previous trading relationships is based on a false memory.

The historian David Olusoga summarised:

> While the empire, especially India, undoubtedly helped
> make Britain rich, even at the height of our imperial power
> we traded more with Europe and the United States than
> with the colonies. It was to the booming cities of America,
> and to the slave-driven cotton economy of the deep south,
> that British capital surged in the nineteenth century. And
> while much of Africa was painted imperial red on the maps
> that famously hung on every classroom wall, Britain did
> more trade with tiny Denmark than with Nigeria, one of
> her biggest west African colonies.

When such distortions dominate the historical narrative,
foreign policy blunders and political recklessness are inevitable. The case for an honest depiction of Britain's history
cannot be made by refuting all the individual details. Finance professionals have an expression for this – 'boiling
the sea', a futile, inefficient and counterproductive process
that wastes effort and does not achieve the required result.
Building a case to prove the condition of amnesia will be
met with resistance and denialism. The personalisation of
history, its transformation into a matter of loyalty, of propaganda, rather than fact, is not accidental. It shows that the
UK does not have a grip, a consensus on its past.

Writer and Fulbright scholar Simon Akam summarised in
2011 this uneasy historical laundering:

> The twentieth century saw the UK eclipsed as a world
> power. Yet, despite that dramatic abrogation of status – and
> the rapid retreat from empire – Britain passed the century,
> almost uniquely among western European nations, with-
> out experiencing a revolution or a catastrophic military

defeat. The sun went down quietly. Therefore, despite a dramatically changed place in the world, we never had to perform the kind of wholesale reassessment of national values that, say, Germany did after World War II. Germany even invented a uniquely German compound noun to parse the process – Vergangenheitsbewältigung – of coming to terms with the past. Britain did no such thing.

In fact, the opposite happened, British popular culture and popular history became trapped in a sort of reverie of veneration of the past and its protagonists, a cosplay of an earlier version of Britain. Constantly and in futility trying to put the 'great' back in Great Britain.

Popular culture fetishisation

The German comedian Henning Wehn tells a story about the day he first landed in the UK. When he turned on the TV in his room, there was a World War II documentary on. He stumbled back in amazement at the coincidence. 'Look at that, a documentary about World War II. What are the chances?' he remembers thinking, to the laughs of knowing British audiences. 'Now I know: they are 100 per cent.'

Other than the constant loop of such documentaries, the frequency of which reaches its peak between Christmas and New Year's Day, there are the (in some cases actually) sepia-toned dramas set either in colonial territories or during the world wars. In 2017 alone, there were two big budget World War II movies, *Dunkirk* (which could not have been timed better to quench post-Brexit-vote Britain's heroic beach fantasies) and *Darkest Hour*, an(other) elegy of Winston Churchill's skills of oratory and war stewardship. In 2015, British TV station Channel 4 commissioned *Indian Summers*, the most expensive drama in its history. Shot from behind what looked like a nostalgia Instagram filter, the drama was a 'retelling of the birth of modern India', via the medium of alcohol, sex and good-looking British protagonists. A reviewer commented that it made him feel quite partial to some colonisation himself. The myth was being honed into not just one of virtuous origin, but a glamorous one at that.

Another version of this historical onanism is modern-day British saviour dramas, such as the hugely successful *The Exotic Marigold Hotel* franchise. The novelist Nikita Lalwani calls it 'an exercise in British wish-fulfilment'. In the 2011 film, English pensioners who decamp to India for relief from their financially pressured conditions back home end up rescuing the hapless Indian protagonist, his hotel, and sorting out his love life. It is essentially a modern-day story of colonialism, one that is paternalistic and self-deprecating, while at the same time servicing the warm nostalgia for British empire. To this genre was added the 2017 TV series *The Good Karma Hospital*, which finds a junior doctor beginning a new chapter of her life in southern India following heartbreak in the United Kingdom. Both titles poke fun at the setting as a sort of passive lower life form location in which the protagonist can go through their journey. Raj exoticism is now an established part of British popular culture.

It seems like the further away empire is in the past, the more Britain wants to recapture it. Capitalism is a skilled sniffer dog and it quickly identified and tapped into this historical revivalism by providing everything from TV dramas to restaurants.

One such colonial chic establishment in London is the restaurant Dishoom, modelled on the cafes Parsis ran in India. In 2015 it was voted by Yelp reviewers as the best restaurant in the UK. The food is perfectly fine, as is the service, but the clincher is the ambience. A secondary effect of history rendered as celluloid is that there is now a distinct aesthetic. Walking into Dishoom feels like stepping on to a movie set, the acceptable face of colonial India, white-brushed for British punters. Gymkhana, a higher-end restaurant of the same style, is all wicker, fans and cocktails in iron beakers. It is just the right side of tasteful. Empire chic has crept up in less carefully calibrated guises all over London.

In 2017, I went for dinner at a new establishment in the East End of London, an area until the late noughties known for its old-school, cheap South Asian curry houses. It dawned upon one of my fellow diners, a woman of Caribbean origin, that there was something off about the decor. I looked up and immediately spotted it – the tobacco leaves. The motif was everywhere, in a room with bamboo chairs and period artwork featuring stern white men on horses surveying the diners. 'I think . . .' she paused. 'I think this is meant to be a slavery-era tobacco farm.'

The British writer Stuart Jeffries called this empire chic 'a wave of colonial nostalgia' where 'Britons time-travel to the era when the people of this rain-soaked dot in the dismal north Atlantic raped, traded, pillaged and murdered their way to running the biggest empire the world has ever seen.' In a country where years of austerity imposed by a right-wing government have increased poverty and homelessness, this colonial stature porn is jarring. Between 2010 and 2018, rough sleeping in England had risen by 169 per cent. In February of 2019, the number of children living in poverty was predicted to hit a record high in the same year. In 2018, use of food banks reached a historical peak as benefits failed to cover basic costs. Britain's historical and cultural projection is increasingly at odds with its reality.

This bankable nostalgia is not a fad, it is a culmination. And it is not just a part of popular culture sewn together along with all the pieces of a nation's quilt; it is singularly defining. It is more a melancholia than nostalgia, adding a state of loss to that of longing. The jeopardy is when that tips into attempts at restoration, of recapturing a past that not only never existed, but in which for the few to flourish, many suffered and perished, including Britons. Not every British person who fought in the war survived till the end of the movie and yet the nation has imprinted itself on the image of the sole surviving protagonist.

This pugnaciousness comes with a defensive insecurity. I spoke to Professor Paul Gilroy, author of *After Empire,* on the day that Theresa May announced that a Brexit divorce text had been agreed by the UK and the EU. Many Members of the British Parliament were not happy with the terms. The announcement was immediately followed by two Brexiters in her government objecting to the text while summoning the language of national subjugation. Boris Johnson said that the arrangement would reduce the country to the status of 'colony' of the European Union. Jacob Rees-Mogg, never to be outdone in the hyperbole stakes, went further and announced that the PM had accepted that the UK would become 'not a vassal state but a slave state'. Professor Gilroy pointed out that this echoed Enoch Powell, an MP who, in the 1960s, warned, in his famous 'Rivers of Blood' speech, that one day 'the black man will have the whip hand over the white man'.

This recurring theme, Gilroy observed, was 'an interesting reversal. And in that reversal is the guilt of the imperial power. It's all coded into that.' Essentially, the British state had been engineered for so long to be at war and to expand. He said: 'The British state is a machine for running and exploring the world which doesn't work very well when it comes to the business of the modern nation.'

And so empire and war mythology are not flaws in the machine of British politics, they are the machine, one that was not repurposed once its functions ceased. The education gap is a function of a wider state of arrest. Unable to move on, to go through its own 'Vergangenheitsbewältigung', the country remains stuck in the loop that has been demonstrated in different ways since the Brexit vote – unable to find the real fights to slake its appetite, it picked them. And those fights bring with them all the protagonists from the past: authoritarian leaders, jingoism, xenophobia and internal conflict.

In choosing to 'leave' Europe, Britain's myth of exceptional strength and historical achievement has disconnected it from reality. It is departing a union on the basis that the nation's success is down to some sort of uniquely magical and virtuous British quality that will subordinate the elements to its will, just as in the past the small island through pluck, bravery and guile took over and 'civilised' the world. It is a near perfect example of how, when taken too far, myths lead to self-harm.

Making America great 'again'

'Again'. In that word is encapsulated all of America's myth of history and its jeopardies. When was this previous 'again' exactly? It is an imaginary place, a selective collage of past greatest hits. 'Again' here means the return to a state of superiority. It means to purify and consolidate once more, behind a vision of America that is orderly at home, dominant and destructive abroad. All this happens while maintaining the contradictory shibboleths of the American dream internally

THE MYTH OF VIRTUOUS ORIGIN

and the freedom bringing externally. Both at home and abroad, this myth has made America less secure. Its foreign meddling has, both pre- and post-9/11, created blowback, from Afghanistan to Iraq, that is still claiming lives. Its internal contradictions collapse under their own weight. A country that said 'give me your poor, your huddled masses' is the same country that is in Trump's America separating children from their parents at the border, often forever, and banning legally resident Muslims from entering the country. It is this sense of an inherently good America that gives moral cover to its fundamental, in fact, defining inequalities. A mythical white and superior America, in which individual liberty thrives and where, as the historian Thomas A. Bailey put it, 'the rags to riches dream of a millionaire's blank check [can be found] in every working man's lunch box'.

America's externally supremacist attitude cannot be divorced from an internally supremacist one. There is a totem pole. America sits on top of it globally and a certain type of American sits on top of it domestically. 'Again' is a coded appeal to a desire to purge contemporary society of elements that challenge those with historical status; immigration, equal rights for women, cultural accommodation, all the developments that diminish the spoils of entitlement. And it is a message to the rest of the world, that American military might and interventionism is back.

Externalisation is an important component of the appeal 'again'. Since World War I and after the Great Depression in the 1930s, America has derived its self-worth, after being dragged out of its isolationism by the 1941 Japanese attack on Pearl Harbor, from engaging in military campaigns and standoffs. The country adopted its own version of Cecil Rhodes's belief that civil war at home is to be avoided by engaging in imperialist ventures. Imperialism is both a commercial boon and a fillip, a valve that can be loosened or tightened, to relieve pressure as required.

It is terrifying to be on the other end of that. The Monica Lewinsky/Bill Clinton scandal broke when I was at university in Khartoum in 1998. I remember watching the news coverage on Al Jazeera and flinching when the newsreader said the Arabic word for 'sexual relations', my face burning as my father and his brothers pretended they did not hear. A few weeks later, I was in the yard of our house when suddenly, the earth trembled and the windows vibrated. I remember thinking it was perhaps the sound and impact of a car tyre exploding, a common event in the heat of Sudan, but it shook the house.

The next morning, we heard that a pharmaceuticals factory called Al-Shifa had been bombed by the Americans. It seemed so far-fetched that for hours I did not believe it, thinking that it was just government chicanery or something more banal, like faulty factory wiring. Sudan was not at war; Khartoum was a peaceful, sleepy city that had never seen open combat. The country was on a terror blacklist but it seemed implausible that it was conducting terrorism business right in the centre of the city, and certainly not anything that required bombing. But the Al-Shifa plant had in fact been taken out on the direct orders of President Clinton. The strike was allegedly in retaliation for Osama bin Laden's bombings of the US embassies in Kenya and Tanzania. The Clinton administration, on flimsy evidence, had eliminated one of Sudan's major medical suppliers. It claimed that the plant was 'actually a disguised chemical weapons factory' and that 'soil samples taken outside the plant had shown the presence of a substance known as Empta, whose only function was to make the nerve gas VX'.

The plant, it was claimed, 'was heavily guarded . . . and it showed a suspicious lack of ordinary commercial activities'. Some US officials even claimed that bin Laden had financed it. It all turned out to be false. During the political fallout of the bombing, I could not get the timing out of my mind. The missiles coincided with Lewinsky's testimony before a grand jury.

Whether the attack was intended to overlap with the Lewinsky Congressional hearing or, in haste, to appear to be doing something at a time when America was rattled by previous terrorist attacks, the Al-Shifa bombing was for the benefit of audiences back home, rather than for its intended, sloppily cobbled together reported 'purpose'. We – me, standing in the yard as the missiles struck – were a headline to galvanise Americans at home. It's a hard lesson to forget. To feel the earth move beneath your feet and know that your entire life and world are collateral damage, a stage for a man far away, a man who was feeling helpless because of a bombing that your country had nothing to do with, and cornered because he did not turn down the offer of fellatio from a young intern.

This random aggression wasn't a one-off. In 1998, a letter was sent to President Clinton from people associated with the neo-conservative think tank Project for the New American Century (PNAC) (as already mentioned in Chapter 4, the breadcrumb trail leads to the think tank, and then to the money). Formed in early 1997, PNAC's purpose, once the fancy descriptions were stripped away, was to maintain American hegemony in the world. Almost a decade after the fall of the Soviet Union, something was needed, in the absence of communism, to give the US a sense of purpose 'again'. Many of the letter's signatories were to, three years later, join the Bush administration. The founder members included Donald Rumsfeld, Paul Wolfowitz and Dick Cheney. The letter said:

> We are writing you because we are convinced that current American policy toward Iraq is not succeeding, and that we may soon face a threat in the Middle East more serious than any we have known since the end of the Cold War . . . We urge you to seize that opportunity, and to enunciate a new strategy that would secure the interests of the US and our friends and allies around the world. That strategy should aim, above all, at the removal of Saddam Hussein's regime from power.

The 1991 Iraq War had not gone far enough.

The organisation's members felt that the end of the Cold War, in the early 1990s, had been a lost opportunity for the United States to press the advantage it had as the by default only super power in the world. The idea was that the US should project itself decisively and pre-emptively (in case China, Germany or Japan got any fresh ideas), and establish a sort of Orwellian 'war is peace' Pax Americana. After 1989, defence expenditure in the US, as a proportion of GDP, began to fall. By the year 2000, US spending on defence was at its lowest since World War II. PNAC wanted this to change, lobbying for an increase in spending and even for a new outfit called 'US Space Forces' to patrol the globe. (Suggesting a 'Space Force' was something Donald Trump was mocked for once he was elected, but the notion was a serious one made by Republican hawks decades prior to his presidency. He is no aberration.)

In 2000, in a chilling report, PNAC members wrote that the process of repositioning the US was a 'process of trans-formation' and that was 'likely to be a long one, absent some catastrophic and catalysing event – like a new Pearl Harbor'. They got their wish. America got its catastrophic and catalytic wake-up. Exactly one year after the report was published, the terrorist attacks of 9/11 happened. Not only did this give such hawks a second stab at the orgy of the first Gulf War, where Saddam was dominated in a 100-hour Desert Storm and the Arabian Gulf was liberated and secured, it also gave them their opening to press the advantage. For many, 9/11 was a rebuke to those who believed that there should be limits on the US in the global arena. For America to be strong and safe, it had to be everywhere.

Writing in *Salon* in 2018, the political writer Tom Engelhardt described the shock, followed by the rush of bloodlust. 'Like their confrères in 1991,' he wrote, 'the top officials of George W. Bush's administration were initially stunned by the event, but soon found themselves swept up in a mood of soaring optimism about the future of both the Republican Party and American power. Their dream, as they launched what they called the Global War on Terror, would be nothing short of creating an eternal Pax Republicana in the United States and a similarly never-ending Pax Americana first in the Greater Middle East and then on a potentially planetary scale.'

In the way Britain has been warped by empire, so has America been warped by the Cold War. The cultural projection that was required made a historical rewriting not only necessary, but a tool of war. And so America's fundamental myth splits into two. The first is the story of Anglo-Saxons striving for self-governance and individual liberty once they had fled draconian Europe. Everything conveniently begins in early seventeenth-century New England, although

Englishmen settled in Virginia at least two decades before that. Perry Miller, an American Pulitzer prize-winning Harvard historian and co-founder of the field of American studies, dominated the field of colonial studies. According to fellow historian Francis T. Butts, his work was 'widely held to provide the standard interpretation of the development of New England culture'. After his death, however, Miller's canon fell subject to criticism that he was forcing coherence, in order to extrapolate something about American character. By his own admission, he divulged: 'I wanted a coherence with which I could coherently begin.'

Historian Michael Zuckerman wrote that in doing so Miller 'made whole colonies disappear with the wave of a wish' and that 'he suggested that early New England afforded an embodiment of American cultural processes "an ideal laboratory. . . . Chiefly valuable for its representative quality . . . a sort of working model for American history."'

These working models of American history were reproduced for every era, each reifying the innate nobility, piety and enterprise of the American prototypical cell. The United States' historical curricula are divided along partisan lines, in which the role of slavery in the American Civil War is downplayed. A 2018 study by the Southern Poverty Law Center's Teaching Tolerance discovered that Civil War literacy among US high school students was poor, with only 8 per cent citing slavery as the central cause of the war. Overall, only 44 per cent were aware of the fact that slavery was legal in all colonies during the American Revolution. Less than half knew that slavery was ended formally only after a constitutional amendment. The stress on individual liberty as the motor of American exceptionalism only works if society is free and flat. The whole idea of America does not work if slavery, both synthetic in the form of indebted Europeans and free labour from Africa, becomes too central to the story. Much like Donald Trump, America is not a self-made man, it is a country that benefited from a trust fund gifted to it by cheap labour and exploitation, a trust fund that created such low margin wealth that its dividends are still being distributed today.

The latest working model of American history was forged in the furnaces of the War on Terror, whereby a conveniently cartoonish villain, hiding in a lair in the mountains and villages of Afghanistan and Pakistan, hated America for its freedom. America patted itself on the back for hunting him down and executing him, while ignoring the millions of Muslims whose lives were lost as America lashed out incoherently. Muslims and Islam provided an ersatz communism, a group of values and characters out of villain central casting against which America's superiority can come into relief and which will give it the excuse to extend itself further, penetrate deeper into the affairs and lands of other nations. This is the second part of America's foundational myth.

This impulse is not a right-wing or conservative one. Bill Maher chest-bumps with other liberals over their muscular liberalism when it comes to Islam and is the most outspoken non-right-wing opponent of the religion. Among many other statements, he has called Islam 'the motherlode of bad ideas', suggested that 'if Muslim men could get laid more, we wouldn't have this problem', called Islam the only 'religion that acts like the mafia that will fucking kill you if you say the wrong thing' and said that 'the Muslim world has too much in common with ISIS'. No media organisations were less sceptical and more supportive of the Iraq War than the liberal *New York Times*. The association between Islamophobia as a continuation of America's totem pole history and the bloody campaigns waged against Muslim countries was never made.

America's account of its history is a fiction that serves only to uphold the irreconcilable contradictions between its self-perception and its reality – a nation built on structural inequality at home and domination abroad. The call to make America great 'again', by voting in a man who stands for none of its alleged values and embodies all of its hypocrisies, is the inevitable culmination of that fiction.

This is the danger of reaching to the past – it informs action and ideology. The past is a simple place; it provides simple solutions to complex, intractable problems. In a sense, there is no 'again', whatever the country or people. There was never a moment in time where a specific culture thrived because it had struck on some golden formula for prosperity and equality. Whether it was the Islamic empire, the Ming dynasty or the Roman empire, none flourished without slavery, disenfranchisement, oppression of women and authoritarianism. Most civilisations are, in relative terms, more advanced than the last in technology and law, but not more advanced in absolute terms. What they all share is a denial of that fact. There is no 'again' for America, or any other nation.

What is striking is that whether it is Britain being reduced to a 'vassal' state of the EU or a United States that has been defanged by the effect of global climate treaties, security and trading alliances, the story is of decline but somehow of no humility. Doublethink is a strong feature of what is required to sustain a myth. A main feature of this doublethink, is the ability to maintain a grievance of humiliation that does not dent self-belief. The way to sustain this contradictory state of defeat and superiority is to avoid confronting the heart of the failure. And so it is easier for a British person to blame the EU and immigrants for their impoverishment than the Conservative government's austerity programme of the decade that preceded Brexit, an austerity that resulted in the visit of a UN poverty envoy in 2018, a tour usually reserved for developing countries. It is also just much simpler to do so. It is a choice between 'I am poor because I am unfortunate' (a wretched state), 'I am poor because of a right-wing government and rigged capitalist world order' (a trapped state) and 'I am poor because of others less deserving, external governments and politicians who are too weak to stand up for me' (a victim state). In the last case, something can be done. You are a victim, but it is not your fault, it is not a feature of the politics you live in, you have volition to change the politicians who conspire against you, leave global treaties, kick out foreigners and be great again.

The tool – the 'balance sheet' and 'context'

In Berlin stands a museum named the Topography of Terror. An outdoor and indoor exhibition, it is a simple retracing of the administrative side of Nazism and the work of its branches of enforcement – the SS and the police. Chronologically displayed, visitors can trace the rise of the Third Reich through to the end of World War II. It is an experience that is hard to describe if one has not visited. Even though there is an audio tour and a thorough description of all the exhibits, there is an absence of narrator. Everything is relayed in the most neutral, factual way, from the copy of the original Final Solution decree, to the mugshots of German resistance members. In the clinical, non-editorialised way the exhibition is presented, history is delivered in all its vivid and banal detail. For a guide or narrator to abhor it would be to consign it to a different time when horrible things happened; to excuse it would be to put too much distance between the present and the past. In doing neither, the purpose of the museum has been achieved – what we learn is that it can happen again.

There are three ways of looking at history – as a source of pride, as a source of shame or as a series of events that inform the present. When history becomes part of identity, when it becomes about a virtuous origin that gives a people an exceptional character, it is no longer history. You can tell when this is happening because history storytellers come into it, discounting this and inflating that, asking for context and a fair appraisal of the good as well as the bad. This is the balance sheet tool. It sets up a false premise, the purpose of which is to turn history into something else, into an achievement, a thing that says something about the quality of a nation's present character. Once the balance sheet tool is wielded it turns history into an account from two sides, trapping those who would like history simply to be demythified in a binary where there can only be two accounts – history as virtuous origin or history as shame.

In 2017, Oxford moral and pastoral theology professor Nigel Biggar created a useful illustration of how this tool works. He said that the British should have 'pride' in their past and, that if they were taught to believe what the 'strident anticolonialists' said, that could lead to a feeling of guilt which makes the public 'vulnerable to wilful manipulation'. The British empire, according to Biggar, was 'morally mixed'; he asserted that 'just like that of any nation state, pride can temper shame'.

He continued: 'Pride at the Royal Navy's century-long suppression of the Atlantic slave trade, for example, will not be entirely obscured by shame at the slaughter of innocents at Amritsar in 1919. And while we might well be moved to think with care about how to intervene abroad successfully, we won't simply abandon the world to its own devices.'

At the time, Biggar was leading a balance sheet project on 'Ethics and the Empire' with the purpose of analysing the impact of Britain's imperial past. Several historians signed a letter objecting to his position, and predictably (see Chapter 3) this was presented as silencing of Biggar by a liberal cabal who want to bury the truth by persecuting a vocal minority. As is usually the case, Biggar was the one who was actually in the majority.

'There is something ironic about an Oxford theologian being portrayed as persecuted for arguing that Britain should be proud of its imperial past,' wrote James McDougall, an Oxford historian, 'when 59 per cent of the population agree with him.'

Biggar's approach is tool thinking, in that it is not, in fact, about the actual issue at all and more about how to win an argument about supremacy. History is not about how people feel; it cannot be appraised in neat algorithms. For example, if the British introduced the railways in India but millions died in the Bengal famine, how many dead Indians equal a railway?

The personalisation of history makes it a matter of loyalty, of propaganda rather than of fact. British politician Michael Gove called attempts to correct the score merely 'versions of the past designed to belittle Britain'. British culture is trapped in a binary, between history as pride and history as disgrace. Correction does not have to end in self-flagellation though, merely recognition. It is only because history has been so warped and sewn into the fabric of identity that its refutation must come at the expense of that identity.

Another fallacy flows from balance sheet reasoning – that of 'context' – the idea that things were just different all the way back then. This justification for not appraising historical characters and events in their full moral dimension is selective and, in many cases, just plain wrong. It assumes that at any given time there was a uniform and time-specific set of ethics. How change ever came about if this is true is a mystery. Those who say US slavery was just a feature of the times, present slavery as a universally agreed upon thing, one around which there was no argument and no controversy, no opposition, no ethical protest and, in fact, no civil war. This ironically and inadvertently erases the efforts of those, both white and black, who pushed the moral panic button. Anti-slavery campaigners' efforts would play much better in the story of America's exceptionalism than a fairy tale of cruelties that were visited with no ill intent or awareness, because those were the values of the time. The 'It was a different time' context fallacy is used to excuse all sorts of bigotries, both in the past and in the current day. It takes for granted that there is always such total consensus around prejudice, that people just weren't to know that racism was wrong. It washes even less if applied in the present. A small-town homophobe or racist grandparent cannot claim ignorance: they are just choosing not to learn.

The same applies to the history of imperialism, whereby voices who spoke out against it within Britain are left out of the 'context' explanation. And of course, the voices of the enslaved and colonised themselves, too, who had a thing or two to say about their status and treatment.

The false premise of the balance sheet corners the well-meaning into reifying it. There is a reason that both in the UK and the US, the culture wars over history found their flashpoint in inanimate statues. In the UK, it has been the statues of Cecil Rhodes and Admiral Nelson which, some argued, extolled their racist and imperialist beliefs. In the US, a tussle about confederate statues in Virginia saw what became a defining event of the Trump presidency – the Charlottesville riots in which three died. Those who defend the monuments are, at worst, using them as ways to uphold supremacy and, at best, have tied history so much to current day national worth that questioning it destabilises the present.

Greatness again, but only for the few

Gore Vidal once described his country as the United States of Amnesia. 'We learn nothing because we remember nothing,' he wrote. If I may paraphrase, we learn nothing because we remember only some things. I am keen though, to stress that the solution to how history cherry-picking informs present day superiority complexes is not in engaging in another exercise of score settling. One of the dangers of the myth of a virtuous origin is that it drags everyone into balance sheet thinking. History is not a story, despite that being implied by the very word. It is not a narrative, not a discussion, not a debate. It is a matter of facts. What is important is that they are presented, rather than relitigated.

All other approaches are dead ends. What is required is an addendum to the histories already written, captured in sculpture, popular culture and education. What is required is the Berlin Topography approach. If there were an honest fulsome education there would be no need for history to be contested via the medium of statues. It is only because there is such a gap, such a vacuum of ignorance, that notions of nationalism and exceptional origin keep creeping into the realm of history.

In 2013 when then British prime minister David Cameron visited the site of the 1919 Amritsar massacre, when British Indian Army troops were ordered to open fire on a crowd of peaceful demonstrators, he expressed regret but no apology. Despite the outrage this caused, he stuck with his refusal to apologise. His approach illustrated the two different ways these accounts can be treated.

'I think the right thing is to acknowledge what happened, to recall what happened, to show respect and understanding for what happened.' So far so good, but then Cameron went on to say: 'That is why the words I used are right: to pay respect to those who lost their lives, to remember what happened, to learn the lessons, to reflect on the fact that those who were responsible were rightly criticised at the time, to learn from the bad and to cherish the good.'

To learn from the bad and cherish the good. That is the myth of virtuous origin, that the bad came with the good, and that the good really is the heart of it, a place that exists in the past, and which can be recaptured.

Both the United States and Britain are in the process of being cannibalised by an 'again' that only ever applies to a certain demographic, a certain class. 'Again' is about a return to exclusivity. That cultivation of nostalgia for the past is a dangerous thing, argues Rajiv Joseph, a US dramatist of Indian ancestry, who wrote the recent play *Guards at the Taj.*

'To view the Raj nostalgically, from my perspective, relates to Trump's "Let's make America great again", which really means: "Let's get back to being led by white males." In the US, there's a certain nostalgia for the white male perspective, and the same it seems to me is true of films and TV about India. There's always going to be the perspective that those were the good old days. But, of course, they weren't.'

CHAPTER 6

The myth of the reliable narrator

'Here's the secret: they're not that smart.'
Michelle Obama

On the day of the 2016 American presidential election, I called a New York-based journalist who was covering the campaign and caught him just as he was about to walk out of his apartment and onto the streets of the city to soak up the atmosphere.

'Trump is going to get his ass kicked,' he said, 'and I wanna be there to see it.' I laughed, told him I was jealous, then went to bed.

When I woke up only a few hours later it was still the middle of the night in London, but it looked very much like Donald Trump was not in any way getting 'his ass kicked'. I called the journalist again.

'It's not looking good,' he said. I am sure I heard his voice catch.

What followed was a liberal media-wide crisis of confidence, one that roiled the liberal establishment in general. The polls, the reporters on the ground, the *New York Times* swingometer all said, in mutual consensus, that Trump was, as my journalist friend had repeated, going to get his ass kicked. Later the next day, I sat with some other journalists in a London pub. It was a fractious evening. An argument broke out over whether Hillary Clinton was a flawed candidate. In another tense exchange someone objected to a declaration that Trump had a 'good instinct'. What was really going on among this group of friends and colleagues, was that no one knew what was going on.

An almost identical scenario had unfolded a few months earlier. On the night of the EU referendum in the UK, I went to bed after hearing Nigel Farage, the face of the Leave campaign, make a pre-concession speech. I woke up to a country that had voted to leave the EU. I plugged the radio into my ears as I left for work because it was all happening so fast. David Cameron resigned as prime minister before I had even caught the bus.

Later that day, the media was in a vortex, setting up then spiking interviews and front pages as it tried to adjust to the new tune that it had not picked up. For a few days, it seemed implausible that no one had resigned from any media establishment that failed to see it coming. As a columnist, it felt surreal to just start writing explainers for what happened, when I had not written a single piece expecting it to. It was the media version of working at a bank on a day the market crashed and the stock price went to zero. The media was caught packaging ideas and repackaging them to the extent that they became completely disembodied from the ground – its own version of sub-prime mortgages. When the real world came knocking, the ideas were worthless, and no one knew or remembered how the process had worked in the first place. An editor in the US told me that the atmosphere in his newsroom was as if there had been an assassination.

The same applied to my colleagues. How could we carry on as normal? What was the media for? There were two paths to be taken at this moment – reckoning with all the ways the media is not separate enough from power in its body and thinking, or denying that there was a problem.

We took the denial route. There was no wholesale appraisal of how we failed to do the one job we were tasked to do – report and explain the facts, as opposed to echoing back industry and political class conventional wisdom. The same thing happened in the British general election of 2017, when Labour Party leader Jeremy Corbyn was derided by almost all mainstream pundits and columnists, only to perform wildly better than expected at the ballot box and rob the government of its majority. A few mea culpas were issued but, all in all, nothing changed. This is the norm, the myth of the reliable narrator. Plagiarism and falsification are red lines, but gullibility and lapses in moral judgement are par for the course. The fact that we did not see it coming meant not that there needed to be serious introspection, but that no one could have possibly seen it coming. There is a certain 'honour among thieves' element to it all, a certain impunity of tenure, which means that accountability is absent.

The Iraq War remains a helpful illustration of this. While some of those politicians who launched and supported military intervention have been marred, if not punished, the ecosystem that forced through their warmongering has not, despite admissions that mistakes were made.

In 2004, the *New York Times* issued a mea culpa, stating that the editors had 'found a number of instances of coverage that was not as rigorous as it should have been.' They said: 'In some cases, information that was controversial then, and seems questionable now, was insufficiently qualified or allowed to stand unchallenged. Looking back, we wish we had been more aggressive in re-examining the claims as new evidence emerged – or failed to emerge.' The

...iat accounts of Iraqi defectors were re- ...ernment officials, the neutrality of which ...*mes* simply assumed; consequently, they re- ...ls' claims about weapons of mass destruction ...ncient question.

... same year, the *Washington Post* issued a similar apology in a 3,000-word front-page article. The newspaper said that it 'did not pay enough attention to voices raising questions about the war'. Leonard Downie, the *Post*'s executive editor, said: 'We were so focused on trying to figure out what the administration was doing that we were not giving the same play to people who said it wouldn't be a good idea to go to war . . . Not enough of those stories were put on the front page. That was a mistake on my part . . . the voices raising questions about the war were the lonely ones. We didn't pay enough attention to the minority.'

The *New Republic*, which had broken with the left-wing orthodoxy in supporting the Iraq War, also issued an apology. 'We feel regret, but no shame. . . . Our strategic rationale for war has collapsed.'

It took some individuals a little bit longer to humble themselves. Multiple Pulitzer prize winner and *New York Times* writer Thomas Friedman, a man who has built a homestead on the wrong side of history, came out in 2006 to say: 'It is now obvious that we are not midwifing democracy in Iraq. We are babysitting a civil war . . . That means "staying the course" is pointless, and it's time to start thinking about Plan B – how we might disengage with the least damage possible.' Three years earlier, he was calling for France to be voted 'Off the Island' (i.e. out of the Security Council) for its impudence in daring to oppose America's war. Fareed Zakaria wrote in 2015, 'I was Wrong on Iraq'. The same noises came from *Washington Post* columnists David

Ignatius and Richard Cohen. Most of these statements came with a caveat that these journalists could not have known better, because government spokespeople were assumed to be credible.

In 2013, before ISIS arose from the war swamp to meddle with this neat appraisal, the British *Times* columnist David Aaronovitch wrote: 'Ten years after the war began, the country is more secure and democratic. The alternative was Syria on steroids.' The *Observer* writer Nick Cohen, in the same year, also issued a similar doubling down when he wrote, 'ten years on, the case for invading Iraq is still valid'.

There was a wholesale failure on the part of those media organisations, journalists and pundits (ostensibly neutral and unaligned ideologically with the Bush administration or Tony Blair's government) to separate themselves from the agenda of power. This rendered them indifferent to the fate of millions of Iraqis. There was a lack of rigour, a default of gullibility, a moral narcissism and a haste to publish without proper investigation.

Where are most of these people now? Failing upwards, for the most part. Friedman is still at the *New York Times* and continues to write the kind of articles that betray a fondness of power at the expense of the truth. In 2018, a few months before the Saudi regime assassinated the journalist Jamal Khashoggi in its Istanbul consulate, Friedman spent some time with the Saudi crown prince, returning to write a paean on the modernising leader who was directing the 'Arab Spring' from 'the top down'. Fareed Zakaria was busted up from his position as *New York Times* columnist to be anchor on an eponymous CNN global affairs show; Aaronovitch and Cohen still have their columns.

Judith Miller, the main *New York Times* journalist on the WMD beat, was not disciplined even after the 2004

..e negotiated a private severance pack-
..*York Times* after becoming embroiled in
..urt case.

..he Iraq War generation of liberal journalists
..osequent thriving to widen the lens on a media
sce.... , even when forced into moments of self-reflection,
rarely follows through into action. As David Uberti observed
in Chapter 3, the impunity of Iraq War peddlers points essentially to a media oligarchy. Whether it was the Iraq War, Brexit or Donald Trump's election, what has never really been reckoned with is the media's role in reproducing the very myths that, when they finally took shape, bewildered its own members. The media wrote all the stories that have led to our age of discontent.

How can you separate bellicose muscular liberalism from the war-underwritten exceptionalism of Anglo-America? How can you separate the promotion and acceptance of casual misogyny and sexism from the election of Donald Trump? How can you separate lazy rote thinking on freedom of speech from its instrumentalisation by bigots and hate preachers? How can you separate a hardwired belief in the superiority of a nation's values from the bigotries that engenders? You cannot. The myths need narrators. The stories need storytellers. They cannot be replaced, new stories cannot be written, if the bench of voices that we continue to appoint, that we continue to vest with authority, is not questioned at least – and retired at most.

The main problem is homogeneity. Politically, the opinion-making class is overwhelmingly centre, right of centre or right-wing. Demographically, it is overwhelmingly white, male and upper or middle class. This results in a world view that is ideologically establishmentarian, unlikely to question the status quo and overly respectful of the offices of power. Received wisdom runs the show. On such received wisdom, and before a UK general election in 2017, where the Conservative Party was expected to win comfortably, the *Guardian* columnist Gary Younge wrote: 'The political class imparted as much to the media class, and the media class duly printed and broadcast it. The political class, drawn for the most part from the same social class as their media counterparts, then took those articles and bulletins and presented them as evidence. The wisdom was distributed to all who mattered. Those who did not receive it did not, by definition, matter. Within this fetid ecosystem the air was too stale for new ideas to grow.' The Conservatives had a disastrous election, lost their majority and hobbled into government by way of a coalition.

In 2009, a report commissioned by the then prime minister Gordon Brown warned that journalism in the UK had 'become one of the most exclusive middle-class professions of the 21st century'. It has only worsened since. There was absolutely no path to me – a non-white, immigrant with no networks in the media – becoming a writer and columnist if I had not synthetically created my own trust fund, delayed my preferred career choice by a decade and taken a job in the finance industry that enabled me to write in the evenings and weekends and eventually fund the first few years of freelance, unpredictable, less-than-minimum-wage work. Those that started out with me have since either left the profession or have managed to sustain a precarious living by way of being sponsored in various forms by parents and partners. In the United States, a similar exclusion is obvious. Research in 2016 by the American Society of News Editors concluded that women and people of colour still made up a small fraction of American newsrooms. An NPR report on the study warned of the danger of this, concluding that 'a

typical white, male-centric newsroom, means critical stories will continue to go unreported and news analysis will
remain unbalanced'.

Even after a decade in the industry, I am still shocked by
how exclusive British journalism is. I ended up in a rather
unexpected place after leaving finance, an industry that has
a bad reputation for being elitist, for journalism. I swapped
a diverse work environment in terms of class, race and academic background, for one that was white, male and almost
exclusively Oxbridge educated. Not only did my new media
colleagues almost all go to Oxford or Cambridge, they often
had attended the same colleges at Oxford or Cambridge.

White men of a certain class dominate the public debate.
This cohort does the job of myth narration with the instinct
of a state propagandist. The fixation on pedigree, the her-
meticism of the opinion-forming class, has created a group
of public intellectuals, from journalists to authors, that are
only equipped to do one thing, uphold the status quo. What
is valued is not intelligence and inquiry, but regurgitation in
order to provide reassurance and comfort. The new stories
that need to be told need new narrators. This is not to suggest that whiteness and maleness should disqualify a voice
and render it invalid, but rather that the current crop of
public voices is not made up of reliable narrators.

This chapter will list examples of such narrators (across
the political spectrum) of the myths detailed in the previous
chapters, point out the uniformity of, and flaws in, their
logic and survey the public opinion-making scene. These
narrators often use the tools and techniques mentioned in
the earlier chapters to advance the myths. See if you can
spot them.

Virtuous origin

Of all the unreliable narrators, those that chronicle popular history are the most flagrant in their lack of neutrality. The appetite for nation-aggrandising accounts of history is fed by a school of popular historians that is both biased and fundamentally unqualified for the job. The Anglo-American exceptionalism discussed in the previous chapter seeks comfort in the myths of the past and also reassurance about the future. It looks for guarantees that something unique about Britain and the US's civilisational victory means there will be no decline. Their values combined with their Spartan strength anoints them as the world's benign but unhesitant patrons in perma-empire.

Niall Ferguson is this school's eminence grise, building a career on feeding this sense of importance and need for justification of immoral foreign policies. His credentials are, on the face of it, impeccable. Educated at Oxford and Cambridge, he has researched or taught at, among others, Harvard, Stanford and the London School of Economics. Author, documentary maker, *Times* columnist and all-round telegenic history raconteur, Ferguson has appointed himself as an expert on empire and the success of Western civilisation. Ferguson is a man whose own personal empire experience was rather charmed. His first memories were of an idyllic Nairobi and he hailed from a family of empire beneficiaries, his grandfather peddled alcohol to indigenous tribes in South America. Ferguson debuted in Oxford as a defender of empire and on that path he was set. His fondness for the moral stamina required to civilise extended to a zealous support of the Iraq War. 'Let me come clean', he wrote in a 2003 *New York Times* article entitled 'The Empire Slinks Back', just as events were tilting towards an abattoir that over the next decade would claim hundreds of thousands of lives. 'I am a fully paid-up member of the neoimperialist gang.' That declaration and the subsequent trajectory of the Iraq War, did not, as previously highlighted, have an impact on Ferguson's credentials as sage and fortune teller.

He went on to say: 'Twelve years ago – when it was not at all fashionable to say so – I was already arguing that it would be "desirable for the United States to depose" tyrants like Saddam Hussein. "Capitalism and democracy," I wrote, "are not naturally occurring, but require strong institutional foundations of law and order. The proper role of an imperial America is to establish these institutions where they are lacking, if necessary . . . by military force."'

He is nostalgic about the British empire and frustrated at America's demurring from it. American empire, according to him is one 'that does not speak its name'. The country 'should admit its imperial status and realise it must stay in Iraq at least 10 years if it is to finish the job'. On the success of the West, he believes it is down to six 'killer apps' that have distinguished the West from others, among them are 'work ethic' and 'competition'.

Despite his chosen empire specialisation, Ferguson is not a historian of empire or prognosticator of the trajectory of civilisations, but a historian of economics. His views on empire and post-imperial foreign intervention are not that of a specialist, but an ideologue.

His lack of qualification and his bias did not stop him becoming such an authority on empire that he was solicited by the British Conservative Party to overhaul the history school curriculum, one that Ferguson himself believed was bound to be 'Eurocentric' because the world was 'Eurocentric'. What children should be taught, according to Ferguson, is the 'big story' of the last 500 years which is 'the rise of western domination of the world'.

On this cooperation, the historian William Dalrymple told *The Times of India* that the Conservative Party's approach fell short. 'I believe Cameron is interested in getting Niall Ferguson on this. Niall's a thorough historian and a very clever and amusing gadfly – but he's also the most pro-empire voice in academia. We need more neutral efforts to educate the British so they can squarely face the bad parts of the period.' In 2017, on the subject of a YouGov poll that surveyed sentiments about empire, Ferguson tweeted: 'I won. Most [Brits] think the British Empire is more something to be proud of (59%) rather than ashamed of (19%).'

There is a symbiosis here, a chicken and egg dynamic. There is an appetite for such accounts of history that inspire pride, that is then fed by more such accounts. Historians such as Ferguson become brands, institutions that create their own markets, which then must be catered to by providing more blustery, feel-good pseudo-history.

This personalisation inevitably creates problems, as the man becomes the ball. Inability to separate his work from himself, while demanding that his work be seen as objective academia, has led Ferguson to pursue personal vendettas and grudges. He threatened to sue the writer Pankaj Mishra for giving him a bad book review in 2011. In 2018, he stepped down from a key position at a Stanford free speech programme after leaked emails revealed that he had urged a group of Republican students to conduct 'opposition research' on a left-wing student. You will recall from Chapter 3 the rather arbitrary commitment to free speech that proponents such as Ferguson enjoy. (I hope this particular author will be spared as I have fact-checked Ferguson's record exhaustively and do not have the funds to respond to a case of libel, but one can never rest assured. Imperialist muscle comes encased in thin skin.)

Ferguson's belief in Western dominance involves a lot of complaining, sensitivity and even paranoia that white men are under unprecedented assault. A fetish for empire is actually an insecurity about loss of status.

It is why this man of many academic sinecures had devolved into writing screeds in his *Times* column, based on flimsy evidence and straw man premises. In 2018, in order to make a point about the demonisation of the white male, he wrote: 'the process of indoctrination starts early. My six-year-old son stunned his parents the other day when we asked what he had been studying at school. He replied that they had been finding out about the life of Martin Luther King Jr. "What did you learn?" I asked. "That most white people are bad," he replied. This is America in 2018.'

It is rather worrying that someone who is willing to draw such a conclusion from the pronouncements of a six-year-old, and furthermore use that conclusion to make a wider point about contemporary society, is vested with the trust and confidence to write an authoritative account of history.

Nigel Biggar, who we met in the last chapter, advocating for the merits of empire, has similarly appointed himself in a position that he is not technically qualified for. A professor of theology rather than empire, he has nonetheless taken it upon himself to assume the impartiality of scientist, when really he is an ideologue.

The unfortunate side effect of this is the pigeonholing of new voices, those that are coming up as new narrators, in a position that is dedicated to rebutting these historical ideological fictions, rather than going about the urgent business of a non-contested history. David Olusoga and Kehinde Andrews are both black British historians who have done a fine job in challenging such narratives, but the dynamic inadvertently sets it up as an equal fight of two accounts. It is not. This is an additional complication of narrator dominance – it exhausts and confounds the flourishing of new voices by restricting their ability to expand, to create a body of work that is not restricted to constantly responding to and challenging myths. And even this effort, to expand the knowledge bank, as Lola and her fellow students tried to do at Cambridge University, is met with resistance.

Ferguson also has strong views on #MeToo. The ghettoisation of women or people of colour in 'their lane' in publishing and journalism is not an issue for him. If one is 'an' authority, they are then 'the' authority, moving from economic history to empire, to Islamism, to sexual politics and consent. On the latter he has this to say:

'I wonder: do we risk sliding into a kind of secular sharia, in which all men are presumed to be sexual predators and only severe punishments can prevent routine rape? Will one-to-one work meetings between a male and a female co-worker soon be a thing of the past? What next? A more general segregation of the sexes? How the Islamists must be enjoying all this.'

Gender equality

It is hard to believe, but Ferguson's whiplash-inducing observation on sexual politics, one that goes from wondering where it's all going, to imagining a world where Islamists are enjoying seeing gender segregation in the West in four sentences, is among the least outrageous written on the subject of consent. It is a competitive field, where again, several men of similar pedigree and disparate specialisations in the media have been comfortable to opine on the acceptable boundaries for women. Here all the tools to divert from the seriousness of the problem were unsheathed.

Douglas Murray's reach for the overcorrection I mention in Chapter 1, where he concluded that the consequence of this new sexual counter-revolution was no sex at all. Murray's credentials are also impeccable and his status in the British media scene is platinum. He is a nominee of the prestigious Orwell Prize and a frequent guest and panellist on TV and radio shows. His last book, *The Strange Death of Europe*, was a bestseller. A gay man who has dedicated his career to pointing out the threats to the European peace posed by immigrants and particularly Muslims, he did not hesitate to veer into the lane of female consent and its risks.

'Feminism isn't producing guides for helping men. It is producing manifestos for torturing them,' he declared. He is very concerned about the 'moral panic' of sexual inquisitions, urging us to calibrate our responses carefully. This is a consideration he does not extend to his own conflation of Muslims and other immigrants, one used to tap into fear of Islamic terrorism so that it may be used as justification for fear of non-white immigrants. In his book, he argues that Europe is in mortal danger, with catastrophe only preventable by taking a harder line against outsiders who wish to move in and go around being non-Christian and not integrating.

On consent, he wisely called for caution on 'the worrying elision of the criminal and the minimal in the current wave of sexual-assault allegations', yet does not hesitate to indulge in such conflation himself. Indeed, his entire position on immigration is based on argument by elision.

He sagely observed the uncomfortable truth that sometimes 'false accusations do happen', but again, does not extend that modulation to his assertion that, as an example

of the unmitigated wickedness of immigrants, in 2009 immigrants were responsible for all reported rapes in Oslo.
The truth was this figure only referred to 'assault rapes'
(rapes committed by a stranger) and not the many more
incidents of domestic rape committed by Norwegians. He
later amended this to 'all attempted grab rapes'. He engages
in further 'elision' on Swedish rape figures, insisting that
the country has the highest level of rape in Europe because
it has one of the highest levels of migration. He does not
account for the fact that Sweden broadened its rape definition in the mid-noughties to encompass acts which would
be considered assault or bodily harm in other countries. In
2011, the Inter Press Agency reported that 'the number of
reported rapes in this Nordic country has increased dramatically in recent years, especially after the Swedish Sexual
Crimes Act was reformed in 2005.' It also predicted that
'the fact that the definition had been broadened could soon
be seen in the rape statistics – the number of reported rapes
more than doubled between 2004 and 2009, a year when
almost 6,000 cases were reported.' A Crime Survey made by
BRÅ, the Swedish National Council for Crime Prevention,
showed that there were no indications of an increase in the
actual number of people who fell victims to sexual crimes
between 2005–8.

The issue of sexual harassment and consent brings out
in Murray an admirable nuanced recognition of the way
power dynamics play out. 'When people and institutions
are riding strong', he wrote in 2017, 'they benefit from a
presumption of innocence. When they are riding weak, or
on the way down, almost any allegation can be accepted
as true.' This clear-sightedness fails him when he glosses
over other power dynamics entirely, claiming: 'Those who
believe Europe is for the world have never explained why

this process should be one way: why Europeans going anywhere else in the world is colonialism whereas the rest of the world coming to Europe is just and fair.' I highly doubt that the difference between invading annexers on the hunt for loot and geopolitical status, and immigrants who are leaving their homes due to economic or political distress has never been 'explained' to Murray or anyone else.

What could be the reason for this selectivity? For this waxing and waning of intellectual rigour, largesse and nuance? Obviously, Murray is no neutral observer; he is a conservative gentrified xenophobe who was nonetheless given the opportunity to expand on these views in the pages of the *National Review*, the *Spectator* and on the airwaves.

Mail on Sunday columnist Peter Hitchens, further distinguished than Murray by being a winner of the Orwell Prize, continues this peculiar trend of seeing Islamic purdah as the natural extension of the #MeToo movement. One solution to the whole intractable problem, if sanity does not intervene, is 'the niqab, the burka and the segregation of the sexes' he says. The title of one of his pieces on this subject warned women that there is nothing to be gained from all this 'squawking' about sex pests, apart from a niqab. Charles Moore, *Daily Telegraph* columnist and former editor of the *Daily Telegraph*, the *Sunday Telegraph* and the *Spectator*, chimed in with the most energetic use of the overcorrection tool to state that the scandal that overtook Westminster when certain MPs were accused of improper conduct meant that 'women are now on top', adding 'I pray they share power with men, not crush us'. Michael White, a distinguished journalist who served as associate editor at the *Guardian* and as political editor, was, for some reason, asked to comment on the BBC on the matter and said that female journalists complaining about inappropriate conduct from male MPs were not only not victims, they were 'predators', 'clever attractive women looking for stories' 'who can play the power game to poor old ugly backbenchers with bad breath'.

It seems personal, doesn't it? For these writers, something like #MeToo threatens their whole ecosystem, if not them personally. There is too much proximity to power, too little accountability and thus too much vested in the status quo. Their awards, high-profile roles, columns and publishing deals should give them comfort that their voices are validated and recognised. They are still sought after and solicited, all the while claiming that they are victims, en route to obsolescence because of political correctness.

The political correctness crisis

Complaints about political correctness are often faked victimhood. In the *Boston Globe* in 2018, Niall Ferguson wrote that 'it is not very fashionable to be a man these days, especially a white one'. This damning conclusion he drew after arranging a conference of historians and failing to include a single woman. Those women he did invite were unable to attend, although he concedes that he should have 'tried harder' to find other female speakers. He did not and, consequently, perhaps not entirely unreasonably, media coverage was negative, with the *New York Times* calling the conference 'too white and too male'. This was enough to make Ferguson feel like he was persecuted and he proceeded to preach about his persecution in the pages of his *Times* column, the *Boston Globe* and in his position as 'Senior Fellow at The Hoover Institution at Stanford University'. In both instances when he came under fire, for trying to dig up dirt on a student in order to discredit him and for failing to include women in a history conference, he conceded that he made lapses in judgement. And yet, according to him, his treatment was the 'racism of the anti-racists', 'the sexism of the anti-sexists'. He complained about white men being unfashionable while owning the catwalk.

This is a common contradictory posture, one which takes the mere questioning of power to be its utter annihilation. This argument fails before it is even made, sabotaged by the facts that those who claim to be victims are in almost total control of the media and the means of cultural production. The bestselling American author Lionel Shriver said on a 2018 BBC radio programme that in the UK, white men are on the bottom rung, 'below Jews', because they are considered to be powerful, and we are only in the business of 'privileging the disadvantaged'. This conviction that criticism is equal to victimisation is a cornerstone of the PC myth promoter's logic, because it is a way to avoid engaging with that criticism and also maintaining unquestioned entitlement. Shriver for example, has become radicalised into becoming an anti-PC activist after being questioned about cultural appropriation in one of her novels, *The Mandibles*, criticised by one reviewer for portraying an America that is 'straight and white' and for depicting the only black character in a bestial state, incontinent, demented and on a leash. There is a thorny but also potentially fruitful conversation to be had about the limits of authorship and where they intersect with cultural or racial tender spots. Personally, I think there should be as few limits as possible – and preferably none – because there is jeopardy of a chilling effect, that good novels are not written because writers fear a backlash. Limiting authors to only what they know or have experienced in fiction also reinforces the minority ghetto in publishing as an unintended consequence. Nevertheless the question of sticking to what you know or have experienced is an interesting cultural juncture of contemporary discourse and should be navigated. But to Shriver, this is 'politically correct censorship' which threatens to turn the world of publishing into a 'timid, homogeneous, and dreary' place, one which she encourages her fellow authors to push back against.

Shriver is right, but not in the way she imagines. The US writer Roxane Gay completed a study in 2012, backed up by Poynter research, which showed that almost 90 per cent of books reviewed in the *New York Times* in 2011 were by white authors. In 2013, the literary website the Open Book crunched the *New York Times* top ten bestseller numbers and revealed that out of 124 authors on the list only three were by non-white authors and not one was African American. Of the three books and book series by these writers, only one had a main non-white character, who was half Latina. In 2017, the *Sunday Times* top ten bestselling hardback non-fiction chart did not include any writers who weren't white. In the UK, the Writing the Future research reported in 2015 on the effect of ghettoising minority voices in either confessional non-fiction or literary fiction about race or colonialism. The result is an under representation of black and ethnic minority British writers in the bestselling writing genres. The problem is in the ranks of publishing as well, according to the report, only 8 per cent of UK publishing comes from a black and ethnic minority background. Timid, homogenous, and dreary, indeed.

When it comes to Shriver herself, she is a live testament to the paranoia of political correctness. She wages a campaign against obsolescence from the stable perch of her publishing numbers. PC has clearly not stopped her from being published to make way for writers of colour, from being a columnist in the pages of the *Spectator* magazine (which has no non-white writers or columnists), making her points about the chilling effect of PC at keynote speeches at writing festivals or, indeed, winning the Orange Prize for Fiction (now the Women's Prize for Fiction). She sees a celebration of otherness at the expense of quality everywhere, seizing on a voluntary form sent by Penguin Random House to literary agents asking for information on their publishing pipeline. The email cites the publisher's 'new company-wide goal': for 'both our new hires and the authors we acquire to reflect UK society by 2025.' This, she believes, goes against a publisher's role which is to 'promote and sell fine writing'. Penguin Random House is eschewing quality, 'drunk on virtue'. I am not sure if Shriver's success has mercifully insulated her from the competitiveness of the publishing industry, but there are no charities there. A Penguin Random House editor I spoke to when the form was being written said that it was merely sound financial planning on the part of management, publishing good books that reflect society means more sales.

This is the heart of it, that Shriver believes the homogeneity of publishing accidentally overlaps with a certain demographic, rather than is artificially produced by a complex system of levers, pulleys, trapdoors and dead ends that raises some and blocks others. Fine writing is everywhere, including in her own novels – sometimes you just have to put a little more effort into finding it. Meritocracy, the myth-supporting argument I wrote about in Chapter 1, is used by Shriver to great effect. If you have made it, you are simply good at what you do. If not, you're substandard. Life is simple on the planet of meritocracy. It's a place where successful people can bask in the fantasy that their success is entirely down to their unique talent and graft, without luck or privilege intervening. Meritocracy as an argument is privilege laundering, its believers emerge on the other side of it clean and shorn of context. It also allows people to abdicate responsibility, duty or guilt towards others less fortunate. They're just not as good, you see.

Shriver's is a common position, of writers panicking about their demise at the hands of people that are invisible. *Guardian* journalist Simon Jenkins complaining, in 2017, that all the black women were getting the jobs and the party invites from a column in a roster that included not one single black female staff columnist, is an example already mentioned in Chapter 4. Niall Ferguson in *The Times* lamenting the demise of the white male and Lionel Shriver in the *Spectator* both continue to declare the extinction of their tribe from publications and industries that have no representation of those people who are allegedly taking over.

The free speech crisis

In the autumn of 2018, I was shortlisted for a journalism award, one that I had won the year before. The category was 'Society and Diversity Commentator of the Year' and on the shortlist were also my *Guardian* colleague Gary Younge and three *Times* writers. One was Melanie Phillips, a columnist who had over the years made statements about immigrants and Muslims that, in my view, were incendiary. Her inclusion made a mockery of an award category celebrating 'society and diversity'. Among many other offences, she wrote that 'mass immigration' is 'convulsing Europe' and that since it is mostly 'composed of Muslims, it is therefore hardly surprising that anti-immigrant feeling is largely anti-Muslim feeling'. 'The sheer weight of numbers', she stated, 'plus the refusal to assimilate to Western values, makes this an unprecedented crisis for Western liberalism.'

In 2009, on the occasion of the resignation of the Bishop of Rochester, Phillips wrote that he was 'one of the very few inside the church to make explicit the link between Christian and British values, and to warn publicly that they are being destroyed through the prevailing doctrine of multiculturalism'.

In her 2006 book *Londonistan*, Phillips claimed that Islam is 'an ideology that itself is non-negotiable and forms a continuum that links peaceful, law-abiding but nevertheless intensely ideological Muslims at one end and murderous jihadists at the other'. She believes that the British establishment is 'transfixed by the artificial division it has erected between those [Muslims] who actively espouse violence and those who do not'.

After a brief deliberation, my colleague Gary Younge and I decided to withdraw from the prize. We sent a polite email to the award organisers, in which we went to great lengths to spell out that we required nothing but that our names be withdrawn. We stated that: 'we would like to draw a clear distinction between those viewpoints with which we disagree and those which we fundamentally object to on account of their bigotry and divisiveness. We believe that Phillips's body of work falls among the latter.'

The organisers refused to withdraw our names, defended Phillips and stated that they 'cannot retrofit clear and fair rules', forcing us to go public with the withdrawal. What ensued was a bewildering blizzard of vilification, anger and disdain, much of it coming from other journalists who had decided that our request to be withdrawn was a violation of freedom of speech. Some of these responses were prompted behind the scenes by the award organisers.

Matthew d'Ancona of the *Guardian* wrote in *GQ*

magazine that our request was 'testing the fundamentals of free speech'. There was a familiar use of the slippery slope tool when he added, 'those who call for names to be withdrawn, platforms to be withheld and speech to be curtailed are always confident that the measures taken will suit their particular value-system'. At the end of his piece, he quoted, of all people, Frederick Douglass, stating that Douglass's commitment to free speech grasped that it was the friend of minorities, something which myself and Gary had missed, by objecting to the onslaught against minorities in the British media.

We were called bullies, thin-skinned, censors. Claire Fox writing in *Quilette,* said that our request was 'a snapshot of a broader censorious atmosphere in relation to views that don't neatly fit into today's prevailing orthodoxies'(clearly she had missed the mainstreaming of Islamophobia and immigrant bashing). Journalist Matthew Parris called it 'no-platforming'. On the day of the award ceremony, Gary and I were attacked in absentia. The journalist George Monbiot, who attended the ceremony, tweeted that he was 'disturbed' to hear our decision to withdraw 'repeatedly denounced from the platform as "censorship", "rudeness" and even "bullying"'. Apart from publishing the letter we sent to the organiser Julia Hobsbawm, Gary and I did not comment, respond or write on the matter, despite the hail of accusations.

Two things became clear. The first was that the definition of what was a free speech issue and what was not, had become entirely arbitrary and meaningless. The second was that journalists who had made a career out of their libertarian free speech credentials were selective in their commitment, and had fallen into the trap of thinking free speech did not apply to those responding to someone else's right to speak. We were not asking that Phillips be removed, we were not asking that the shortlist be relitigated, we were simply objecting to a writer's views and did not wish to share a shortlist with her. I didn't even feel like I had a choice. But free speech crisis mythology demands that legitimate objection to what has become, in the UK at least, a real crisis of xenophobia and Islamophobia be seen as a failure to hold steadfast to the principle of free speech. *The Times* journalist David Aaronovitch and former chair of Index on Censorship helpfully demonstrated this muddled thinking. In response to the *Guardian*'s former editor on social media, Aaronovitch asked what the judges could have done. 'Quietly lose her nomination? Nobble the judges?' He understood, he added, our desire not to be on the shortlist, but that desire will now *obviously* (emphasis mine) 'become a free speech question because of the dilemma I posed you in my first tweet'. When challenged on the universality of his position, cracks began to appear. One of Melanie Phillips's flagship beliefs is that Islamophobia as a concept does not exist and has been invented to chill criticism of Islam and Islamic practices. According to Phillips, the view that Islamophobia is a prejudice against Muslims as a people is 'a fiction to shut down debate'. On this, Aaronovitch was questioned by Jonathan Portes, professor of economics at King's College, London. 'Would you genuinely take the same stance with someone who claimed that anti-Semitism literally didn't exist, because it was a concept invented solely to protect Jews from legitimate criticism? If you can honestly answer yes, we should all accept you're sincere (agree or not).'

The answer was not 'yes'. Aaronovitch replied, 'As it happens I don't agree with this in practice. I perceive a prejudice against Muslims – amounting to Islamophobia – as being real. But it IS an argument. The existence of anti-Semitism really isn't.' In the thread, he went on to say: 'for many perfectly reasonable people a read-across from anti-Semitism to Islamophobia has to be argued, not axiomatically stated. Why? I've explained already. Because Jews are a race/people and Muslims are a faith. I'm prepared to argue with them.'

Forgive me for the lengthy quotations, but this is how myths are perpetrated, not via bold, clumsy statements, but fine dissembling that one must sift through to find the nugget of disingenuousness. Aaronovitch had decided, arbitrarily, that to claim Islamophobia was a fiction was something which was open to debate and not beyond the pale, and he based that on his view that technically (tools like a technicality), Muslims were not classified as a race/people, even though they are treated like a race/people.

It was a classic of the genre, a mess. People were intent on shoehorning our withdrawal request into the category of free speech when it was nothing of the sort. It was about Islamophobia and xenophobia and how the gentrification and rewarding of both makes the world a more dangerous place for those who will not be saved from a hate crime by pleading with the assailant about technicalities. A more dangerous place for those Muslims who cannot tweet thread away a knife assailant when coming home from the mosque, who cannot halt the snatching of the hijab from a woman's head by arguing to their attackers that Muslims are not a race. Our withdrawal was about the simple right to object to the increasing threat faced by Muslims and immigrants, and the media's complicity in that. But the free speech moral panic klaxon worked. The articles written, social media condemnations posted and, on the day, denouncements of myself and Gary from the award ceremony podium successfully created a free speech 'event' by refusing to acknowledge that response to hate speech is free speech. When the whole affair was over, all the free speech caricatures had been drawn – Phillips and the award organisers as martyrs, Gary and I as censors and liberal journalists as the bearers of the free speech torch. What was not discussed at any great length was the incendiary language against Muslims and immigrants, or how it affects them. The accusations of cowardice and thin skin were particularly perplexing and upsetting. They are tools in their own way. We were not going to have a wrestling match with Melanie Phillips – we were going to sit in a five-star hotel in Mayfair and have a nice breakfast in a room in which she might have been. For me, in hindsight, withdrawing from the prize was quite a hard thing to do and the fear that I would be labelled as some backward troglodyte who didn't understand free speech was real. Gary and I both spent days triangulating between the *Guardian* editors and each other, trying to craft the language of withdrawal as carefully as possible. And yet even this was used against us, as if our anger were not swift and righteous enough, and therefore implied a calculated photo op. D'Ancona wrote: 'while I acknowledge Gary and Nesrine's right to follow their respective consciences, there was much that puzzled me about this. Why, for instance, had they waited eight days since the announcement of the shortlist?' If we had withdrawn immediately, it would have been an unconsidered hissy fit. When we took our time, it was taken to be a cynical move, too slow to suggest real outrage. There was no way to win, except perhaps to keep our mouths shut. That trap is the biggest success of the free speech myth – and the ironic chilling effect is not recognised.

There is only one perceived way to register objection of abhorrent views, which is to take them on. This is a common narcissism in the media. Free speech proponents lean into the storm, they take on the bad guys and vanquish them with logic. Bret Stephens of the *New York Times*, a star Pulitzer prize-winning columnist poached from the *Wall Street Journal* in 2017, flatters himself often in this light, while falling apart with rage at most of the criticism he receives. In response to an objection that the *New York Times* had written an article about a Nazi that seemed too sympathetic, he wrote: 'A newspaper, after all, isn't supposed to be a form of mental comfort food. We are not an advocacy group, a support network, a cheering section, or a church affirming a particular faith – except, that is, a faith in hard and relentless questioning.' He called disagreement 'a dying art'. This was rich from someone who left social media because it was too shouty, only to return sporadically to hurl insults at his critics. In June 2017, Stephens publicly forswore Twitter, saying that the medium debased politics and that he would 'intercede only to say nice things about the writing I admire, the people I like and the music I love'.

In response to criticism of an article of his that misread the success of Democrats in the midterms (and which had to be quietly amended, twice, after more results came in, invalidating his thesis), Stephens tweeted at statistician Nate Silver of 538, 'too bad you're a Twitter troll'. Unprovoked, he tweeted at James Zogby, founder and president of the Arab American Institute, who took issue with a chef calling hummus Israeli food, saying it was part of a history of 'cultural appropriation' and a systematic effort to erase Palestinian history and culture. Stephens fired back at him: 'Hummus seems to have first been mentioned as a Cairene food in the thirteenth century or so. Maybe Maimonides came up with it. Who knows? Who cares? Why not just enjoy it instead of declaring "cultural genocide" and making a fool of yourself?'

He called ex-Obama aide Tommy Vietor an 'asshole' (a tweet which he later deleted after it was flagged as inappropriate by the *New York Times*). In response to a tweet by a *Times* colleague who deleted a tweet he received flack for and admitted was not crafted well, Stephens said: 'This. Is. Insane. And must stop. And there is nothing wrong with your original tweet, @EricLiptonNYT. And there is something deeply psychologically wrong with people who think there is. And fascistic. And yes I'm still on Twitter.'

A dying art indeed.

There is also a synergy between the media, academics and political writers. The free speech myth serves many purposes, often it is erected as a moral shield for risible ideas, one which some members of the media are bamboozled into raising because of their inability to look past their commitment to free speech in the abstract. In 2018, Canadian academic Eric Kaufmann and British academic Matthew Goodwin set up a debate and called it: 'Is rising ethnic diversity a threat to the West?' It was met with an outcry in objection to the fact that 'ethnic diversity' implied race, rather than immigration, which is what the academics claimed they were discussing. Again, this objection was framed as virtue 'signalling' and censoriousness.

David Aaronovitch, who sat on the panel, conceded that the title was inflammatory. 'Sure,' he wrote in his *Times* column, 'one of the participants in the diversity debate has a book to sell and perhaps because of this the event was given a deliberately provocative title' (which seems like an excuse worse than the original crime, but there we are). He called a facetious picture of the panellists with the headline 'Are Dinner Party racists a threat to democracy?' 'libel' (this is libel, while suggesting that ethnic diversity is a threat to Western civilisation is free speech) and dismissed the rest of the criticism as that of a 'Twitter mob'. Finally, Aaronovitch concludes in his column that 'ironically and tragically, this idiocy by the liberal left allows the far-right to pose as the champions of free speech and therefore as champions of true British aspirations'. The organisers of the debate had their moral shield, the debate went ahead under a different heading and Goodwin and Kaufmann, to continue their scam, wrote a piece after it was held called 'What happened when we tried to debate immigration'. (They didn't 'try', they did.)

Goodwin and Kaufmann are added to a growing list of people who concede a mistake was made, but both refuse to be humble about it and will not own their positions. Free speech is a useful tool for such dissimulation.

Damaging identity politics

The problem of 'not owning' a position is best exemplified by the identity politics myth. No myth employs so many euphemisms for excusing the mobilisation of majority white populations against the interests of minorities. Even in the process of writing this book, since I finished work on Chapter 4, a new euphemism has arrived, 'diversity politics', as coined by Matthew Goodwin and Eric Kaufmann when they had to change their debate title from 'Is rising ethnic diversity a threat to the West?' It was a rare honour to see a euphemism come to be right in front of your eyes. 'White-shift' is another, the title of Eric Kaufmann's book in which he makes the argument that there is, indeed, a white identity politics, but that it is OK. He claims that Western politics is being forged by 'the tug of war between white ethno-traditionalism and anti-racist moralism' and that white people should be allowed to assert their 'racial self-interest'.

This parsing of words is a common skill shared by analysts and influential thinkers on identity politics whose blind commitment to the myth inevitably ends in a skewed advocacy, rather than dispassionate analysis.

David Goodhart, a bestselling author and founder of *Prospect* magazine (I list narrator's achievements to underscore their recognition, influence and reach, as opposed to their objective excellence, as these are two separate things, but more on that later), is a master parser.

'White interest,' he argues, is fair and unjustly demonised. But, like Douglas Murray, his largesse and finely tuned language lapses when it is race-related interest of any other sort. What underpins Goodhart's thesis, one to which, in fairness to him, he is no fair weather convert, having floated the defence of 'own kind' politics as far back as 2004, is the exception for whiteness. In an article for *Prospect* entitled 'Too Diverse?', Goodhart argues that diversity undermines the social contract, because it is harder for people to contribute to a blind pool of resources if they feel that those who benefit are struggling in ways they can't relate to. It is an homage to the shared kinship of ethnicity. He calls it a 'calculus of affinity', where we relate better to those we literally relate to, either by actual kinship, or racial affiliation. It is the 'glue of ethnicity', humans are 'social, group-based primates with constraints on their willingness to share', some expressions of racism 'can be read as declarations of dismay at the passing of old ways of life'. This sort of anthropological elevation of ethnic solidarity as a natural and unavoidable part of life is one that Goodhart can make without being accused of excusing or apologising for racism, but the problem is that he does not apply it universally.

He has little time for it when it comes specifically to black British people. He went for black MP David Lammy, who had linked the Windrush scandal, where the government violated the citizenship status of Afro-Caribbean origin British citizens by deporting them, to institutional racism. Goodhart accused Lammy of 'uncritical channelling of black anger and victimhood'. He called a summation of this immigration scandal by the black British artist Akala on the BBC a 'racial grievance outburst'. He is particularly galled by the black British inner city, observing in 2011 that: 'the nihilistic grievance culture of the black inner city, fanned by parts of the hip-hop/rap scene and copied by many white people, has created a hardcore sub-culture of post-political disaffection. The disaffection is mainly unjustified.'

On this double standard, engaging with Goodhart, a man so distinguished by book sales and think tank positions, is to fall into a quicksand of equivocation and logic that stalls once it comes anywhere near the proximity of its natural conclusion. When I challenged him on his inconsistent position, he responded: 'How does it help black inner city youth to be told white society is implacably hostile to you, and to dress up a big admin failure at HO [the Home Office] as further proof of racist intent? Surely it deepens culture of disaffection, education/economic failure which itself feeds gang/knife violence.'

He then went on to concede that: 'Windrush would have been less likely if there had been people of Caribbean background at the top of HO. No one knew how many legit ppl might get caught in error (yes there were warnings), it was not a priority. That still doesn't make it an act of racist intent.'

This is a very neat encapsulation of the problem with such narrators, the irresponsible intellectual dressing up of what is really a personal belief, even an ideology, as detached observation. Goodhart will in one breath advocate for a discount for tribal behaviour, up to and including racism, because that's just how we are made. But in another breath, he will deny other groups that very right. Not only that, he will advocate for a discount for white tribal behaviour when it comes to merely imagined or intangible grievances, something as abstract as resisting 'risk-pooling' in a welfare state for others who don't look or behave like you (he does not pause to answer the obvious question this begs, which is why non-whites don't suffer from this risk-pooling aversion too?). At the same time, he will argue that sure, more people of Caribbean background at the top of the Home Office would have minimised the risk of maltreatment of others of similar background, but that is not a grievance that means anything or should go anywhere because it wasn't based in 'intent'.

Some are just innocent primates hardwired to behave a certain way, others not only can, but should, fight the sense that their tribes are under assault, and civilise themselves by rising above it. Some are helpless, others have agency. He extends ethnic kinship justification for white populations who have a perceived sense of loss, for something as intangible as the passing of an old way of life, but not to those populations that are experiencing real and tangible harm due to their ethnic or racial classification. He goes one step further, in blaming tribal ties among minorities for triggering a sort of jealous tribalism in white majorities, just by existing. 'The "thickest" solidarities,' he writes, 'are now often found among ethnic minority groups themselves in response to real or perceived discrimination. This can be another source of resentment for poor whites who look on enviously from their own fragmented neighbourhoods as minorities recreate some of the mutual support and sense of community that was once a feature of British working-class life.' For Goodhart to be satisfied, it seems that ethnic minority groups must either disappear altogether, or dissolve their (natural, 'primate') loyalties, so as not to antagonise anyone.

According to Goodhart, what is important is not the original issue (racism, disenfranchisement, incarceration), but the 'effects of accentuating those stories', which may be 'counterproductive for the people they want to support'. The stories you hear about yourself can affect how your life pans out. On black inner-city youths, Goodhart claims they 'will not get a job if you don't give a shit and have been taught by the culture around you that you are a victim of a racist society'.

It is encouraging that Goodhart correctly focuses on the power of stories and how they can shape a culture. It is a shame that he has dedicated his own power as storyteller to promote a myth, which is that the political tribal behaviour of minorities is indulgence (something which he also applies to concerns about sexual harassment at work, a 'metropolitan' fixation). In the same way the myth of free speech works, the myth of a disruptive and narcissistic identity politics is a call for quietism.

We need new voices

It is important to note at this point, that this is not an exhaustive selection of narrators, merely a selection of the most prominent, lauded and respected. The purpose is to demonstrate that there is a monopoly of voices, hailing from an increasingly exclusive background, that dominates storytelling.

It would be less of a problem if they acknowledged or expressed their limitations and/or lack of neutrality. It would

also be less of a problem if they were presented and pack-
aged that way by those institutions that employ them, but
across the board their voices and authority are considered
the default. Their influence not only filters down to mainstream opinion, but upwards to politics. For politicians, the
media is both a disseminator to the public and an interme-
diator between them and the public. Those parties, leaders
and political programmes that are considered electable are
made so by elites. These elites are not distant enough from
such leaders and programmes, and vet and elevate those
who reflect their own image and self-interest. The lack of
neutrality, this undeclared interest in the status quo, goes
some way in explaining the sensitivity to challenge and
the strange, blatantly clear inconsistencies in thought. Introspection, openness to questioning, and elegance of logic
spring naturally from positions of honesty, no dissembling
is required. No threats of libel or resorts to abuse. But when
the spread of ideas is so narrow, what occurs is the elevation of a diligent, high output mediocrity, generally quick to
anger, and maudlin self-pity. There is a reason that Jordan
Peterson has become the box office 'intellectual' of our time.
He is myth ground zero, indulging in the trickery of preach-
ing the most regressive common themes about gender, race
and religion, while feigning that this is in fact a new and
challenging thing. His success does not prove that there is
an appetite for his ideas because they have been blacklisted
by the mainstream media, it proves that there is already
fertile ground for all these myths.

I am not suggesting that there is a coordinated cabal and
that everyone is complicit, that there are no hardworking,
well-intentioned journalists and pundits who try and sometimes succeed in testing their assumptions, but that there
is a media analogue of the patriarchy. The mediarchy, if

you will allow the crude coinage. In this mediarchy, there is groupthink born of uniformity in pedigree, and a proximity to power via shared networks and values, which means that instead of reflecting reality, it distorts it, instead of embracing change, it resists it. It is set up as a massive lacuna, all other faults can be seen except its own. It has only just occurred to me, through no deliberate design, that almost every single one of the voices profiled above, male, female, gay and straight, has weighed in with a word or two against the tide of sexual consent reappraisal.

Impunity expands that lacuna. When journalists face no consequence for failing to do their jobs, when they are too aligned with power, when their backgrounds and networks insulate them from vast swathes of the population, myth regurgitation becomes a risk. Representation is the first solution to this monopoly of ignorance. We need fewer white, fewer male and fewer affluent voices. It is easy, in fact inevitable, that the media 'missed' the rise of white right-wing terrorism – those that are affected by it, and in fact have been warning about it, are absent from its newsrooms and columns. Is it a surprise that the Brexit vote happened, when immigrants, so lacking in positions of reporting and influence in the British media, could be presented as a threat rather than an integrated part of Britain? Is it a surprise that with an ideological bent that skews right of centre, conversations about economic solutions to inequality are dominated by scapegoating of immigrants, rather than an examination of the capitalist status quo?

In 2016, a City University study found that the British media is 95 per cent white, 86 per cent university educated and 55 per cent male, with women overwhelmingly occupying junior roles. In the middle of an Islamophobia crisis, 0.4 per cent of British journalists are Muslim. British columnists are the most exclusive, with only four current affairs staff columnists of colour in the mainstream British press – only one of them is female and none of them is Muslim. For myth projection to end, for the necessary change to happen, schemes to foster and integrate those from different backgrounds are vital. But most importantly what is required is a reappraisal. We need to step back and allow the myth of reliability, of neutrality, of non-alignment with a political and economic elite, to fall away from those voices we vest with authority. They are not only letting down those not of their own ilk, they are letting their own kind down, unable to explain the world in an objective manner or anticipate how it is changing. They will continue to be blindsided by the rise of populism and the virility of authoritarianism that, as has become clear since 2016, turns on the media first. There is a boomerang effect built into myths. They are bad for everyone.

AFTERWORD

New tools for new stories

'No one knows what a more democratic and inclusive culture would be like. It is fatuously omniscient to assume it would be worse than what we already have. The attempt of reactionaries to shut people down shows both fear and stupidity. But it's too late: they will be hearing from us.'

Hanif Kureishi

The boomerang effect – myths are bad for everyone

Myths are bad for everyone, because not all who believe in myths can win. Myths are sustained by giving the illusion of relative status. Because not everyone can be at the top of the pyramid, those further down have to believe that they are further up. But they are still downstream from those in power, still stuck reproducing harmful patterns, still struggling, while believing that the problem is someone else who is trying to take their position.

Myths eat their loved ones.

The success of a myth depends on how well it can convince enough people that they are exempt from its consequences. A myth creates winners and losers; it convinces its adherents that they are the winners. Patriarchy continues to thrive because enough men believe that they are winning, despite the system exerting such pressures on them that in

the United States men are 3.5 times more likely to die by
suicide than women. In the UK, suicide is the single biggest
killer of men under the age of forty-five. Such a high rate
of male suicide may be superficially associated with economic factors such as recent recessions, unemployment and
austerity, but research by the UK-based charity Samaritans
cited the specifically male elements of economic struggle as
the trigger. Men, the report concluded, measure themselves
against a 'gold standard' which prizes power, control and
invincibility. Men in mid-life are particularly prone to a
sense of futility, as the decline of traditional male industries
means that they 'have lost not only their jobs but also a
source of masculine pride and identity'. They also do not
develop the emotional ducts to process these challenges
and are 'overwhelmingly dependent on a female partner for
emotional support'.

The men convicted for assault or murder of a female partner are not winning; the boys emptying semi-automatics in
their high schools because they were rejected by girls are
not winning; the collateral damage – the children, the innocent bystanders, their murdered partners – are not winning.
The myth of gender equality does not only deny the pain of
women, it denies that of men.

The same can be said of all the other myths, they
boomerang inevitably. Trashing the culture of political
correctness only foments one where everyone's sensitivities
are trampled upon, not just those who myth believers think
don't deserve special treatment. The reception of Trump's
taste for insults is a good illustration of how those who
elected him were sick of a political correctness that coddled
the feelings of those lower down the status pole. But they
now have to contend with a president who is not saving
his non-PC 'honesty' for Mexican immigrants or Muslims,

but disabled people, war heroes (John McCain, a 'dummy'), the Supreme Court ('a mess'), his own Republican Party ('stupid'), the FBI, the CIA, US allies all over the world and various politicians and media personalities, to whom he refers in terms of their physical or intellectual capabilities. 'Like a dog' is one of his favourite insults.

In 2016, the Southern Poverty Law Center (SPLC) registered a surge in playground bullying in American schools. The frequency that Trump's comments transmitted was picked up – Muslims, Jews and immigrants were targeted by both school children and their teachers. The research collected 5,000 comments and stories. Twenty per cent mentioned Trump, which was five times more than all the other politicians cited in the survey put together. Based on this, the SPLC gave the phenomenon a name, 'The Trump Effect'. In 2017, BuzzFeed News uncovered 54 incidents in which high school students either explicitly mentioned Trump, or used a Trump message or policy (such as the Muslim ban) to harass a classmate. But it didn't stop at Muslims and Jews, it expanded to bullying girls, students of different sexual orientation and ultimately into targeting students who simply did not support Trump. Violence and damage to school property increased and the overwhelming majority of educators 'saw a negative impact on students' mood and behavior following the election'. As Trump himself would say, so much winning.

Similarly, free speech absolutism creates a polarisation, a race to the bottom where licence is confused with freedom, where free speech is used as a technical excuse to commodify the spectacle of pain. When conspiracy theorist Alex Jones was kicked off digital platforms for suggesting that the Sandy Hook massacre was fabricated (among other theories) he asked, 'Now, who will stand against tyranny and who will stand for free speech?' Shortly after, a defamation suit was brought against him (one of many) – his defence was the First Amendment. Even though the court concluded that his free speech rights were not being violated because there should be an effort to balance 'freedom of expression with the safeguarding of people's reputations', liberal free speech advocates were not convinced. On his TV show, US liberal talk show host Bill Maher indignantly said, 'We're losing the thread, of the concepts that are important to this country. . . . Either you care about the real American shit or you don't. I don't like Alex Jones, but Alex Jones gets to speak.'

How did we get here? To a place where a man like Alex Jones can make a career out of harassing the parents of children shot to death in school massacres, and this strange strain of free speech masochism still support him? We are here because the free speech crisis myth has been allowed to be warped and corrupted as its targets – the snowflakes, the women, the queers – were not sacred cows. And so now its tentacles extend to grieving parents, even to strangers who can find themselves suddenly at the centre of a conspiracy theory video which has been doctored and posted online. Once free speech is associated with the right to denigrate, it corrodes sensitivity to all. In his book, *The Harm in Hate Speech*, professor of law and philosophy Jeremy Waldron spells out this blowback theory.

The very point of hate speech, he says, 'is to negate the implicit assurance that a society offers to the members of vulnerable groups – that they are accepted . . . as a matter of course, along with everyone else'. Purveyors of hate 'aim to undermine this assurance, call it in question, and taint it with visible expressions of hatred, exclusion and contempt'. It would seem that the slippery slope when it comes to free speech doesn't curve towards more curtailing of speech, but more licence for it in a way that makes everyone vulnerable to whichever free speech hitman is on the loose.

In addition to this downward spiral of privileging speech over dignity, free speech absolutism today just creates a toxic atmosphere for everyone. To fall for the myth that curbing or curating abusive or hateful speech constitutes a crisis simply contributes to a wider cultural corruption. The popularisation of abusing human beings for whatever end – ideological, personal or just cynical – is the actual free speech crisis. The exploiting of free speech to set up roll-up roll-up circus performances is contributing to an extremism that is lucrative for everyone, from the BBC and CNN to Alex Jones.

Every day you can tune into a number of debates where a truth and an untruth are pitted against each other, with the untruth spokesperson's presence legitimised by the cop out of free speech, and often marketed in such terms. In early 2019, *Today*, BBC radio's most highbrow news programme hosted a debate where a student was berated for not being able to handle 'unfashionable views' because he refused to be taught by a professor who wrote 'homosexuality is bestiality' in an academic journal. The next step on from the merely 'unfashionable' is the downright martyred. As mentioned in Chapter 2, when Sam Harris hosted the author of *The Bell Curve*, Charles Murray, the episode was given the title 'Forbidden Knowledge'. In 2018, in keeping with the fashion, a group of academics created a journal that allows for anonymous publication and called it *The Journal of Controversial Ideas*.

On a large scale, these emissions can pollute the environment, poisoning the atmosphere for everyone, sometimes literally, where climate change deniers are invited to push 'facts' that are nothing but opinions, but are lent a veneer of legitimacy by being allowed on to a platform in the first place. Regulation in this case is a far cry from censorship, it is simply a responsibility. The same way it is a responsibility when it comes to other matters such as false advertising, or not declaring an interest in a product one is selling. When someone on Instagram gushes about a product and then marks it with the hashtag #ad, this is simply a compliance with commercial laws that protect consumers from being sold an item without knowing that the seller is being paid. This is a far higher bar than is being set by most media organisations when they host lobbyists or guests with a record of non-factual messaging. Jeremy Waldron, who is regarded as one of the world's leading experts on legal philosophy, writes that it is only 'natural to think that the law should be involved – both in its ability to underpin the provision of public goods and in its ability to express and communicate common commitments.' After all, he reminds us: 'Societies do not become well ordered by magic.'

And so, as if also by magic, it is expected that fixating on the expressions of identity politics of the 'other' will not create a friendly environment for the growth of dangerous supremacist identitarians, who end up targeting not only minorities. They are murdering white British MPs, white journalists and plotting to kill white American Democratic politicians and white, high-profile, left-wing figures.

'We willingly turned the other way on white supremacy because there were real political costs to talking about white supremacy,' the national-security strategist P.W. Singer said to the *New York Times* magazine in 2018. While we hyperventilate about cultural appropriation and 'oppression Olympics', what the writer Amy Chua describes as the attempt by different minority groups to extract more rights and special treatment, white supremacist groups have been gathering momentum away from the limelight. Peddling an identity politics myth that focuses on the behaviour of minorities not only creates division where there is none and dismisses legitimate grievances, it also gives ideological fodder to white identitarian movements while giving them cover.

In the United States, the identity that has posed the most serious threat to internal security did not come from outside the country. White supremacists and far-right extremists have killed more people since 9/11 than any other group of domestic extremists. A report by the Anti-Defamation League's Center on Extremism revealed that the overwhelming majority, 71 per cent, of politically motivated extremist deaths in the US in the ten years preceding 2017 were at the hands of far-right or white-supremacist ideologues. The proportion of such crimes committed in the same timeframe by Islamic extremists, the focus of the country's counter-terrorism strategy? Just 26 per cent.

But the excepting of whiteness still runs so deep that these numbers have had little effect on the country's counter-terrorism approach, which is still focused primarily on jihadists. Between 2002 and 2017, according to the Stimson Center, the United States' spend on counterterrorism, channelled mainly to investigating foreign and US born jihadis, was $2.8 trillion. In that period, attacks by Muslim extremists resulted in 100 deaths. Between 2008 and 2017 alone, domestic extremists killed 387 people.

In that light, what sense does it make that the first national security measure taken by the Trump administration was to ban visitors from Muslim countries? None at all. It's dog whistling while Rome burns. The boomerang effect is evident in the profiles of the dead. They are Heather Heyer, mowed down at a far-right rally in Virginia in 2017. They are MP Jo Cox. They are Taliesin Myrddin Namkai-Meche and Rick Best, two men stabbed to death on a train in 2017, when intervening to prevent a racist attack. It is not only black churches, mosques, Sikh temples and synagogues which are being targeted. The white identity politics is growing more feverish, but it is not new. Data gathered between 1986 and 2016 by Ryan Jerome LeCount of Hamline University decouples it from Trump, proving that 'what it means to identify with the liberal or conservative "team" for US Whites is increasingly bound up with one's racial politics'.

Racial politics also backfire in other less obvious but in aggregate, life-shortening ways. In *Dying of Whiteness: How the Politics of Racial Resentment is Killing America's Heartland*, author Jonathan Metzl argues that the cultural associations of 'whiteness' encourage white people to adopt political views, such as opposition to gun laws or the Affordable Care Act, that reduce their own life expectancy.

'They could look at the wealthy persons or corporations or donors who were actually causing policies that were worsening their lives, or they could look at the people they believed were taking away their resources,' Metzl summarised in a *Vox* interview. 'And they chose, electorally, to look at the latter – and that's hurting nearly everybody.'

And on it goes. That denial is in turn fleshed out by a false recollection of a nation's history. Historical exceptionalism is the most powerful nation building tool and also the most corrosive. It gives a false sense of self, an intoxication of superiority, which leads to wild political adventurism. Those who were shocked by the Brexit vote and who continued to prosecute the case for staying in the European Union through statistics and facts, failed to grasp that Brexit was, in essence, a nativist and jingoistic exercise. It was one rooted in an unrealistic view of the country's prospects outside the EU, based on an aggrandising history. There was not enough time to undo the coding. It would have taken a few more generations of reprogramming to teach the British that their history does not inform their present, that an empire in the past cannot vanquish a strong union of European countries today. That a victory in World War II was not secured by British grit alone, but also alliances with others.

So almost from the day of the vote, the self-harm of the belief in the exceptional apartness of the British became apparent. And still the connections are not made. As warnings came that there might be food shortages, some responded that it may do the country good to go through a spot of hunger. Britain has gone soft you see, in peacetime, and so its lean days of glory might return if it goes through adversity. A Leave voter interviewed by the BBC in early 2019 said that food shortages would make people 'appreciate what they've had'. As businesses packed up and left, taking tax revenue and employment with them, the old thriving in adversity canards were rolled out. In December 2018, the British foreign secretary told the *Sunday Telegraph*: 'I've always thought that even in a no-deal situation this is a great country, we'll find a way to flourish and prosper. We've faced much bigger challenges in our history.'

As warnings that cancer medications might not become available in the case of a hard Brexit, Leave supporters responded in varying forms of pain fetishisation. This is Britain's 'paranoid fantasy' as the Irish writer Fintan O'Toole calls it, that lies behind Brexit. A historical psychosis where Britain finds its finest hour but only through adversity. Where it prevails but only after a Dunkirk or a German blitzkrieg. O'Toole describes it as: 'the fever-dream of an English Resistance, and its weird corollary: a desire to have actually been invaded so that one could – gloriously – resist. And not just resist but, in the ultimate apotheosis of masochism, die.'

The British will literally die in order to close some historical loop, one that the longest period of peacetime and accord in Europe in modern history has interfered with.

And what of our intellectual and political elite? The narrators and curators of public life who hail from the best academic institutions. What of the hundreds of years invested, and lives spent, in the pursuit of science and rational thought? What has belief in this elite's credentials, its neutrality, and its talent achieved? An America where Trump rules the country via incoherent tweets and a Britain which is marching, death cult-like, towards self-immolation. It is impossible after these two events that there can be any review of the intellectual and political complex of these two nations that doesn't involve wholesale fumigation. How has putting faith in members of a certain class, a certain educational background and a certain breeding worked out for us? How have the 'Oxford chums' as the *Economist* put it in a scathing editorial in 2018, worked out for Britain? Those who rise to positions of influence through 'bluff rather than expertise'. 'Britain,' the editorial diagnosed, 'is governed by a self-involved clique that rewards group membership above competence and self-confidence above expertise.' This 'chumocracy' in Britain is everywhere and cross-pollinates between the media and politics, failing upwards and sideways between both careers. Boris Johnson walks away from the mess of Brexit into a six-figure *Daily Telegraph* column, even though as a politician he is ineffective and as a writer he is barely competent. Nick Timothy, one of two advisors to Theresa May who shepherded her party's disastrous post-Brexit election, crashed out of Downing Street only to join the *Telegraph* as a columnist, although it is not clear what his expertise is apart from losing elections that were in the bag. During his time as May's advisor Timothy was drawn to David Goodhart of the Somewheres and Any-wheres. In one of her flagship speeches as prime minister, May said 'if you believe you are a citizen of the world, you are a citizen of nowhere.' The chumocracy is not only an industry network, it is an ideological one.

George Osborne, another Brexit casualty, was rewarded by the clique for the loss of his political position by being handed the editorship of the *Evening Standard* newspaper. Michael Gove, in between cabinet gigs while waiting for the Brexit calculus winds to blow his way, rejoined *The Times* as a columnist and book reviewer. I found myself bemused to be sitting next to him on a weekly BBC news panel of journalists one Saturday, where he was introduced as a *Times* columnist just there to give a journalist's view of the world, even though he was a sitting MP. It is dizzying to watch this revolving door of chumocracy spin as the coun-try's Parliament and politics descended deeper into chaos.

Why do we believe in these people? In these myths? There are no winners here, only the perception of winning.

Myths may look like they are working, but they are not. At least not for anyone apart from the ring-fenced few. Myths are hierarchy stabilisers, in that they keep them going by creating the illusion of status, by concentrating on relative status. If attention can be maintained on how you are better off than someone below you, it can be diverted from the fact that there is someone above you who is either exploiting you, or enjoying more unearned privileges than you. If attention can be maintained on how those below you are coming for your resources, then your eyes are fixed downwards, never upwards. By their very nature, hierarchies only have one small group at the top.

Believing in a myth is sort of like taking part in a Ponzi scheme. You are constantly being told that your stake is accruing, sometimes you might even get a dividend, but ultimately only the scheme owners make any real money. There is no real value created, it eventually collapses, and the money winners abscond with the spoils.

The negative effects of myths are only supposed to affect other people. One of Donald Trump's signature election promises was to build a wall along the Mexico border and that Mexico would pay for it. Once that promise clashed with reality and Trump demanded that the wall be paid for by the US tax payer, he triggered the longest government shutdown in the history of the United States. For the first time, his policies hit those who had voted for him to inflict the pain on others. A prison warden affected by the shutdown interviewed by the *New York Times* in January 2019 put it very well when she said: 'I voted for him, and he's the one who's doing this. I thought he was going to do good things. He's not hurting the people he needs to be hurting.'

He's not hurting the people he needs to be hurting. That in a nutshell is the myth boomerang effect. If a political programme is based on empowering its supporters by appealing to their sense of superiority over the marginalised, it will come for its own supporters at some point. And they are usually those supporters less cushioned by wealth or job security. Sometimes it comes back in obvious ways, such as when a wild promise to erect a wall based on hyper-vilifying of Mexicans and immigrants cannot be executed without hitting you, a hand-to-mouth federal government employee, in the pocket. Others in more subtle ways.

The same bewilderment can be seen in Brexit voters who

are horrified at the impact of the very thing they voted for. A depreciating pound means holidays are more expensive, imports are more costly and inflation higher. EU citizen flight impacted the NHS, already under severe pressure and, by 2019, one-third of British companies were planning to relocate after Brexit or had already shifted operations in preparation for a hard Brexit. There was even shock at the fact that loss of freedom of movement will impact British travellers the same way it does Europeans. But Brexit was only supposed to hurt the other people, the immigrants who were allegedly swarming in. Again, the nature of these things is that those who sold the myths, the policies, the promises, will be the ones who are relatively immune from their consequences.

Even in the period that it has taken to write the previous chapters, the velocity of the myths has intensified. There is little in this book that is unique to Britain or the United States. The myths of different cultures are surprisingly familiar. What is special about the current age where myths have taken such hold, is their aggressive mutation – there are just so many more ways for them to be disseminated. The anthropologist Claude Lévi-Strauss argued that myths develop in order to 'resolve collective problems of classification and hierarchy, marking lines between the inside and the outside, the Law and its exceptions, those who belong and those who do not' and that they are based on a structure that recurs across cultures and eras. But that does not mean that we resign ourselves to the inevitability of their perversion.

Legend has it that the moment it became clear that Donald Trump was winning, around 3 a.m. Eastern time, David Remnick of the *New Yorker* sat down and wrote his now famous piece, 'An American Tragedy', in one sitting. It started with the assertion: 'The election of Donald Trump to the Presidency is nothing less than a tragedy for the American republic, a tragedy for the Constitution, and a triumph for the forces, at home and abroad, of nativism, authoritarianism, misogyny, and racism.' Remnick, in the small hours of that morning, came ever so close to the heart of it. He had no time for those who were waiting in the wings, rightly predicted, to normalise Trump, to stress the innate decency of the American people and minimise the darkness that elected him. But at the end of the piece, once Remnick is spent and his affection for his desecrated America rises again, he ends on a note of exceptionalism.

'But despair is no answer. To combat authoritarianism, to call out lies, to struggle honorably and fiercely in the name of American ideals—that is what is left to do.'

It does not occur to Remnick, even as he warns against the complacencies of belief in an inherently virtuous America, that maybe the forces of nativism, authoritarianism, misogyny and racism, do in fact, also embody America. Who is to say which set of these competing ideas is the definitive one? We must start earlier – the American Tragedy was happening all along.

None of the things that myths preach against, from defensive identity politics activism to the necessity of political correctness, would be necessary in a world where Remnick's cushion of 'ideals' existed. But we are not there yet. The greatest trick a myth can play is to convince people that we are in the best of all possible worlds, that we live in a moral universe.

New tools for new stories

So how do we start? How are these myths to be challenged if they are so ubiquitous? As an op-ed writer in an era where the discourse is made up of point scoring, 'clapping back' and generally trying to annihilate opponents by making 'gotcha' arguments, I ask myself one question that has always served me well. 'Are you trying to make a point or are you trying to get somewhere?' It is an instant corrective. Very often when presented with the question, I found that I was on the path of trying to discredit an idea or a person I disagreed with so fully that I had lost sight of the purpose of the exercise, which should be to further understanding of an issue and for readers to end up somewhere – not necessarily exactly where I wanted, but to a place that was different to where they started. It is why I still miss comment threads: they were a way of measuring that distance. It is easy, especially when faced with bad faith arguments, to fail to stick to this principle. But it is an important one to keep in mind if we are going to get somewhere, rather than just make a point to ourselves and those who already agree with us. What follows are simple strategies that I have tried to employ while thinking about writing this book and throughout writing it. I think of them as good tools, ones that can be used to challenge myths and write new stories, without falling into the traps laid by all the argumentative techniques laid out earlier in the book.

Question

Acknowledgement is the first step – recognising how these stories push narratives and questioning the 'facts' that they present as incontrovertible. What struck me when researching this book, especially the political correctness and free speech crisis chapters, was how quickly premises of arguments fall apart the moment they are subjected to basic scrutiny. Solid evidence that I instinctively felt was rather far-fetched, turned out to be false or, even worse, fabricated. Sometimes it was Chinese whispers, others it was arson, a sort of cultural pyromania where little fires were ignited here and there and then reported on in feigned shock by the perpetrators.

Reputable media organisations used to be above this, but no longer. We are not talking Breitbart here. The *Telegraph* making up details about Lola Olufemi and her group of bandits who want to change the university curriculum was an intentional act to enrage their readers. *The Times* was in such haste to nail a real-life example of political correctness going mad that a veteran journalist with a good reputation made so many mistakes reporting a story about a Muslim foster family that he and his editor were reprimanded by the Independent Press Standards Organisation and the family courts. Even the BBC regularly rehashes clickbait stories about political correctness out of laziness and traffic chasing. Politicians, pundits and opinion makers then repeat the stories and before they have even triggered suspicion in the recipient's mind, they are conventional wisdom. This is not to be taken as an excuse to dismiss all sources as 'fake news', but as a prompt, a reminder to question if it seems, as I will detail below, like there is something behind a story. As mentioned before, the purpose of myths is to hide the real crises, so as to dampen efforts to resolve them. Gender equality is regressing. Speech by those empowered against the weak has never been more free or in demand. Identity politics has, in fact, been brought to bear on minorities by white people. Political correctness protocols are being less and less observed. The belief in a virtuous origin uses history to justify an inglorious present. And our narrators are unreliable.

Look beyond the story

The second step is to understand the purpose of the stories we are told. What are they trying to achieve? The giveaway is that they are framing some sort of rebalancing request by a minority group as an unreasonable demand, or dismissing a request to be spared a moral wound as pathetic. Generally, if a story either implies or expressly suggests the following, approach it with care:

- Demand for special treatment based on identity (e.g. changing curricula along racial lines, taking time off work to perform religious duties, establishing sexual harassment guidelines). Most of the time, as detailed in Chapter 2, reports for such demands are made up.
- Demand for sensitivity due to thin skin, weakness, entitlement (e.g. adding trigger warnings to literature, providing safe spaces at work or academic institutions). The language used in this instance is usually a good tell. It ranges from highbrow accusations of a culture of 'coddling' and 'safetyism', to popular street insults such as 'snowflake', 'soyboy', 'cuck' and, of course, 'triggered'.

The unifying premise of these stories is that things are going 'too far', which is a classic resistance to change response. Such stories chill in two ways: the first is to overestimate the scale of change or threatened change; the second is to make no distinction between the genuine excesses of a movement and the purpose of the movement as a whole. I hope that by now this will sound familiar to you; the dismissal of defensive identity politics by reducing it to skirmishes about cultural appropriation, the snubbing of political correctness by collapsing it into controversies about pronouns and Christmas, the co-option of free speech by smearing all those who object to that co-option as hysterical, the snubbing of those calling for accurate historical accounts as vandals only interested in tearing down statues – the disqualification of a cause by way of its shortcomings, rather than its purpose.

Sure, sometimes students get a bit emotional and carried away, it doesn't mean that we should jettison all concerns about how free speech is abused. Of course, there are some obviously ridiculous manifestations of identity politics where a certain individualistic narcissism takes over, replacing thought for experience. That doesn't make identity a less central factor in determining how a group is enfranchised. It is a valid argument, that tearing down statues might not be the most productive way of going about reappraising inaccurate depictions of history, but it's only one part of the conversation, not the entire discourse. Absolutely, political correctness sometimes does go too far, but in the end it's about the spirit of the discussion, rather than its detail. Dismissing a movement via its outliers is called 'nutpicking', picking out and highlighting the most extreme members of a group as the definitive representative of that group.

A brief experiment I conducted over social media opened my eyes to how, on the whole, most reasonable people can have a legitimate objection to politically correct measures, without that meaning that they subscribe to the moral hysteria that comes along with that. I asked people to give me examples of incidents where they genuinely felt that political correctness had gone too far, urging them to avoid the usual cliches. The top three answers I received were: cultural appropriation, the fashion of demanding only actors who shared an identity of a role can play it (objecting to a straight man playing a gay man for example) and the elimination of trophies at sports day. The polite and informative discussion that followed (still a novelty, I go back to it whenever I am worn down by the constant high-pitched shriek of the internet) taught me something far more important than the detail of the stories people told. It was possible to discuss these things without making them about something else – about Muslims, immigrants, 'lefties' or students. And when it wasn't about something else, most people actually felt more free to say what was on their mind without being afraid that it was to be used as a supporting argument in some position that they do not agree with as a whole. It is possible to believe that banning trophies at sports day in schools is perhaps not a great idea without signing up to the fact that a lobby of disabled campaigners was now driving academic sports policy. My question was not associated with anything, I was just genuinely curious.

So look out for the narrative behind the incendiary example, what Albert Hirschman describes in his 1991 book *The Rhetoric of Reaction* as 'the first reaction'. Conservatism responds to the opening up of societies after social, religious or economic revolutions by nutpicking. The first reaction, described as 'the movement of ideas following (and opposing) the assertion of equality before the law and of civil rights in general', in its fervour did not make a distinction between the positive and negative aspects of the French Revolution. This tradition goes on today, assuming that 'la Révolution est un bloc', defining and smearing movements for change by their excesses.

Do not pick a side

This might be an odd piece of advice, considering how I have just spent a whole book stressing the importance of standing firm in the face of resistance to progress. But myths are not exclusive to a certain political position or ideology, they are just about power. Liberals' narcissism is just as susceptible to myth-making as right-wing superiority complexes. That is why these old stories are so powerful, they speak not to ideology, but something more universal, the elegance of nature's hierarchy, the warm glow of feeling special, or feeling better than others. You will find that weakness everywhere, liberal love of wars in barbaric places that need to be saved is shared happily with hawkish right-wing warmongers.

My motivation for writing this book was triggered by the fear of swapping one set of certainties for another, one set of moral snobbery for another. It's a trap, to fight myths by creating other myths. Although I ended broadly on the left, I found the Anglo-American heritage of leftist thinking so steeped in resistance to the right that it ended up in its own storytelling business. I remember at the beginning of the Syrian civil war being quite speechless with confusion when, in order to pre-empt calls for intervention in the conflict, some on the left began to push some odd line that Bashar al-Assad was really quite popular with the Syrians. The same perplexity hit me when I realised that support for the Muslim Brotherhood in some Arab countries was fashionable in Western left-wing circles, even though that sat entirely uncomfortably with the secular heritage of the left. It took me a while to figure out that the Muslim Brotherhood was seen as the enemy of Arab dictators propped up by Western neo-imperialist regimes, even though the party espoused fundamentally illiberal politics and has, in almost every single country it has secured power or been adjacent to power, including the one in which I grew up, been bad news.

Seek knowledge and foster a non-partisan world view. This might seem like a banal point, but myths thrive by presenting facts as emotion and teasing out emotion as a response.

Argue better, or not at all

Get offline. Or off social media at least. Or if you must, stay for nothing but entertainment value, a newsfeed and engage as little as possible in arguments. Social media lends itself well to misinformation, increasing the velocity of myths and sharpening polarisation. It is basically an uber-tool that lends itself extremely well to short gotcha points and hence to all the individual tools, to straw-manning, diversion and whataboutery.

The reason I say get off altogether is because it's very hard to be on social media and be even marginally interested in politics without getting drawn in. The only conversation that is happening is a fight. And that will eventually draw everyone into making a point, rather than getting somewhere. Everyone is different of course. I am getting better at resisting the draw of arguments (mostly because I argue for a living, and don't particularly want to do it for free, you do enough of that in journalism), but still have felt the binary ping-pong of point and counterpoint and burn and counter-burn beginning to infuse my thought process with mulishness, hostility and factionalism.

When American writer Ta Nehisi Coates left Twitter, he blamed it for being a corruptive force on good writing and thinking. Part of the process of becoming a good thinker and writer, he realised, is controlling what comes in. 'I never had to think about that before,' he said in a 2018 interview. 'But it got to a level of where it's like, oh I can't absorb everything. I actually can't! There are some things I should not know. There are some things I should not see.' He reiterates in the interview that: 'if I don't exert control over what comes in, I will in no way be able to exert control over what comes out. That's like, the writing is so important to me, man.' I would swap the word 'writing' here with 'thinking', and apply it universally. The thinking is so important. If you don't exert control over what comes in, you will in no way be able to exert control over what comes out.

Having said that, I could never deny that social media – and Twitter in particular – has given power to those shut out of the conversation, and acts very often as a sort of vigilante that metes out rough but necessary justice. I could never deny that it is, at the moment, the only tool for myth busting and disinformation outside of mainstream media. It is good that when corporations fail to do their job and hire someone with terrible views that Twitter coalesces into a shifting shoal of small minnows with an awesome power as a body working in tandem, to unearth old tweets, blogs or interviews. It breaks, or tries to break, nepotistic networks. It can be an instant fact-check as well, where experts work tweet in tweet with laymen to nail a climate change statistic or an exaggerated claim about immigration. It is a vast bullshitometer, but it is also vastly imperfect, lending itself to mob frenzies. But all that is proof that there is so much pent-up frustration, so many voices excluded from the conversation, such an urgent need for veracity, so many new stories out there, that sometimes it turns into something of a sinister force, pulling people down just for the sake of it. If you choose to stay online, stay out of arguments. Make your point and move on. Use the platform to disseminate your ideas and challenge others, not in litigating minutiae with strangers.

Tell new stories

The good news (finally) is, that one of the reasons things are getting worse, is that they are getting better. There are simply more people in places which they had previously not been allowed, and this is a threat to those who have always had an advantage. There are more women, more people of colour, more LGBTQ+ people in public life, in the office, in academia and (nominally) in the media. Power is shifting, and with that shift comes discomfort and resistance from those who now have to listen to new ideas and humble themselves, when they have always had an advantage. That is why demographics alone are no guarantee of progress. Only the redistribution of power is.

The strength of myths is not in facts, but in the narrative. It is in the actual stories. The 'facts' myths use are just conduits, devices that transport and plant the myths, like the fronds of a flying dandelion seed. And so it is pointless to fight fake facts, or true but cynically twisted facts, with other facts. It is pointless (believe me, I have been failing at this for years) to fight xenophobia with statistics about how much tax immigrants pay, how little crime they commit or how they are a net good for the economy. But one should know these things, the real facts, in order to write the new stories.

New stories are not just the corrections of old stories, they are visions, certainty that we have a choice, to be open to the fact that for societies to evolve an old order must change. We cannot pick and choose the elements of progress that suit our own demographic or preferences because that eventually breaks down the whole machine. As American philosopher Alfred North Whitehead observed: 'The major advances of civilization are processes which all but wreck the societies in which they occur. Those societies which cannot combine reverence to their symbols with freedom of revision, must ultimately decay either from anarchy, or from the slow atrophy of a life stifled by useless shadows.' The only way to preserve the good, is to allow it to multiply in ever more unfamiliar iterations, rather than jealously guard it.

We need new stories, but we also need to write them ourselves. It will not be easy and it will not happen overnight. But one thing is certain as far as the keepers of the status quo are concerned: it is too late. They will be hearing from us.

NOTES

8   'Something of the momentum of a millennial movement': Adam Kuper, *Anthropolgy and Anthropologists: The Modern British School* (Routledge, Taylor and Francis Group, 1996), 161

9   'Revolutionary men with principles': Nawal El Saadawi, *Woman at Point Zero* (Zed Books Limited, 2015), 119

13   United Nations Annual Gender Inequality Index 2017: http://hdr.undp.org/en/composite/GII [accessed on 22 July 2019]

16   'The pursuit of happiness is a pointless goal': Tim Lott and Jordan Peterson, 'The pursuit of happiness is a pointless goal' (*Observer*, 21 January 2018), https://www.theguardian.com/global/2018/jan/21/jordan-peterson-self-help-author-12-steps-interview [accessed on 22 July 2019]

18   'What was decided among the Prehistoric Protozoa': Patrick Geddes and J. Arthur Thomson (W Scott, 1889, Reproduction), 267

19   'The anatomy of the corpus callosum': Jennifer Robertson (ed.), *Same-Sex Cultures and Sexualities: An Anthropological Reader* (Blackwell Publishing, 2005), 34

19   'The female brain is predominantly hard-wired for empathy': Simon Baron-Cohen, *The Essential Difference: The Truth About the Male and Female Brain* (Basic Books, 2003), 1

19   'Men and women really do think differently, say scientists': Mark Bridge, Tom Whipple, 'Men and women really do think differently, say scientists' (*The Times*, 13 November 2018), https://www.thetimes.co.uk/article/men-and-women-do-think-differently-say-scientists-sex-differences-bbfkhgs3h [accessed on 22 July 2019]

20   'Upon closer inspection of the data': Gina Rippon, 'No, that study doesn't prove that men and women think differently' (*New Statesman*, 20 November 2018), https://www.newstatesman.com/politics/feminism/2018/11/no-study-doesn-t-prove-that-men-and-women-think-differently [accessed on 22 July 2019]

21   'The problem with men': *Newsnight* (BBC Two, 1 November 2017)

22   'The rules are being redrawn': Douglas Murray, 'The consequence of this

new sexual counter-revolution? No sex at all' (*Spectator*, 4 November 2017), https://www.spectator.co.uk/2017/11/the-consequence-of-this-new-sexual-counter-revolution-no-sex-at-all/ [accessed on 22 July 2019]

22 'The journalist Peter Hitchens went down the creative route': Peter Hitchens, 'What will women gain from all this squawking about sex pests? A niqab' (*Mail on Sunday*, 5 November 2017), https://www.dailymail.co.uk/debate/article-5050887/What-women-gain-squawking-sex-pests-Niqab.html [accessed on 22 July 2019]

22 '. . . ironically resigned confusion': Giles Coren, 'A couple of xx's could end my glorious career' (*The Times*, 21 October 2017), https://www.thetimes.co.uk/article/a-couple-of-misplaced-kisses-could-end-my-career-plwzh6n3l [accessed on 22 July 2019]

22 '. . . wondered if women are just hardwired': Rod Liddle, 'It's not victim blaming to suggest there might be two sides to every story' (*Spectator*, 4 November 2017), https://www.spectator.co.uk/2017/11/its-not-victim-shaming-to-suggest-there-might-be-two-sides-to-every-story/ [accessed on 22 July 2019]

22 '. . . #MeToo a "sexual inquisition"': Brendan O'Neill, 'Who will put a brake on this Sexual Inquisition?' (*Spiked Online*, 6 November 2017), https://www.spiked-online.com/2017/11/06/who-will-put-a-brake-on-this-sexual-inquisition/ [accessed on 22 July 2019]

23 '. . . Westminster female reporters': Rachel Wearmouth, 'Ex-Guardian Columnist Calls Female Political Journalists "Predators" Who Trick "Poor Old Ugly" MPs' (*Huffington Post*, 2 November 2017), https://www.huffingtonpost.co.uk/entry/guardian-michael-white_uk_59fa015be4b00c6145e353fc [accessed on 22 July 2019].

23 '. . . nuance between rape and other forms of sexual assault': Bret Stephens, 'When #MeToo Goes Too Far' (*New York Times*, 20 December 2017), https://www.nytimes.com/2017/12/20/opinion/metoo-damon-too-far.html [accessed on 22 July 2019]

23 '. . . sexism in the UK is more "in your face"': 'UN Special Rapporteur Rashida Manjoo says UK has "sexist culture"' (BBC News, 15 April 2014), https://www.bbc.co.uk/news/uk-27034117 [accessed on 22 July 2019]

24 '. . . rapes in London rose by 20 per cent': Lizzie Dearden, 'London sees 20% rise in rape reports in a year, but police admit they "don't understand" reason' (*Independent*, 23 February 2018), https://www.independent.co.uk/news/uk/crime/rape-london-reports-met-police-rise-crime-sexual-assault-a8225821.html [accessed on 22 July 2019]

26 '. . . more women than men enrolled in universities': 'More women than men in Saudi universities, says ministry' (*Al Arabiya*, 28 May 2015), https://english.alarabiya.net/en/perspective/features/2015/05/28/More-women-than-men-in-Saudi-universities-says-ministry.html [accessed on 22 July 2019]

28 '. . . three women a day are killed': National Organization for Women, 'Violence Against Women in the United States: Statistics', https://now.org/resource/violence-against-women-in-the-united-states-statistic/ [accessed on 23 July 2019]

28 '. . . hovering around 38 per cent': World Health Organization, 'Violence Against Women' (29 November 2017), https://www.who.int/news-room/fact-sheets/detail/violence-against-women [accessed on 23 July 2019]

28 'In England and Wales': '900 women have been killed by men in England and Wales over the past 6 years' (*Telegraph*, 7 December 2016), https://www.telegraph.co.uk/women/life/900-women-have-killed-men-england-wales-past-6-years/ [accessed on 23 July 2019]

32 '. . . twenty-seven abortion bans have been enacted': Elizabeth Nash, 'Unprecedented Wave of Abortion Bans Is an Urgent Call to Action' (Guttmacher Institute, 22 May 2018), https://www.guttmacher.org/article/2019/05/unprecedented-wave-abortion-bans-urgent-call-action [accessed on 23 July 2019]

32 '. . . there has been a similar reversal in positive trends': World Economic Forum, *The Global Gender Gap Report, 2017*, http://www3.weforum.org/docs/WEF_GGGR_2017.pdf [accessed on 23 July 2019]

34 'In a 1995 PBS episode of *Think Tank*': 'Has Feminism Gone Too Far?' (*Think Tank* Transcripts, 1995) https://www.pbs.org/thinktank/transcript132.html [accessed on 23 July 2019]

36 '. . . only 7 per cent of cases resulted in a conviction': Kathleen Daly and Brigitte Bouhours, 'Rape and Attrition in the Legal Process: A Comparative Analysis of Five Countries' (University of Chicago, 2010) https://core.ac.uk/download/pdf/143870355.pdf [accessed on 23 July 2019]

39 'An internal company memo': James Damore, 'Google's Ideological Echo Chamber' (July 2017) https://www.documentcloud.org/documents/3914586-Googles-Ideological-Echo-Chamber.html [accessed on 23 July 2019]

40 '. . . advantage blindness': Ben Fuchs, Megan Reitz and John Higgins, 'Do You Have "Advantage Blindness"?' (*Harvard Business Review*, April 2014), https://hbr.org/2018/04/do-you-have-advantage-blindness [accessed on 23 July 2019]

40–1 '. . . research published in *Work and Occupations*': Carroll Seron, Susan Silbey, Erin Cech and Brian Rubineau, '"I Am Not a Feminist, but . . .": Hegemony of a Meritocratic Ideology and the Limits of Critique Among Women in Engineering' (*Work and Occupations*, 45(2), 1 March 2018), 131–67 https://doi.org/10.1177/0730888418759774 [accessed on 23 July 2019]

42 'Franks, the first woman to win the Pulitzer Prize for national reporting': Lucinda Franks, 'My Generation Thought Women Were Empowered. Did We Deceive Ourselves?' (*New York Times*, 9 December 2017), https://www.nytimes.com/2017/12/08/opinion/sunday/women-empowerment-sexism.html [accessed on 23 July 2019]

44 'A 2015 Birmingham University study': Dr Natalie Braber, 'Representation of Domestic Violence in two British Newspapers, *The Guardian* and *The Sun*, 2009–2011' (*ELR Journal*, 2014), 86–104 https://www.birmingham.ac.uk/Documents/college-artslaw/elal/elr-journal/issue-1/ELR-Braber.pdf [accessed on 23 July 2019]

45 '. . . the redistribution of sex': Ross Douthat, 'The Redistribution of Sex' (*New York Times*, 2 May 2018) https://www.nytimes.com/2018/05/02/opinion/ incels-sex-robots-redistribution.html [accessed on 23 July 2019]

46 'previously, pleasantly, progressive': Amy Butcher, 'MIA: The Liberal Men We Love' (Literary Hub, 27 February 2018), https://lithub.com/mia-the-liberal-men-we-love/ [accessed on 23 July 2019]

46 'Men view even small losses of deference': William J. Goode, 'Why Men Resist' (*Dissent Magazine*, Spring 1980), https://www.dissentmagazine.org/ article/why-men-resist [accessed on 23 July 2019]

49 '. . . fathers were as likely as mothers': Gretchen Livingston and Kim Parker, '8 Facts About American Dads' (Pew Research Center, 12 June 2019), https:// www.pewresearch.org/fact-tank/2019/06/12/fathers-day-facts/ [accessed on 23 July 2019]

50 '. . . wielding anti-feminism as a political cudgel': Ishan Tharoor, 'How Anti-feminism Is Shaping World Politics' (*Washington Post*, 30 January 2018), https://www.washingtonpost.com/news/worldviews/wp/2018/01/30/ how-anti-feminism-is-shaping-world-politics/?utm_term=.599465193223 [accessed on 23 July 2019]

52 '. . . it is wrong but natural to protect oneself': Kate Manne, 'Why the Majority of White Women Voted for Trump' (AlterNet, 7 November 2017), https:// www.alternet.org/2017/11/white-women-against-hillary-clinton-logic-misogyny-book/ [accessed on 23 July 2019]

53 '. . . *Harper's Magazine* also uncovered a fixation on complementarity': Seyward Darby, 'The Rise of the Valkyries' (*Harper's Magazine*, September 2017), https://harpers.org/archive/2017/09/the-rise-of-the-valkyries/ [accessed on 23 July 2019]

53 '. . . simply coughing up outrage into a blog will get us nowhere': Germaine Greer, 'The Failures of the New Feminism' (*New Statesman*, 14 May 2014), https://www.newstatesman.com/culture/2014/05/germaine-greer-failures-new-feminism [accessed on 23 July 2019]

54 '. . . partakes in a long moral tradition': Moira Donegan, 'How #MeToo revealed the central rift within feminism today' (*Guardian*, 11 May 2018), https://www.theguardian.com/news/2018/may/11/how-metoo-revealed-the-central-rift-within-feminism-social-individualist [accessed on 23 July 2019]

55 '. . . "smelling salts" and the "fainting couch"': Bari Weiss, 'Aziz Ansari Is Guilty. Of Not Being a Mind Reader' (*New York Times*, 15 January 2018), https://www.nytimes.com/2018/01/15/opinion/aziz-ansari-babe-sexual-harassment.html [accessed on 23 July 2019]

57 'The phrase "politically correct"': Ruth Perry, 'Historically Correct' (*The Women's Review of Books*, Vol. 5 (9), February 1992), 15

57 '. . . racist incidents at UK universities': Eleanor Busby, 'Racist incidents at UK universities have risen by more than 60 per cent in two years, figures show' (*Independent*, 11 June 2018), https://www.independent.co.uk/news/education/ education-news/racism-uk-university-students-campus-nus-incidents-a8390241. html [accessed on 23 July 2019]

58 'They get to create a narrative about me': 'Weekend Woman's Hour: Lola Olufemi, Anne Marie Duff, and David Steel on the 1967 Abortion Act' (BBC Radio 4, 28 October 2017) https://www.bbc.co.uk/programmes/b09bx9fq [accessed on 23 July 2019]

60 '. . . falling over themselves in their rush': Jonathan Yardley, 'Radical revolution on campus, review of *Tenured Radicals: How Politics Has Corrupted Our Higher Education* by Roger Kimball' (*Washington Post*, 6 June 1990), https://www.washingtonpost.com/archive/lifestyle/1990/06/06/radical-revolution-on-campus/66ec7e09-721f-4397-95f1-cdbcd1ffb6e8/?utm_term=.fbfd71691bbf [accessed on 23 July 2019]

62 '. . . political correctness has ignited controversy across the land': Kat Chow, '"Politically Correct": The Phrase Has Gone From Wisdom To Weapon' (*Code Switch*, NPR, December 14 2016), https://www.npr.org/sections/codeswitch/2016/12/14/505324427/politically-correct-the-phrase-has-gone-from-wisdom-to-weapon?t=1562162061694 [accessed on 23 July 2019]

64 '. . . evidence suggests that Trump's grandiose rhetorical style': Lucian Gideon Conway III, Meredith A. Repkea, Shannon C. Houck, 'Donald Trump as a Cultural Revolt Against Perceived Communication Restriction: Priming Political Correctness Norms Causes More Trump Support' (*Journal of Social and Political Psychology*, Vol. 5 (1), 2017), 246

64 '. . . norms of restrictive communication': *ibid.*

65 'Having elevated the powers of PC to mythic status': Moira Weigel, 'Political correctness: how the right invented a phantom enemy' (*Guardian*, 30 November 2016), https://www.theguardian.com/us-news/2016/nov/30/political-correctness-how-the-right-invented-phantom-enemy-donald-trump [accessed on 23 July 2019]

70 'After Brexit, we can give Isil [ISIS] terrorists the justice they deserve': Colonel Richard Kemp, 'After Brexit, we can give Isil terrorists the justice they deserve – and that means the death penalty' (*Telegraph*, 23 July 2018), https://www.telegraph.co.uk/politics/2018/07/23/laws-inadequate-prosecuting-isil-beatles-brexit-can-change/ [accessed on 23 July 2019]

70 '. . . a crushing 60 to 26 margin': Tom Clark, 'Free speech? New polling suggests Britain is "less PC" than Trump's America' (*Prospect Magazine*, 16 February 2018), https://www.prospectmagazine.co.uk/magazine/free-speech-new-polling-suggests-britain-is-less-pc-than-trumps-america [accessed on 23 July 2019]

71 '. . . anti-intellectualism is strongly associated': Matthew Motta, 'The Dynamics and Political Implications of Anti-Intellectualism in the United States' (*American Politics Research*, 2018, 46(3)), 467

73 '. . . longtime libertarians': Jane Mayer, 'Covert Operations: The billionaire brothers who are waging a war against Obama' (*New Yorker*, 30 August 2010), https://www.newyorker.com/magazine/2010/08/30/covert-operations [accessed on 23 July 2019]

74 '. . . two wrongs don't make a right': Harvey C. Mansfield Jr, 'Political Correctness and the Suicide of the Intellect' (The Heritage Foundation, 26 June

1991), 1

74 'We mustn't let things get by that we know are wrong': *ibid.*, 7

75 '. . . no sooner was it invoked as a genuine standard for sociopolitical practice': Ruth Perry, 'Historically Correct' (*The Women's Review of Books*, February 1992), 16

77 'X is for *X-Factor*': Leo McKinstry, 'A to Z of politically correct madness: The Left's "Thought Police" continues to censor language as "manfully" is labelled sexist' (*Daily Mail*, 18 November 2017), https://www.dailymail. co.uk/news/article-5094791/A-Z-politically-correct-madness.html [accessed on 25 July 2019]

78 'N IS FOR . . . NIGGER': James Delingpole, 'The A–Z of political correctness' (*Telegraph*, 15 May 2011), https://www.telegraph.co.uk/comment/ personal-view/8513876/The-A-Z-of-political-correctness.html [accessed on 25 July 2019]

78 'The bus driver won £30,000': Leigh Holmwood and agencies, 'Sun pays £30,000 damages to Muslim bus driver accused of fanaticism' (*Guardian*, 26 February 2009), https://www.theguardian.com/media/2009/feb/26/sun-pays-damages-to-muslim-bus-driver [accessed on 25 July 2019]

78 'She won £11,000 in compensation': Jessica Elgot, 'Daily Mail to pay Kate Maltby £11,000 costs over negative article' (*Guardian*, 23 May 2018), https://www.theguardian.com/media/2018/may/23/daily-mail-to-pay-kate-maltby-11000-over-negative-article [accessed on 25 July 2019]

79 'The Independent Press Standards Organisation (IPSO) ruled': Charlotte Tobitt, 'Daily Mail runs front page IPSO ruling on inaccuracies in Iraq compensation claim report as staff told making similar errors again would "put careers at risk"' (*Press Gazette*, 27 July 2018), https://www.pressgazette. co.uk/daily-mail-runs-front-page-ipso-adjudication-on-iraq-compensation-claims-as-staff-told-making-similar-error-again-would-put-careers-at-risk/ [accessed on 25 July 2019]

80 'it makes no sense ever giving up your own taste': Chris Stirewalt, 'Roseanne Barr and the new political correctness' (Fox News Halftime Report, 29 May 2018), https://www.foxnews.com/politics/roseanne-barr-and-the-new-political-correctness [accessed on 25 July 2019]

81 'the *Daily Mail* is the UK's most complained about newspaper': Dominic Ponsford, 'Daily Mail is officially UK's most complained about newspaper – but regionals most likely to be censured by PCC' (*Press Gazette*, 3 February 2014), https://www.pressgazette.co.uk/daily-mail-officially-uks-most-complained-about-newspaper-regionals-are-mostly-likely-be-censured/ [accessed on 25 July 2019]

83 '. . . political correctness shoots itself in the foot': Tom Clark, 'Free speech? New polling suggests Britain is "less PC" than Trump's America' (*Prospect*, February 16 2018), https://www.prospectmagazine.co.uk/magazine/ free-speech-new-polling-suggests-britain-is-less-pc-than-trumps-america [accessed on 25 July 2019]

84 'I believe that everybody has a right to be in the United States': Adam Serwer,

'The Nationalist's Delusion' (*Atlantic*, 20 November 2017), https://www.theatlantic.com/politics/archive/2017/11/the-nationalists-delusion/546356/ [accessed on 25 July 2019]

86 '. . . the controversy over *The Bell Curve*': Ezra Klein, 'Sam Harris, Charles Murray, and the allure of race science' (Vox, 27 March 2018), https://www.vox.com/policy-and-politics/2018/3/27/15695060/sam-harris-charles-murray-race-iq-forbidden-knowledge-podcast-bell-curve [accessed on 25 July 2019]

86 '. . . this isn't "forbidden knowledge."': *ibid.*

87 '. . . feted in the *New York Times*': Bari Weiss, 'Meet the Renegades of the Intellectual Dark Web' (*New York Times*, 8 May 2018), https://www.nytimes.com/2018/05/08/opinion/intellectual-dark-web.html [accessed on 25 July 2019]

89 'lit the flame': Patrick Wintour, 'Hillary Clinton: Europe must curb immigration to stop rightwing populists' (*Guardian*, 22 November 2018), https://www.theguardian.com/world/2018/nov/22/hillary-clinton-europe-must-curb-immigration-stop-populists-trump-brexit [accessed on 25 July 2019]

89 'populist correctness': Arwa Mahdawi, 'Populist correctness: the new PC culture of Trump's America and Brexit Britain' (*Guardian*, 19 February 2017), https://www.theguardian.com/commentisfree/2017/feb/19/populist-correctness-new-pc-culture-trump-america-brexit-britain [accessed on 25 July 2019]

89 'Offends': Kemp for Governor, campaign ad, https://www.youtube.com/watch?v=-3irfSQZZyw [accessed on 25 July 2019]

90 '. . . caught on tape complaining': David Gilbert, 'Trump Secures Georgia Win for Brian Kemp, Who Wants to "round up" illegals in his pickup truck' (Vice News, 25 July 2018), https://news.vice.com/en_us/article/a3qkv8/trump-georgia-brian-kemp-governor [accessed on 25 July 2019]

90 'If Kemp wins his runoff': Ed Kilgore, '"Political Incorrectness" Is Just "Political Correctness" for Conservatives' (Intelligencer, 17 July 2018), http://nymag.com/intelligencer/2018/07/anti-pc-is-political-correctness-for-the-right.html [accessed on 25 July 2019]

91 'coded cover': Polly Toynbee, 'This bold equality push is just what we needed. In 1997' (*Guardian*, 28 April 2009), https://www.theguardian.com/commentisfree/2009/apr/28/toynbee-equality-bill-welfare [accessed on 25 July 2019]

92 'a matter of replacing one set of authorities and dogmas': Edward W. Said, *Reflections on Exile and Other Essays* (Harvard University Press, 2001), 381

95 'The claim that free speech is under attack': William Davies, 'The free speech panic: how the right concocted a crisis' (*Guardian*, 26 July 2018), https://www.theguardian.com/news/2018/jul/26/the-free-speech-panic-censorship-how-the-right-concocted-a-crisis [accessed on 25 July 2019]

97 '. . . a "wide cross section" of Americans': Maeve Duggan, 'Online Harassment 2017' (Pew Research Center, 11 July 2017), https://www.pewinternet.org/2017/07/11/online-harassment-2017/ [accessed on 25 July 2019]

97 'The picture is not much different in the UK': 'Black and Asian women MPs

abused more online' (Amnesty International UK, 2017), https://www.amnesty.org.uk/online-violence-women-mps

98	'I participated in a *Guardian* survey': Becky Gardiner, Mahana Mansfield, Ian Anderson, Josh Holder, Daan Louter and Monica Ulmanu, 'The dark side of Guardian comments' (*Guardian*, 12 April 2016), https://www.theguardian.com/technology/2016/apr/12/the-dark-side-of-guardian-comments [accessed on 25 July 2019]

101	'Appearing on BBC's *Newsnight*': 'What do far-right extremism and Islamist extremism have in common?' (BBC *Newsnight*, 19 June 2017), https://www.youtube.com/watch?v=XGNEZr11LFE [accessed on 25 July 2019]

103	'Right-wing media blogs as well as mainstream publications': Claire Fox, 'The dangers of illiberal liberalism' (*Economist*, 17 August 2018), https://www.economist.com/open-future/2018/08/17/the-dangers-of-illiberal-liberalism [accessed on 25 July 2019]

104	'. . . led to a spike in racist incidents': Tell MAMA, '"Letterbox" insults against Muslim women spike in wake of Boris Johnson comments' (Tell MAMA, 23 August 2018), https://tellmamauk.org/press/letterbox-insults-against-muslim-women-spike-in-wake-of-boris-johnson-comments/ [accessed on 25 July 2019]

104	'Deplorable to see': Isabel Oakeshott (Twitter, 3:29 p.m., 10 August 10 2018), https://twitter.com/IsabelOakeshott/status/1027924888848396288?s=20 [accessed on 25 July 2019]

105	'the privileging of freedom of speech over freedom to life': Liz Fekete, Director, Institute of Race Relations (Brief Letters, *Guardian*, 25 March 2018), https://www.theguardian.com/world/2018/mar/25/freedom-of-speech-or-freedom-to-life [accessed on 25 July 2019]

106	'has never accepted an absolutist interpretation of freedom of speech': Christopher Wolfe, 'The Limits of Free Speech (Book Review)' (*Review of Politics*, Notre Dame, Ind. Vol. 48, Iss. 1, Winter 1986), 139, https://search.proquest.com/openview/9d9d438f2304ff12be298b07179f651e/1?pq-origsite=gscholar&cbl=1820944 [accessed on 25 July 2019]

108	'The suppression of noxious ideas does not defeat them': Danuta Kean, 'Free-speech groups defend publication of Milo Yiannopoulos memoir' (*Guardian*, 6 January 2017), https://www.theguardian.com/books/2017/jan/06/free-speech-groups-defend-publication-of-milo-yiannoploulos-memoir [accessed on 25 July 2019]

110	'When his comments about pedophilia/pederasty came to light': Roxane Gay, 'All I really need to say' (tumblr, February 20 2017), https://roxanegay.tumblr.com/post/157506508260/all-i-really-need-to-say [accessed on 25 July 2019]

114	'. . . the joint most invited guest': Nick Reilly, 'Nigel Farage is about to set the record for the most Question Time appearances this century' (Yahoo! News, 21 February 2018), https://uk.news.yahoo.com/nigel-farage-set-record-question-time-appearances-century-155615416.html?guccounter=1&guce_referrer=aHR0cHM6Ly93d3cuZ29vZ2xlLm-

NvbS8&guce_referrer_sig=AQAAAD7POnjWq-aPJ8FxLdeplMTPn2t-KzwIxqeEqeVywFBMl6GwkQEQc67pQNvFPNVdRH1pqFxJxv2l2Agl-C7g-Tw5wuk0cYkF1EuOuT8l8ilx_vbSuX78A3Kufu3hatRCURvz0qZdv-75ViU-VripSv2bdvg5Oyc5t9g7vAcI7bbEnda [accessed on 25 July 2019]

116 'Don't you fucking say you're calling me out': Sarah Marsh, 'Steve Bannon calls for Tommy Robinson to be released from prison' (*Guardian*, 15 July 2018), https://www.theguardian.com/us-news/2018/jul/15/steve-bannon-tommy-robinson-released-from-prison-trump-strategist-lbc-radio-interview [accessed on 25 July 2019]

116 'This is exactly the argument they like': Mark Townsend, '#FreeTommy – the making of a far-right English "martyr"' (*Guardian*, 29 July 2018), https://www.theguardian.com/uk-news/2018/jul/29/tommy-robinson-far-right-resurgence-steve-bannon-us-support [accessed on 25 July 2019]

118 'free speech grifters': Mari Uyehara, 'The Free Speech Grifters' (*GQ*, 19 March 2018), https://www.gq.com/story/free-speech-grifting [accessed on 25 July 2019]

118 'Given the myopic focus on liberals': *ibid.*

119 'Free Speech University Ranking': Tom Slater, 'Free Speech University Rankings' (*Spiked Online*, 24 February 2019), https://www.spiked-online.com/free-speech-university-rankings/ [accessed on 25 July 2019]

119 'misleading, ill-informed and worryingly influential': Carl Thompson, 'Free Speech Rankings: misleading, ill-informed and worryingly influential' (*Times Higher Education*, 17 February 2018) https://www.timeshighereducation.com/blog/free-speech-rankings-misleading-ill-informed-and-worryingly-influential [accessed on 25 July 2019]

119 'You'd have to have been living under a rock': Tom Slater, 'The poshos pushing campus censorship' (*Telegraph*, 19 January 2016), https://www.telegraph.co.uk/education/universityeducation/12108340/The-poshos-pushing-campus-censorship.html [accessed on 25 July 2019]

120 '*Spiked* received six figure donations from the Charles Koch Foundation': George Monbiot, 'How US billionaires are fuelling the hard-right cause in Britain' (*Guardian*, 7 December 2018), https://www.theguardian.com/commentisfree/2018/dec/07/us-billionaires-hard-right-britain-spiked-magazine-charles-david-koch-foundation [accessed on 25 July 2019]

120 '. . . overall public support for free speech has in fact, risen over time': Matthew Yglesias, 'Everything we think about the political correctness debate is wrong' (Vox, 12 March 2018), https://www.vox.com/policy-and-politics/2018/3/12/17100496/political-correctness-data [accessed on 25 July 2019]

121 'There is no campus free speech crisis': Jeffrey Adam Sachs, 'There is no campus free speech crisis: a close look at the evidence' (Niskanen Center, 27 April 2018), https://niskanencenter.org/blog/there-is-no-campus-free-speech-crisis-a-close-look-at-the-evidence/ [accessed on 25 July 2019]

123 '. . . suicide by boycott tactic': Stephanie Saul, 'The Conservative Force Behind Speeches Roiling College Campuses' (*New York Times*, 20 May 2017),

https://www.nytimes.com/2017/05/20/us/college-conservative-speeches.html [accessed on 25 July 2019]

123 '. . . a perceived "chilling" of free speech on university campuses': Rachel Pells, 'Anti-terror laws "to blame for campus free speech concerns"' (*Times Higher Education*, 11 January 2018), https://www.timeshighereducation.com/news/anti-terror-laws-blame-campus-free-speech-concerns [accessed on 25 July 2019]

124 '. . . echoed Amos': Benjamin Kentish, 'Universities hit back at Government claims they are restricting free speech' (*Independent*, 10 January 2018), https://www.independent.co.uk/news/uk/politics/university-free-speech-restrictions-hit-back-government-a8152376.html [accessed on 25 July 2019]

124 'speaker disinvitation attempts have a higher success rate': Sean Stevens, Campus Speaker Disinvitation Trends (Part 2 of 2) (Heterodox Academy, 7 February 2017), https://heterodoxacademy.org/campus-speaker-disinvitations-recent-trends-part-2-of-2/ [accessed on 25 July 2019]

126 'Today this speech restriction, tomorrow the Inquisition': Magdalena Jozwiak, 'Internet, Freedom of Speech and Slippery Slope Argument – The Case of the "Right to Be Forgotten"', (SSRN, 22 March 2018), https://papers.ssrn.com/sol3/papers.cfm?abstract_id=3141370#references-widget [accessed on 25 July 2019]

126 'slippery slope arguments are slippery themselves': *ibid.*

128 'Who next?': Kenan Malik, 'Even those with the vilest of views have the right to be heard' (*Observer*, 18 March 2018), https://www.theguardian.com/commentisfree/2018/mar/18/far-right-activists-barred-britain-state-speech [accessed on 25 July 2019]

129 '. . . protest only overseen by official administrators of dissent': Aaron Bastani, 'Peaceful protest will not be tolerated' (*Guardian*, 10 September 2013), https://www.theguardian.com/commentisfree/2013/sep/10/peaceful-protest-anti-fascist-protesters-edl [accessed on 25 July 2019]

132 'If free speech does take precedence': Andrew Marantz, 'How Social-Media Trolls Turned U.C. Berkeley into a Free-Speech Circus' (*New Yorker*, 25 June 2018), https://www.newyorker.com/magazine/2018/07/02/how-social-media-trolls-turned-uc-berkeley-into-a-free-speech-circus [accessed on 25 July 2019]

134 'What makes identity politics a significant departure': Sonia Kruks, *Retrieving Experience: Subjectivity and Recognition in Feminist Politics* (Cornell University Press, 2001), 85

136 'I know for many people that this is a tough decision': Jo Cox, 'Better to improve than leave' (*Batley News* and *Spenborough Guardian*, 26 May 2016), http://www.jocox.org.uk/2016/05/26/newspaper-column-better-to-improve-than-leave/ [accessed on 25 July 2019]

137 '. . . advised Westminster party leaders': David Isaac and Rebecca Hilsenrath, 'A letter to all political parties in Westminster' (Equality and Human Rights Commission, 25 November 2016), https://www.equalityhumanrights.com/en/our-work/news/letter-all-political-parties-westminster [accessed on 25

July 2019]

137 '. . . accused the Commission of instrumentalising': Dominic Lawson, 'The horrific murder of Jo Cox and a contemptible campaign to smear Brexit supporters' (*Daily Mail*, 28 November, 2016), https://www.dailymail.co.uk/debate/article-3977178/DOMINIC-LAWSON-horrific-murder-Jo-Cox-contemptible-campaign-smear-Brexit-supporters.html [accessed on 25 July 2019]

142 'We know that this is false': Asad Haider, 'Mistaken Identity: Race and Class in the Age of Trump' (talk at Elliott Bay Book Company, 3 May 2018), https://www.youtube.com/watch?v=6vaZGh5CIPY [accessed on 25 July 2019]

143 'politics of recognition': Amy Chua, 'How America's identity politics went from inclusion to division' (*Guardian*, 1 March 2018), https://www.theguardian.com/society/2018/mar/01/how-americas-identity-politics-went-from-inclusion-to-division [accessed on 25 July 2019]

143 'To put it bluntly – most of us prefer our own kind': David Goodhart, 'Too Diverse? (*Prospect*, 20 February 2004), https://www.prospectmagazine.co.uk/magazine/too-diverse-david-goodhart-multiculturalism-britain-immigration-globalisation [accessed on 25 July 2019]

143 'The fundamental belief that drove my dad': 'How A Rising Star Of White Nationalism Broke Free From The Movement' (*Fresh Air*, NPR, 24 September 2018), https://www.npr.org/2018/09/24/651052970/how-a-rising-star-of-white-nationalism-broke-free-from-the-movement [accessed on 25 July 2019]

144 'Lilla manages to blame the Trump "whitelash" on liberals': Mark Lilla, 'The End of Identity Liberalism' (*New York Times*, 18 November 2016), https://www.nytimes.com/2016/11/20/opinion/sunday/the-end-of-identity-liberalism.html [accessed on 25 July 2019]

146 'I kind of feel that people are looking down on us': Declan Wash, 'Alienated and Angry, Coal Miners See Donald Trump as Their Only Choice' (*New York Times*, 19 August 2016), https://www.nytimes.com/2016/08/20/world/americas/alienated-and-angry-coal-miners-see-donald-trump-as-their-only-choice.html [accessed on 25 July 2019]

146 'It was lapped up': Nicholas Carnes and Noam Lupu, 'It's time to bust the myth: Most Trump voters were not working class' (*Washington Post*, 5 June 2017), https://www.washingtonpost.com/news/monkey-cage/wp/2017/06/05/its-time-to-bust-the-myth-most-trump-voters-were-not-working-class/?utm_term=.5f63c23a8593 [accessed on 25 July 2019]

146 'Contrary to what some have suggested': Matthew Fowler, Vladimir E. Medenica and Cathy J. Cohen, 'Why 41 percent of white millennials voted for Trump' (*Washington Post*, 15 December 2017), https://www.washingtonpost.com/news/monkey-cage/wp/2017/12/15/racial-resentment-is-why-41-percent-of-white-millennials-voted-for-trump-in-2016/?utm_term=.9e49ac22dd79 [accessed on 25 July 2019]

147 '. . . perceptions of the American economy were influenced': Michael Tesler,

Post-Racial or Most Racial? Race and Politics in the Obama Era (The University of Chicago Press Books, 2016)

148 'The evidence is pretty clear': Michael Tesler, 'Economic anxiety isn't driving racial resentment. Racial resentment is driving economic anxiety' (*Washington Post*, 22 August 2016), https://www.washingtonpost.com/news/monkey-cage/wp/2016/08/22/economic-anxiety-isnt-driving-racial-resentment-racial-resentment-is-driving-economic-anxiety/?utm_term=.1abd02035e0e [accessed on 25 July 2019]

149 'it used to be a pretty good deal': Niraj Chokshi, 'Trump Voters Driven by Fear of Losing Status, Not Economic Anxiety, Study Finds' (*New York Times*, 24 April 2018), https://www.nytimes.com/2018/04/24/us/politics/trump-economic-anxiety.html [accessed on 25 July 2019]

151 'red and yellows': Ben Kamisar, 'Moore laments racial division between "reds and yellows"' (*The Hill*, 18 September 2017), https://thehill.com/homenews/campaign/351194-roy-moore-refers-to-red-and-yellow-americans-in-campaign-speech [accessed on 25 July 2019]

152 'Allegations of racism were a "smear", he responded to his supporters': David Maraniss, 'Duke emerges from loss stronger than ever' (*Washington Post*, 8 October 1990)

152 'Let them call you racists': Eli Watkins and James Gray, 'Bannon: "Let them call you racists"' (CNN Politics, 11 March 2018), https://edition.cnn.com/2018/03/10/politics/steve-bannon-national-front/index.html [accessed on 25 July 2019]

153 'There was no alternative': Simon Cox and Anna Meisel, 'Martin Sellner: The new face of the far right in Europe' (BBC News, 20 September 2018), https://www.bbc.co.uk/news/stories-45572411 [accessed on 25 July 2019]

156 'The Democrats – the longer they talk about identity politics, I got 'em': Robert Kuttner, 'How Democrats Can Make Race a Winning Issue' (*American Prospect*, 4 September 2018), https://prospect.org/article/how-democrats-can-make-race-winning-issue [accessed on 25 July 2019]

157 'pale, male, stales': Simon Jenkins, 'Pale, stale males are the last group it's OK to vilify' (*Guardian*, 15 December 2016), https://www.theguardian.com/commentisfree/2016/dec/15/pale-stale-males-blamed-brexit-trump [accessed on 25 July 2019]

157 'like what it must have been like to be a black person 20 or 30 years ago': Karl McDonald, 'Sir Simon Jenkins: I feel like a black person must have 30 years ago' (*Independent*, 16 December 2016), https://inews.co.uk/inews-lifestyle/people/sir-simon-jenkins-i-feel-like-black-person-must-30-years-ago/ [accessed on 25 July 2019]

158 'which have whipped up racial antagonism': Lionel Shriver, 'Identity politics are – by definition – racist' (*Spectator*, 18 August 2018), https://www.spectator.co.uk/2018/08/identity-politics-are-by-definition-racist/ [accessed on 25 July 2019]

159 'The Calamity Thesis': Adam Serwer, 'The Nationalist's Delusion' (*Atlantic*, 20 November 2017), https://www.theatlantic.com/politics/archive/2017/11/

the-nationalists-delusion/546356/ [accessed on 25 July 2019]

160 'the possessive investment in whiteness': George Lipsitz, *The Possessive Investment in Whiteness: How White People Profit from Identity Politics, Revised and Expanded Edition* (Temple University Press, 2006), vii

161 'The cult of ethnicity and its zealots': C. Vann Woodward, 'Equal but Separate' (*The New Republic*, 15–22 July 1991), 42–3

163 'that they felt pressured into delivering a "certain kind of book"'; Sarah Shaffi, 'Diversity report finds mono-culture prevails in publishing' (*The Bookseller*, 14 April 2015), https://www.thebookseller.com/news/diversity-report-finds-mono-culture-prevails-publishing [accessed on 25 July 2019]

164 'actively committed to struggling': Combahee River Collective, 'A Black Feminist Statement' (Combahee River Collective, 1977), 210

164 'We realize that the only people who care enough': *ibid.*, 212

164 'If Black women were free': *ibid.*, 215

165 'in the eyes of the identity politics critics': Jonathan Dean, 'Who's afraid of identity politics?' (LSE blog, 9 December 2016), https://blogs.lse.ac.uk/politicsandpolicy/whos-afraid-of-identity-politics/) [accessed on 26 July 2019)

167 'In the atmosphere of wilful indifference': Janet Reitman, 'U.S. Law Enforcement Failed to See the Threat of White Nationalism. Now They Don't Know How to Stop It' (*New York Times*, 3 November 2018), https://www.nytimes.com/2018/11/03/magazine/FBI-charlottesville-white-nationalism-far-right.html [accessed on 25 July 2019]

168 'There is simply no electoral benefit': Sean McElwee, 'If liberals don't embrace identity politics, they will lose' (The Outline, 17 January 2018), https://theoutline.com/post/2953/if-liberals-dont-embrace-identity-politics-they-will-lose?zd=1&zi=6ioipdib [accessed on 25 July 2019]

171 'Americans' sketchy understanding': Nancy Isenberg, *White Trash: The 400-Year Untold History of Class in America* (Atlantic Books, 2017), 13

172 'in order to save the 40 million': Pankaj Mishra, 'How colonial violence came home: the ugly truth of the first world war' (*Guardian*, 10 November 2017), https://www.theguardian.com/news/2017/nov/10/how-colonial-violence-came-home-the-ugly-truth-of-the-first-world-war [accessed on 25 July 2019]

174 'They were not there on holiday': Simon Akam, 'Left Behind' (*The New Republic*, 21 May 2011), https://newrepublic.com/article/88797/british-empire-queen-elizabeth-india-ireland-africa-imperial [accessed on 25 July 2019]

176 'But the research also found': Sally Weale, 'Michael Gove's claims about history teaching are false, says research' (*Guardian*, 13 September 2016), https://www.theguardian.com/world/2016/sep/13/michael-goves-claims-about-history-teaching-are-false-says-research [accessed on 25 July 2019]

177 'an inherent bias in the curriculum that runs the other way': The Secret Teacher, 'Secret Teacher: the emphasis on British history is depriving students of balance' (*Guardian*, 26 May 2018), https://www.theguardian.com/teacher-network/2018/may/26/secret-teacher-history-bias-school-fear-student-future [accessed on 25 July 2019]

179 'Anyone who suggests that the United Kingdom cannot be trusted': Department for Exiting the European Union and The Rt Hon David Davis MP, 'David Davis' speech on the future security partnership' (GOV.UK, 6 June 2018), https://www.gov.uk/government/news/david-davis-speech-on-the-future-security-partnership [accessed on 25 July 2019]

179 'The first Eurosceptic': Jonathan Isaby, 'Jacob Rees-Mogg identifies the three historical heroes from his constituency who will be his political inspiration' (Conservative Home, 8 June 2010), https://www.conservativehome.com/thetorydiary/2010/06/jacob-reesmogg-identifies-the-three-historical-heroes-from-his-constituency-who-will-be-his-politica.html [accessed on 25 July 2019]

179 'we survived our break from Europe': Giles Fraser, 'The English Reformation was the first Brexit – we survived our break from Europe then, and we'll do so again' (*Telegraph*, 18 August 2018), https://www.telegraph.co.uk/news/2018/08/14/english-reformation-first-brexit-survived-break-europe-do/

179 'showed the world what a free people could achieve': Michael Gove, 'EU referendum: Michael Gove explains why Britain should leave the EU' (*Telegraph*, 20 February 2016), https://www.telegraph.co.uk/news/newstopics/eureferendum/12166345/European-referendum-Michael-Gove-explains-why-Britain-should-leave-the-EU.html [accessed on 25 July 2019]

180 'it will be like Dunkirk again': Andrew MacAskill, Anjuli Davies, '"Insecurity is fantastic," says billionaire funder of Brexit campaign' (Reuters, 11 May 2016), https://uk.reuters.com/article/uk-britain-eu-donations-hargreaves/insecurity-is-fantastic-says-billionaire-funder-of-brexit-campaign-idUKKCN0Y22ID [accessed on 25 July 2019]

180 'Thirty-five years ago this week': Owen Bennett, '"We Will Go To War With Spain Over Gibraltar"' Warns Ex-Tory Leader Lord Howard (*Huffington Post*, 2 April 2017), https://www.huffingtonpost.co.uk/entry/gibraltar-war-falklands-lord-howard_uk_58e0ed0ee4b0c777f788130f [accessed on 25 July 2019]

180 'unbelievable that within a week': George Parker, Jim Brunsden, Ian Mount, 'Gibraltar tensions bubble over into British war talk' (*Financial Times*, 2 April 2017), https://www.ft.com/content/391f0114-17a1-11e7-a53d-df09f373be87 [accessed on 25 July 2019]

180 'a colossal military disaster': 'Great Speeches of the 19th Century: Winston Churchill, "We shall fight on the beaches" (*Guardian*, 20 April 2007), https://www.theguardian.com/theguardian/2007/apr/20/greatspeeches1 [accessed on 25 July 2019]

180 'miracle of deliverance': *ibid.*

182 'you must take the decision which is fraught with risk': Harry Yorke, 'Boris Johnson likens Brexit dilemma to Churchill's defiance of Hitler' (*Telegraph*, 6 December 2018), https://www.telegraph.co.uk/politics/2018/12/06/boris-johnson-likens-brexit-dilemma-churchills-defiance-hitler/ [accessed on 25 July 2019]

183 'make me an offer': Lucy Pasha-Robinson, 'Angela Merkel "ridicules Theresa

May's Brexit demands during secret press briefing"' (*Independent*, 29 January 2018), https://www.independent.co.uk/news/world/europe/angela-merkel-theresa-may-brexit-demands-press-briefing-davos-eu-talks-a8183436.html [accessed on 25 July 2019]

183 'France and England will never be powers comparable to the United States': 'An affair to remember' (*Economist*, 27 July 2006), https://www.economist.com/node/7218678 [accessed on 25 July 2019]

184 'betrayed our relationship': Boris Johnson, 'The Aussies are just like us, so let's stop kicking them out' (*Telegraph*, 25 August 2013), https://www.telegraph.co.uk/news/politics/10265619/The-Aussies-are-just-like-us-so-lets-stop-kicking-them-out.html [accessed on 25 July 2019]

185 'While the empire': David Olusoga, 'Empire 2.0 is dangerous nostalgia for something that never existed' (*Guardian*, 19 March 2017), https://www.theguardian.com/commentisfree/2017/mar/19/empire-20-is-dangerous-nostalgia-for-something-that-never-existed [accessed on 25 July 2019]

185 'The twentieth century saw the UK eclipsed': Simon Akam, 'Left Behind' (*The New Republic*, 21 May 2011), https://newrepublic.com/article/88797/british-empire-queen-elizabeth-india-ireland-africa-imperial [accessed on 25 July 2019]

187 'an exercise in British wish-fulfilment': Nikita Lalwani, 'The Best Exotic Marigold Hotel: an exercise in British wish-fulfilment' (*Guardian*, 27 February 2012), https://www.theguardian.com/commentisfree/2012/feb/27/best-exotic-marigold-hotel-compliance [accessed on 25 July 2019]

188 'a wave of colonial nostalgia': Stuart Jeffries, 'The best exotic nostalgia boom: why colonial style is back' (*Guardian*, 19 March 2015), https://www.theguardian.com/culture/2015/mar/19/the-best-exotic-nostalgia-boom-why-colonial-style-is-back [accessed on 25 July 2019]

189 'reduce the country to the status of "colony"': Guy Faulconbridge, 'Boris Johnson says Brexit deal will make Britain an EU colony' (Reuters, 13 November 2018), https://www.reuters.com/article/us-britain-eu-johnson/boris-johnson-says-brexit-deal-will-make-britain-an-eu-colony-idUSKCN1NI16D [accessed on 25 July 2019]

189 'not a vassal state but a slave state': Nick Clegg, 'On Brexit, Jacob Rees-Mogg is right: Britain risks vassal status' (*Financial Times*, 27 January 2018), https://www.ft.com/content/be44ff5a-028e-11e8-9e12-af73e8db3c71 [accessed on 25 July 2019]

191 'the rags to riches dream of a millionaire's blank check': Thomas A. Bailey, *Essays Diplomatic and Undiplomatic of Thomas A. Bailey* (Appleton-Century-Crofts, 1969), 2

192 'actually a disguised chemical weapons factory': Nathan J. Robinson, 'Bill Clinton's Act of Terrorism' (*Jacobin*, October 2016), https://www.jacobinmag.com/2016/10/bill-clinton-al-shifa-sudan-bombing-khartoum/ [accessed on 23 July 2019]

194 'We are writing you because' : Muhammad Sahimi, 'The Push for War with Iran' (PBS *Frontline*, 27 October 2011), https://www.pbs.org/wgbh/pages/

frontline/tehranbureau/2011/10/analysis-the-push-for-war-with-iran.html [accessed on 23 July 2019]

194 'process of transformation': Donald Kagan, Gary Schmitt, Thomas Donnelly, 'Rebuilding America's Defenses, Strategy, Forces and Resources for a New Century' (A Report of The Project for the New American Century, September 2000), 51

195 'Like their confrères in 1991': Tom Engelhardt, 'In the heart of a dying empire (*Salon*, 30 September 2018), https://www.salon.com/2018/09/30/in-the-heart-of-a-dying-empire_partner/ [accessed on 25 July 2019]

196 'widely held to provide the standard interpretation': Francis T. Butts, 'The Myth of Perry Miller' (*The American Historical Review*, Vol. 87, No. 3, June 1982), 665

196 'I wanted a coherence with which I could coherently begin': Michael Zuckerman, 'Myth and Method: The Current Crises in American Historical Writing' (*The History Teacher*, Vol. 17, No. 2, February 1984), 224

196 'made whole colonies disappear': *ibid.*

196 'Civil War literacy among US high school students': 'SPLC report: U.S. education on American slavery sorely lacking' (Southern Poverty Law Center, 31 January 2018), https://www.splcenter.org/news/2018/01/31/splc-report-us-education-american-slavery-sorely-lacking [accessed on 25 July 2019]

200 'the British should have "pride' in their past'": Nigel Biggar, 'Don't feel guilty about our colonial history' (*The Times*, 30 November 2017), https://www.thetimes.co.uk/article/don-t-feel-guilty-about-our-colonial-history-ghvstdhmj [accessed on 25 July 2019]

201 'There is something ironic about an Oxford theologian': James McDougall, 'The history of empire isn't about pride – or guilt' (*Guardian*, 3 January 2018), https://www.theguardian.com/commentisfree/2018/jan/03/history-empire-pride-guilt-truth-oxford-nigel-biggar [accessed on 25 July 2019]

204 'I think the right thing is to acknowledge': 'David Cameron marks British 1919 Amritsar massacre' (BBC News, 20 February 2013), https://www.bbc.co.uk/news/uk-politics-21515360 [accessed on 25 July 2019]

204 'To view the Raj nostalgically': Stuart Jeffries, 'Visions of India: how film and TV romanticises life after the Raj' (*Guardian*, 17 June 2017), https://www.theguardian.com/film/2017/jun/17/how-film-and-tv-romanticises-life-in-india-after-the-raj?page=with%3Aimg-5\ [accessed on 25 July 2019]

207 'found a number of instances of coverage': 'From The Editors: The Times and Iraq' (*New York Times*, 26 May 2004), https://www.nytimes.com/2004/05/26/world/from-the-editors-the-times-and-iraq.html [accessed on 25 July 2019]

208 'did not pay enough attention to voices': Gary Younge, 'Washington Post apologises for underplaying WMD scepticism' (*Guardian*, 13 August 2004), https://www.theguardian.com/world/2004/aug/13/pressandpublishing.usa [accessed on 25 July 2019]

208 'We feel regret, but no shame': The Editors, 'Were We Wrong?' (*The New Republic*, 28 June 2004), https://newrepublic.com/article/67651/

were-we-wrong [accessed on 25 July 2019]

208 'It is now obvious': Thomas Friedman, 'Time for Plan B' (*New York Times*, 4 August 2006), https://www.nytimes.com/2006/08/04/opinion/04friedman.html [accessed on 25 July 2019]

208 'Off the Island': Thomas L. Friedman, 'Vote France Off the Island' (*New York Times*, 9 February 2003), https://www.nytimes.com/2003/02/09/opinion/vote-france-off-the-island.html [accessed on 25 July 2019]

208 'I was Wrong on Iraq': Fareed Zakaria, 'Iraq war was a terrible mistake' (CNN, 26 October 2015), https://edition.cnn.com/2015/10/26/opinions/zakaria-iraq-war-lessons/index.html [accessed on 25 July 2019]

209 'Ten years after the war began': David Aaronovitch, 'Now we know why it was right to invade Iraq' (*The Times*, 21 February 2013), https://www.thetimes.co.uk/article/now-we-know-why-it-was-right-to-invade-iraq-b9tsvq7l2xz [accessed on 25 July 2019]

209 'ten years on, the case for invading Iraq is still valid': Nick Cohen, 'Ten years on, the case for invading Iraq is still valid' (*Observer*, 3 March 2013), https://www.theguardian.com/commentisfree/2013/mar/03/10-years-right-invaded-iraq [accessed on 25 July 2019]

209 '"Arab Spring" from "the top down"': Thomas L. Friedman, 'Saudi Arabia's Arab Spring, at Last' (*New York Times*, 23 November 2017), https://www.nytimes.com/2017/11/23/opinion/saudi-prince-mbs-arab-spring.html [accessed on 25 July 2019]

211 'The political class imparted as much to the media class': Gary Younge, 'We were told Corbyn was "unelectable". Then came the surge' (*Guardian*, 6 June 2017), https://www.theguardian.com/commentisfree/2017/jun/06/jeremy-corbyn-unelectable-political-climate [accessed on 25 July 2019]

211 '. . . one of the most exclusive middle-class professions': Patrick Wintour, 'Student fees for those who live at home should be axed – report' (*Guardian*, 19 July 2009), https://www.theguardian.com/politics/2009/jul/19/fees-home-students-axed [accessed on 25 July 2019]

211 '2016 research by the American Society of News Editors': ASNE, 'Table 0 – Employees By Minority Group', https://www.asne.org/content.asp?contentid=147 [accessed on 25 July 2019]

212 'a typical white, male-centric newsroom': Tal Abbady, 'The Modern Newsroom Is Stuck Behind The Gender And Color Line' (*Code Switch*, NPR, 1 May 2017), https://www.npr.org/sections/codeswitch/2017/05/01/492982066/the-modern-newsroom-is-stuck-behind-the-gender-and-the-color-line [accessed on 25 July 2019]

213 'Let me come clean': Niall Ferguson, 'The Empire Slinks Back' (*New York Times Magazine*, 27 April 2003), https://www.nytimes.com/2003/04/27/magazine/the-empire-slinks-back.html [accessed on 25 July 2019]

214 '. . . bound to be "Eurocentric" because the world was "Eurocentric"', Charlotte Higgins, 'Rightwing historian Niall Ferguson given school curriculum role' (*Guardian*, 30 May 2010), https://www.theguardian.com/politics/2010/may/30/niall-ferguson-school-curriculum-role [accessed on 25 July 2019]

215 'I believe Cameron is interested': Srijana Mitra Das, 'Jallianwala Bagh massacre: David Cameron's apology that wasn't?' (*The Times of India*, 21 February 2013), https://timesofindia.indiatimes.com/india/Jallianwala-Bagh-massacre-David-Camerons-apology-that-wasnt/articleshow/18603655.cms [accessed on 25 July 2019]

215 'I won': Niall Ferguson (Twitter, 6:22 p.m., 20 July 2017), https://twitter.com/nfergus/status/888086778732728320?lang=en [accessed on 25 July 2019]

216 'the process of indoctrination starts early': Niall Ferguson, 'White men are bad; even a six-year-old tells me so' (*The Times*, 1 April 2018), https://www.thetimes.co.uk/article/white-men-are-bad-even-a-six-year-old-tells-me-so-hgbnpm809 [accessed on 25 July 2019]

217 'I wonder: do we risk sliding': Niall Ferguson, 'Stop harassment but don't slide into secular sharia' (*The Times*, 26 November 2017), https://www.thetimes.co.uk/article/stop-harassment-but-don-t-slide-into-secular-sharia-zj53ckj28 [accessed on 25 July 2019]

218 'Feminism isn't producing guides': Douglas Murray 'The consequence of this new sexual counter-revolution? No sex at all' (*Spectator*, 4 November 2017), https://www.spectator.co.uk/2017/11/the-consequence-of-this-new-sexual-counter-revolution-no-sex-at-all/ [accessed on 25 July 2019]

218 'the worrying elision of the criminal': Douglas Murray, 'Sexual Power Dynamics: Examining the Missing Part of the Story' (*The National Review*, 28 November 2017), https://www.nationalreview.com/2017/11/sexual-power-dynamics-sexual-assault-missing-part-story/ [accessed on 25 July 2019]

218 'false accusations do happen': Douglas Murray, 'What the Bishop Bell Case Reveals about Our #MeToo Moment' (*The National Review*, 20 December 2017), https://www.nationalreview.com/2017/12/bishop-bell-case-what-it-reveals-about-metoo-moment/ [accessed on 25 July 2019]

219 'immigrants were responsible for all reported rapes': Douglas Murray, *The Strange Death of Europe*, first edn (Bloomsbury, 2017), 56

219 'the number of reported rapes in this Nordic country': Andreas Lönnqvist, 'Rape, As Sweden Redefines It' (Inter Press Service, 7 February 2011), http://www.ipsnews.net/2011/02/rape-as-sweden-redefines-it-2/ [accessed on 25 July 2019]

219 'no indications of an increase': *ibid*.

219 'When people and institutions are riding strong': Douglas Murray, 'What the Bishop Bell Case Reveals about Our #MeToo Moment' (*The National Review*, 20 December 2017), https://www.nationalreview.com/2017/12/bishop-bell-case-what-it-reveals-about-metoo-moment/ [accessed on 25 July 2019]

219 'Those who believe Europe is for the world': Douglas Murray, *The Strange Death of Europe* (Bloomsbury, 2017), 296

220 'this scandal shows that women are now on top': Charles Moore, 'This scandal shows that women are now on top. I pray they share power with men, not crush us' (*Telegraph*, 3 November 2017), https://

www.telegraph.co.uk/news/2017/11/03/scandal-shows-women-now-top-pray-share-power-men-not-crush-us/ [accessed on 25 July 2019]

221 'it is not very fashionable to be a man these days': Niall Ferguson, 'White men are bad?' (*Boston Globe*, 2 April 2018), https://www.bostonglobe.com/opinion/2018/04/02/white-men-are-bad/LrBxRAPJ1bgiiTZOp6ri8I/story.html [accessed on 25 July 2019]

222 'privileging the disadvantaged': *Any Questions?* (BBC Radio 4, 31 March 2018), https://www.bbc.co.uk/programmes/p062x1z7 [accessed on 25 July 2019]

223 '. . . almost 90 per cent of books': Roxane Gay, 'Where Things Stand' (*The Rumpus*, 6 June 2012), https://therumpus.net/2012/06/where-things-stand/ [accessed on 25 July 2019]

223 '. . . out of 124 authors on the list': Jason T. Low, 'Where's the Diversity? The NY Times top 10 bestsellers list' (The Open Book Blog, 10 December 2013), https://blog.leeandlow.com/2013/12/10/wheres-the-diversity-the-ny-times-top-10-bestsellers-list/ [accessed on 25 July 2019]

223 '. . . the *Sunday Times* top ten bestselling hardback non-fiction chart': 'The Sunday Times Bestsellers of the Year 2017' (*Sunday Times*, 24 December 2017), https://www.thetimes.co.uk/article/the-sunday-times-bestsellers-of-the-year-2017-ldqr8lt9n?ni-statuscode=acsaz-307 [accessed on 25 July 2019]

224 'new company-wide goal': Lionel Shriver, 'Great writers are found with an open mind' (*Spectator*, 9 June 2018), https://www.spectator.co.uk/2018/06/when-diversity-means-uniformity/ [accessed on 25 July 2019]

225 '"mass immigration" is "convulsing Europe"': Melanie Phillips, 'How the West Was Lost' (*Spectator*, 11 May 2002), http://archive.spectator.co.uk/article/11th-may-2002/14/how-the-west-was-lost [accessed on 25 July 2019]

226 'one of the very few inside the church': Melanie Phillips, 'When a bishop has to leave the Church of England to stand up for Christians, what hope is left for Britain?' (*Daily Mail*, 29 March 2009), https://www.dailymail.co.uk/debate/article-1165719/MELANIE-PHILIPS-When-bishop-leave-C-E-stand-Christians-hope-left-Britain.html [accessed on 25 July 2019]

226 '. . . Islam is "an ideology that itself is non-negotiable"': Jackie Ashley, 'The multicultural menace, anti-semitism and me' (*Guardian*, 16 June 2006), https://www.theguardian.com/politics/2006/jun/16/media.politicsphilosophyandsociety [accessed on 25 July 2019]

226 'testing the fundamentals of free speech': Matthew d'Ancona, 'The Comment Awards 2018 show that feelings matter more than facts' (*GQ*, 22 October 2018), https://www.gq-magazine.co.uk/article/the-comment-awards-2018-show-that-feelings-matter-more-than-facts [accessed on 25 July 2019]

227 'a snapshot of a broader censorious atmosphere': Claire Fox, 'The Comment Awards Fiasco' (*Quillette*, 25 October 2018), https://quillette.com/2018/10/25/the-comment-awards-fiasco/ [accessed on 25 July 2019]

227 'no-platforming': Matthew Parris, 'In Defence of Nick Clegg' (*Spectator*, 27 October 2018), https://www.spectator.co.uk/2018/10/

in-defence-of-nick-clegg/ [accessed on 25 July 2019]

227 'repeatedly denounced from the platform as "censorship"': George Monbiot (Twitter, 10:32 a.m., 16 November 2018), https://twitter.com/georgemonbiot/status/1063379279281573888 [accessed on 25 July 2019]

228 'Quietly lose her nomination? Nobble the judges?': David Aaronovitch (Twitter, 11:09 p.m., 12 October 2018), https://twitter.com/DAaronovitch/status/1050871122915409920 [accessed on 25 July 2019]

228 'become a free speech question': David Aaronovitch (Twitter, 7:26 a.m., 13 October 2018), https://twitter.com/DAaronovitch/status/1050996208783777792?s=20 [accessed on 25 July 2019]

228 'a fiction to shut down debate': Melanie Phillips, 'Islamophobia is a fiction to shut down debate' (*The Times*, 7 May 2018), https://www.thetimes.co.uk/article/islamophobia-is-a-fiction-to-shut-down-debate-wwtzggnc7 [accessed on 25 July 2019]

228 'Would you genuinely take the same stance': Jonathan Portes (Twitter, 2:17 p.m., 13 October 2018), https://twitter.com/jdportes/status/1051099535127302144?s=20 [accessed on 25 July 2019]

228 'As it happens I don't agree': David Aaronovitch (Twitter, 4:00 p.m., 13 October 2018), https://twitter.com/DAaronovitch/status/1051125449521356800?s=20 [accessed on 25 July 2019]

231 'A newspaper, after all': Bret Stephens, 'Free Speech and the Necessity of Discomfort' (*New York Times*, 22 February 2018), https://www.nytimes.com/2018/02/22/opinion/free-speech-discomfort.html [accessed on 25 July 2019]

231 'intercede only to say nice things': Bret Stephens, 'How Twitter Pornified Politics' (*New York Times*, 23 June 2017), https://www.nytimes.com/2017/06/23/opinion/how-twitter-pornified-politics.html

231 'too bad you're a Twitter troll': Bret Stephens (Twitter, 2:56 a.m., 9 November 2018), https://twitter.com/BretStephensNYT/status/1060727768151924736?s=20 [accessed on 25 July 2019]

231 'Hummus seems to have first been mentioned': Bret Stephens (Twitter, 8:49 p.m., 26 December ember 2017), https://twitter.com/BretStephensNYT/status/945758524000362496?s=20 [accessed on 25 July 2019]

231 'He called ex-Obama aide Tommy Vietor an "asshole"': Joe Concha, 'NY Times's Bret Stephens deletes tweet calling ex-Obama aide "an asshole"' (*The Hill*, 11 January 2018), https://thehill.com/homenews/media/368586-ny-times-bret-stephens-deletes-tweet-calling-ex-obama-aide-an-asshole [accessed on 25 July 2019]

232 'This. Is. Insane': Bret Stephens (Twitter, 4:41 a.m., 16 February 2018), https://twitter.com/BretStephensNYT/status/964359114338914304?s=20 [accessed on 25 July 2019]

232 'one of the participants in the diversity debate': David Aaronovitch, 'Illiberal left plays into hands of the far right' (*The Times*, 25 October 2018), https://www.thetimes.co.uk/article/illiberal-left-plays-into-hands-of-the-far-right-qwwcwvrmd [accessed on 25 July 2019]

233 'What happened when we tried to debate immigration': Matthew Good-win and Eric Kaufmann, 'What Happened When We Tried to Debate Immigration' (*Quillette*, 8 December 2018), https://quillette.com/2018/12/08/what-happened-when-we-tried-to-debate-immigration/ [accessed on 25 July 2019]

233 'the tug of war between white ethno-traditionalism': Kenan Malik, 'White identity is meaningless. Real dignity is found in shared hopes' (*Guardian*, 21 October 2018), https://www.theguardian.com/commentisfree/2018/oct/21/white-identity-is-meaningless-dignity-is-found-in-shared-hopes [accessed on 25 July 2019]

234 'Too Diverse?': David Goodhart, 'Too Diverse?' (*Prospect*, 20 February 2004), https://www.prospectmagazine.co.uk/magazine/too-diverse-david-goodhart-multiculturalism-britain-immigration-globalisation [accessed on 25 July 2019]

235 'uncritical channelling of black anger': David Goodhart (Twitter, 1:29 p.m., 12 May 2018), https://twitter.com/david_goodhart/status/995279834753495040 [accessed on 25 July 2019]

235 'racial grievance outburst': David Goodhart (Twitter, 4:42 p.m., 12 May 2018), https://twitter.com/David_Goodhart/status/995328243065675776?s=20 [accessed on 25 July 2019]

235 'the nihilistic grievance culture': David Goodhart, 'The riots at the end of history' (*Prospect*, 9 August 2011), http://www.prospectmagazine.co.uk/2011/08/the-riots-at-the-end-of-history/ [accessed on 25 July 2019]

235 'How does it help black inner city youth': David Goodhart (Twitter, 2:52 p.m., 13 May 2018), https://twitter.com/David_Goodhart/status/995663062433783808?s=20 [accessed on 25 July 2019]

235 'Windrush would have been less likely': David Goodhart (Twitter, 3:19 p.m., 13 May 2018), https://twitter.com/David_Goodhart/status/995669746619207680?s=20 [accessed on 25 July 2019]

236 'The "thickest" solidarities': David Goodhart, 'Too Diverse?' (*Prospect*, 20 February 2004), https://www.prospectmagazine.co.uk/magazine/too-diverse-david-goodhart-multiculturalism-britain-immigration-globalisation [accessed on 25 July 2019]

237 'will not get a job if you don't give a shit': David Goodhart, 'The riots at the end of history' (*Prospect*, 9 August 2011), http://www.prospectmagazine.co.uk/2011/08/the-riots-at-the-end-of-history/ [accessed on 25 July 2019]

237 '. . . a "metropolitan" fixation': David Goodhart (Twitter, 4:12 p.m., 5 November 2017), https://twitter.com/David_Goodhart/status/927207074278313984 [accessed on 25 July 2019]

239 '. . . the British media is 95 per cent white': Neil Thurnan, 'Does British Journalism Have a Diversity Problem?' (City University London, full results published in May 2016 by the Reuters Institute), https://drive.google.com/a/guardian.co.uk/file/d/0B4lqRxA4qQpjakl1UEd5WEFlRGc/view?usp=sharing [accessed on 25 July 2019]

242 '. . . men are 3.5 times more likely to die by suicide': Helene Schumacher,

'Why more men than women die by suicide' (BBC.com, 18 March 2019), http://www.bbc.com/future/story/20190313-why-more-men-kill-themselves-than-women [accessed on 25 July 2019]

242 'the decline of traditional male industries': Jacqui Thornton, 'Men and Suicide, Why it's a Social Issue' (Samaritans in partnership with Network Rail, 2016), 8

243 'The Trump Effect': 'Hate at School' (Southern Poverty Law Center, 2 May 2019), https://www.splcenter.org/20190502/hate-school [accessed on 25 July 2019]

243 '54 incidents in which high school students': Albert Samaha, Mike Hayes, Talal Ansari, 'Kids Are Quoting Trump To Bully Their Classmates And Teachers Don't Know What To Do About It' (BuzzFeed News, 6 June 2017), https://www.buzzfeednews.com/article/albertsamaha/kids-are-quoting-trump-to-bully-their-classmates [accessed on 25 July 2019]

244 'We're losing the thread': Jacqueline Thomsen, 'Bill Maher criticizes social media bans: "Alex Jones gets to speak"' (*The Hill*, 18 August 2018), https://thehill.com/policy/technology/technology/402450-bill-maher-on-social-media-bans-alex-jones-gets-to-speak [accessed on 25 July 2019]

244 'is to negate the implicit assurance': Stanley Fish, 'The Harm in Free Speech' (*New York Times*, 4 June 2012), https://opinionator.blogs.nytimes.com/2012/06/04/the-harm-in-free-speech/ [accessed on 25 July 2019]

245 'unfashionable views': Joe Lo, 'Today Show presenter: Being against gay rights is "legitimate" and "acceptable"' (Left Food Forward, 10 January 2019), https://leftfootforward.org/2019/01/today-show-presenter-being-against-gay-rights-is-legitimate-and-acceptable/ [accessed on 25 July 2019]

246 'natural to think that the law should be involved': Stanley Fish, 'The Harm in Free Speech' (*New York Times*, 4 June 2012), https://opinionator.blogs.nytimes.com/2012/06/04/the-harm-in-free-speech/ [accessed on 25 July 2019]

246 'We willingly turned the other way': Janet Reitman, 'U.S. Law Enforcement Failed to See the Threat of White Nationalism. Now They Don't Know How to Stop It.' (*New York Times*, 3 November 2018), https://www.nytimes.com/2018/11/03/magazine/FBI-charlottesville-white-nationalism-far-right.html [accessed on 25 July 2019]

247 'A report by the Anti-Defamation League's Center on Extremism revealed': 'ADL Report: White Supremacist Murders More Than Doubled in 2017' (ADL.org, 17 January 2018), https://www.adl.org/news/press-releases/adl-report-white-supremacist-murders-more-than-doubled-in-2017 [accessed on 25 July 2019]

247 '. . . according to the Stimson Center': 'Stimson Study Group On Counterterrorism Spending: Protecting America While Promoting Efficiencies and Accountability' (Stimson, May 2018), 7, https://www.stimson.org/sites/default/files/file-attachments/CT_Spending_Report_0.pdf Stimson [accessed on 25 July 2019]

248 'what it means to identify with the liberal or conservative': Ryan Jerome LeCount, 'Visualizing the Increasing Effect of Racial Resentment on Political

Ideology among Whites, 1986 to 2016' (*Socius*, 20 September 2018), 2

248 'They could look at the wealthy persons': Sean Illing, 'How the politics of racial resentment is killing white people' (Vox, 19 March 2019), https://www.vox.com/2019/3/19/18236247/dying-of-whiteness-trump-politics-jonathan-metzl [accessed on 25 July 2019]

249 'I've always thought that even in a no-deal situation': Edward Malnick, 'Jeremy Hunt: UK will "flourish and prosper" if it walks away from the EU without a deal' (*Telegraph*, 15 December 2018), https://www.telegraph.co.uk/politics/2018/12/15/jeremy-hunt-uk-will-flourish-prosper-walks-away-eu-without-deal/ [accessed on 25 July 2019]

249 'appreciate what they've had': Siobhán O'Grady, 'One possible consequence of no-deal Brexit: Fresh-food shortages and higher prices' (*Washington Post*, 29 January 2019), https://www.washingtonpost.com/world/2019/01/29/one-possible-consequence-no-deal-brexit-fresh-food-shortages-higher-prices/?utm_term=.25f11e0fc007 [accessed on 25 July 2019]

249 'the fever-dream of an English Resistance': Fintan O'Toole, 'The paranoid fantasy behind Brexit' (*Guardian*, 16 November 2018), https://www.theguardian.com/politics/2018/nov/16/brexit-paranoid-fantasy-fintan-otoole [accessed on 25 July 2019]

250 'How have the "Oxford chums"': Bagehot, 'The elite that failed' (*Economist*, 22 December 2018), https://www.economist.com/britain/2018/12/22/the-elite-that-failed [accessed on 25 July 2019]

252 'I voted for him, and he's the one who's doing this': Zack Beauchamp, '"He's not hurting the people he needs to be": a Trump voter says the quiet part out loud' (Vox, 8 January 2019), https://www.vox.com/policy-and-politics/2019/1/8/18173678/trump-shutdown-voter-florida [accessed on 25 July 2019]

253 '... one-third of British companies': Philip Inman, 'One in three UK firms plan for Brexit relocation, IoD says' (*Guardian*, 1 February 2019), https://www.theguardian.com/politics/2019/feb/01/one-three-uk-firms-activate-plans-move-operations-abroad-no-deal-brexit-iod-survey [accessed on 25 July 2019]

253 'resolve collective problems of classification': Timothy N. Laurie, 'Becoming-Animal Is a Trap for Humans: Deleuze and Guattari in Madagascar' in *Deleuze and the Non-Human* (Palgrave Macmillan, 2015), 151

254 'The election of Donald Trump to the Presidency': David Remnick, 'An American Tragedy' (*New Yorker*, 9 November 2016), https://www.newyorker.com/news/news-desk/an-american-tragedy-2 [accessed on 25 July 2019]

256 '... a veteran journalist with a good reputation': Brian Cathcart, '"Muslim Fostering": Times Journalism Utterly Discredited' (*Byline*, 7 September 2018), https://www.byline.com/column/68/article/2281 [accessed on 25 July 2019]

259 'the movement of ideas following': Albert O. Hirschman, *The Rhetoric of Reaction – Perversity, Futility, Jeopardy* (Belknap Press, 1991), 132

261 'I never had to think about that before': 'Why Is This Happening? With

Chris Hayes' (27 November 2018), https://www.nbcnews.com/think/opinion/understanding-state-american-democracy-ta-nehisi-coates-podcast-transcript-ncna940696 [accessed on 25 July 2019]

263 'The major advances of civilisation': Alfred North Whitehead, *Symbolism: Its Meaning and Effect* (Fordham University Press, 1985), 88

ACKNOWLEDGEMENTS

My thanks go to David, whose unwavering enthusiasm for this book never failed to pick me up when I was flagging, and for his wise counsel in helping me transition to full-time writing. To Lizzie for her indefatigability as friend, honest reader of messy drafts, and rare intellect. To Karolina for positively dragging this book out of me. To Jenny for being an ally. And to Mary and Pankaj for an unflagging confidence in me that I am not sure I am worthy of – I hope never to disappoint them. And finally to Declan, who under difficult circumstances continued to offer me an oasis; generously and graciously spinning a quiet, peaceful nest in which I could write.

INDEX